THE
NEW
AMERICANS

THE
NEW
AMERICANS

Cecyle S. Neidle

Foreword by Oscar Cargill

TWAYNE PUBLISHERS

A DIVISION OF G. K. HALL & CO., BOSTON

To Ned, Meg, Louise, and Betsy,
some of whose grandparents
experienced the hardships
described herein

This book contains testimony about America by people stemming from diverse European backgrounds, who were not native Americans. Most of them became Americans; some did not, but all lived among us long enough to form definite opinions about America. All included here made their views of America known. As the searchlight passes over more than three hundred years of our history, our country, its people, its way of life, are sometimes seen in the glow of approbation, sometimes in shadow, and frequently in sunlight and shadow. We see the process by which aliens became Americans, and we note the reactions of those who were drawn back to their homelands. Some of the comments are objective, some haughty, some condescending, and some heartwarmingly appreciative. The observations of some of these people are herewith presented.

Foreword

When the U.S.S.R. can produce a book comparable to this, filled with expressions of the realized hopes of immigrants and refugees who have become dedicated and distinguished citizens, then, and then only, will the United States have real cause for alarm. All history provides no greater contrast than the Berlin Wall to keep disaffected citizens *in* and our quota system to keep ardent would-be citizens *out*, both probably mistaken policies, if not in other ways comparable. The truth is, the American immigrant is nearer in motivation to the pioneers of our settlement than are the seventh generation descendants of those pioneers. He is a man on the move, of disciplined will and high imagination, while still the unspoiled child of destiny and faith. He is a man who believes in the American net of law and order with its large interstices. And he is the necessary irritant in our complacency. He wants us to be what he expected us to be.

Save in minor and absurd ways, save in times of what some call national emergency, America has never been a land of compulsions, but if I had not Justice Holmes's belief in "the open market place of ideas," I would be inclined to compel certain colleagues and friends to read *The New Americans*, this admirably titled volume. To him of the dismal view, of whom there are presently too many, I would commend complete immersion. To those who think their blood is the only genuine American stream, despite the somewhat yellowish aspect of its red corpuscles, I'd commend immersion in the strong detergent writings of Ben Franklin or Thomas Jefferson. To those who think the compositions of a lofty being called the "pure artist" are alone consequential I'd compel memorizing and recitation after the old-time practice of the country school with the McGuffey reader, for I suspect that they lack humility. More seriously, I think that every true student of American history, literature, and culture should be acquainted with the testimony in this book, the moving testimony of the immigrant who has "stayed"—as the great majority have, to his and our patent advantage. That is, I would make it that tenderest form of compulsion, "required reading," in any course that dared prefix the word "American" to its content.

But, of course, the best students of our society, the most earnest ones, are not necessarily in the academic procession. To such independent readers and searchers, and particularly to those abroad, I recommend the guidance supplied by Mrs. Neidle in this book. No one knows her subject so well as she, perhaps not even the U. S. Commissioner of Immigration. Out of an enormous quantity of material covering the extent of our history she has made a very wise and illuminating selection. And what a range of personalities, employments, talents, professions, and genius her book represents. The well-informed American will find, I dare say, some few personalities and large contributors to our history and culture (as I have) of whom he has never heard before but whom he must respect and honor. If there are omissions from this distinguished array, they are deliberate in order to avoid duplication of substance or the printing of material that is too familiar, like that of such transient visitors as Charles Dickens and Alexis de Toqueville. A feature not to be overlooked is the inclusion of a number of comparisons by immigrants of the countries they have left to the nation they have come to—a subject not much entered into elsewhere. Mrs. Neidle's general introduction with its broad survey of immigration, with its causes and consequences, is scholarly and astonishingly complete. Her designation of the periods in the story of immigration are sensible and will probably not undergo much modification as time passes. For those who find America too complex to capsulate, that is, complex beyond most countries, she provides a formula for a beginning: Why not start with the "new" Americans who are possibly the best Americans and the most typical? They have a common denominator: They all *believe*, and they are in the process of becoming the majority.

Oscar Cargill

Ohio University,
Athens, Ohio.

Acknowledgments

It is a privilege to acknowledge my obligation to Professor Gay Wilson Allen of New York University, who guided the initial effort with unusual patience and courtesy and whose counsel was always available to me thereafter; Professor Oscar Cargill of New York University, for giving of his time so generously in reading the whole manuscript and for supplying the kind of penetrating criticism and suggestions for which he is known; Professor Robert D. Cross of Columbia University, for reading the partial manuscript and contributing his valuable opinion, and last but not least, Professor Sigmund Diamond of Columbia University, who read the manuscript and offered invaluable counsel in regard to structure and content.

I also wish to thank the following publishers who have given their permission to use material to which they hold the copyrights: Barnes & Noble for *The Journal of Jasper Danckaerts;* The University of Chicago Press for *Atoms in the Family* by Laura Fermi; Dorrance & Company for *From Steerage to Congress* by Richard Bartholdt; Doubleday & Company for generously supplying the names and addresses of copyright holders; Dodd, Mead & Company for *I Am a Woman—And a Jew* by Elizabeth G. Sterne; E. P. Dutton & Company for *Seventy Years of Life and Labor* by Samuel Gompers; Estate of Albert Einstein for *Out of My Later Years* by Albert Einstein; Harcourt, Brace & World, Inc., for *America is in the Heart* by Carlos Bulosan; Harper & Row for *Laughing in the Jungle* by Louis Adamic, *A Lost Paradise* by Samuel Chotzinoff, *An American in the Making* by Marcus E. Ravage, and *America and the New Epoch* by Charles P. Steinmetz; Houghton Mifflin Company for *The Promised Land* by Mary Antin, *The Autobiography of Andrew Carnegie* by Andrew Carnegie, *A Far Journey* by Abraham Mitrie Rihbany, and *The Memoirs of Henry Villard* by Henry Villard, and for permission to include several poems by Archibald MacLeish; the McGraw-Hill Book Company for *The Heart is the Teacher* by Leonard

Covello; The Macmillan Company for *Under the Shadow of Liberty* by Edward Corsi, *A Dreamer's Journey* by Morris Raphael Cohen, *Pascal d'Angelo, Son of Italy* by Pascal d'Angelo, *Loose Leaves from a Busy Life* by Morris Hillquit, *The Soul of an Immigrant* by Constantine Panunzio, *Immigrant's Return* by Angelo Pellegrini, *The Making of an American* by Jacob A. Riis, *The Inside Story of an Outsider* and *You Still Have Your Head* by Franz Schoenberner; Alfred A. Knopt, Inc., for *A Lost Paradise* by Samuel Chotzinoff, *Living My Life* by Emma Goldman, and *The Domestic Manners of the Americans* by Frances Trollope; Meredith Press for *First Papers* by Martin Gumpert, *My India, My America* by Krishnalal Shridharani, and *A Woman's Quest* by Marie E. Zakrszewska; University of Minnesota Press for *Woman at Work: The Autobiography of Mary Anderson* by Mary Anderson and Mary Winslow; J. B. Lippincott Company for *This is my America* by Stoyan Christowe; Liveright Publishing Corp. for *Up-Stream* by Ludwig Lewisohn; Norwegian American Historical Association for *The Log Book of a Young Immigrant* by Laurance M. Larson; G. P. Putnam's Sons for *Autobiography* by John Cournos; Fleming H. Revell Company for *From Alien to Citizen* by Edward Steiner; Reynal & Company for *Felix Frankfurter Reminisces* by Felix Frankfurter; Vanguard Press for *Doctor for the People* by Michael Shadid; Ives Washburn, Inc., for *My American Adventure* by Erna Barschak; New York Folklore Society for permission to reprint portions from the article "Immigrant's Idyll" by Maurice Hindus. Excerpts from the following works are protected by copyright and have been reprinted here by special permission of Charles Scribner's Sons: *From Immigrant to Inventor* by Michael Pupin; *Persons and Places* and *The Middle Span* by George Santayana; and *Reflections On America* by Jacques Maritain.

I also acknowledge the courtesy of Mrs. Oscar Ameringer, Mr. Cary W. Bok, Mrs. Thomas K. Finletter, Mr. Maurice Hindus, Mr. Carl Christian Jensen, Mr. David C. de Jong, Mrs. Louise Lewisohn, Mr. Henry Morgenthau, Jr. And—to all who showed an interest in this work, my deepest appreciation and thanks.

CECYLE S. NEIDLE

TABLE OF CONTENTS

THE
NEW
AMERICANS

PART ONE

GENERAL INTRODUCTION

She's a tough land under the corn mister;
She has changed the bone in the cheeks of many races;
She has winced the eyes of the soft Slavs with her sun on them;
She has tried the fat from the round rump of Italians;
Even the voice of the English has gone dry
    and hard on the tongue and alive in the throat speaking:
She's a tough land under the oak-trees mister:
It may be she can change the word in the book
As she changes the bone of a man's head in his children:
It may be that the earth and the men remain . . .
                  "Background With Revolutionaries"
                     Archibald MacLeish

1

American Beginnings

> "America is neither a land nor a people,
> A word's shape it is, a wind's sweep—
> America is alone: many together,
> Many of one mouth, of one breath,
> Dressed as one—and none brothers among them:
> Only the taught speech and the aped tongue."
>
> *"American Letter"*
> Archibald MacLeish

The assertion that America is a nation of immigrants is a truism that cannot be refuted. America was settled by Europeans, and despite the addition of Negroes and some Orientals, the character of our immigration has remained predominantly European. William Faulkner was aware of it when he spoke of immigration to the North in his novel *Intruder in the Dust* as "the coastal spew of Europe." The South received comparatively little foreign influx, which is held to have been one of the causes of its insularity. Americans, it has been observed, "have no organic past, only ambiguous memories of European derivations."[1] * In comparison with a time span comprising several thousand years of recorded history and millennia of unrecorded history, during which countless generations followed one another in unbroken succession, the annals of the oldest American families, barely exceeding three hundred years—at most fewer than twenty generations—must be considered to be short. It is this fact which gives to the definition of a foreigner as one "who came over on the boat after I did,"[2] a specific aptness.

The first efforts at colonization in North America, begun at the end of the sixteenth century, while the first Elizabeth was Queen of England, proved to be failures. (The Queen was a shareholder in some of those ventures.) From the first successful attempts—in 1607 in the South, and in 1620 in the North—the population movement was continuous, albeit uneven. At mid-

---

*Numbered references will be found at the end of this section.

century an American historian declared: "by 1949 the nature of the population had changed so much that only a minority could feel genuinely old stock; the typical American, if such a person could really be found, was a third generation immigrant."[3] Up to 1820 incoming aliens found no bars of any kind at American ports of entry. Accurate records were not kept until 1820, when ship captains bringing immigrants were required to furnish to the customs, lists of passengers and other information.

The total number of foreign-born who entered the United States between 1776 and the present is held to be nearly thirty-nine million.[4] The first immigrant depot was Castle Garden. It had been an amusement place until it was taken over by the State of New York in 1855. In 1892 Ellis Island became the main clearing house for immigrants under the aegis of the federal government. Twenty-five million passed through its gates between its inception and the time it was closed in 1954.[5] The year that brought the greatest influx was 1907, when a daily average of five thousand aliens crowded Ellis Island, straining the capacity of the depot and the patience of immigration officials. Ellis Island is now a national shrine. The Statue of Liberty dates from 1885 and is a gift of the French people in commemoration of the hundredth anniversary of American independence. The loftiest statue in the world, it became the symbol of welcome to millions of newcomers. Many wept at the sight of her and at the same time experienced an affirmation of the hopes that had caused them to leave home, family, and friends in order to follow a distant dream.

Free and unhindered entry into our land has passed into the limbo of history. Since 1929 the influx of aliens has been so drastically reduced that pictures of shawled immigrants carrying bundles and followed by queues of children in strange-looking clothes have become as much a part of the American past as Indians in war paint and feathers. Now that most European aliens have become absorbed into the mainstream of American life, questions about them and their reactions to American life seem more pertinent than ever. Who were these newcomers to our land? What manner of lives did they lead in our country? How did they react to our way of life?

We have ample information about the lives of foreigners in our midst. Much of it is documentary evidence, written by newcomers to America—immigrants as well as visitors and travelers

—which conveys in their own words their impressions, the hopes and frustrations of immigrants, and their efforts to surmount their handicaps. It is with this kind of direct information that this book concerns itself. The difference between the reactions of visitors and those who came to make their homes in this country is pointed out by a twentieth century entrant:

> If you have come to a new continent to live there permanently, you have feelings entirely different from those of an occasional tourist behind whose enchanted curiosity rests the knowledge that he will return to the intimate familiarity of his established home elsewhere. For if you have come to stay, you have to realize that, whatever you see, whatever the given conditions are, you have to put up with them permanently. Your body, your mind, have to adjust themselves to whatever you find. There is something final in *that* knowledge.[5]

This necessity to readjust, to accept a different status and changed living conditions, caused all immigrants a great deal of anguish and privation, at least in the beginning. All faced the struggle for acceptance and, when coupled with the struggle for a livelihood, it was sufficient, in Thomas Paine's words, "to try men's souls." Some became triumphantly successful; others never overcame their handicaps. In the words of Louis Adamic* all helped to "feed the roots of America's . . . greatness."

---

* Louis Adamic, *Laughing in the Jungle* (New York, 1932).

2

One-Way and Two-Way Traffic Across the Atlantic

Even before the Revolution travelers braved the hazards of a trip across the seas to satisfy their curiosity about life in the English colonies. One was Peter Kalm, a Swedish scientist, pupil of Linnaeus, who was sent here by the Swedish Academy during the middle of the eighteenth century. This two-way traffic was to increase considerably during the nineteenth century. Europeans were apt to be impressed with the progress, the industry of the people, the expanding frontier, the fact that there were no beggars and little thievery, which they attributed to the enviable circumstance that there was sufficient work for all. Their attention was apt to be arrested by the spirit of independence and assertiveness ("I am as good as you are"), which they recognized as a corollary of the spirit of equality and democracy. They were not expected to approve of this American characteristic, since it was in direct contradiction to the prevailing *Zeitgeist*. What shocked and revolted most visitors were the concomitants of slavery—the sight of people in chains weeping and filling the air with lamentations. One of the shrewdest and most objective commentators was Alexis de Toqueville, who was sent here by the French government in 1831—during The Age of Jackson. The outcome was *Democracy in America,* which saw publication in France in 1835 and in America in 1838. It is considered to contain the most apt and authoritative comments on social conditions in America and on our political and administrative system.

When De Tocqueville observed that "the happy and the powerful do not go into exile," he was referring to those who were taking the "one-way trip" across the ocean, to reestablish themselves in America, hopefully, with more success than they had had in Europe. Sixty years before De Tocqueville another Frenchman, Hector St. John de Crevecoeur, who lived among us for almost twenty years before he returned to his natal place —France—had come to the same conclusion. Crevecoeur's com-

18

ment was that "the rich stay in Europe, it is only the middling and the poor that emigrate." These statements have the backing of historic fact and common sense. Immigrants usually belonged to "the annals of the poor," to the down-trodden, the misfits, the ne'er-do-wells, who were forced to alter the course of their lives from sheer necessity. Even those who were induced to take the step of relocating themselves by a high love of adventure, or who brought money with them with which to acquire land, or who came to fill special posts as technical experts, tutors, craftsmen, or ministers—cannot be classified as of "the powerful." Another earmark shared by those who ventured into the unknown, especially during the days when the voyage across the ocean was full of peril, was courage—of the kind required of astronauts today.

A special group deserves to be placed in rubrics—those whom religious or political persecution drove out of their natal places. Religious persecution brought not only the Separatists, Puritans, Catholics, and Quakers from England, German Pietists from the Rhineland, Huguenots from France, the Stavanger Quakers from Norway, but furnished continuous pressure for emigration throughout the nineteenth and twentieth centuries. The Jews from Russia, Poland, and Roumania, who came after the eighteen-eighties, were sufferers from religious persecution, as was the large group of Hitler victims during the nineteen-thirties and forties. During the nineteenth century there were also Protestant groups from Holland and Sweden who preferred emigration to enforced acceptance of religious dogmas of which they disapproved. Political persecution was responsible for bringing French refugees during the French Revolution and for depositing two waves of Germans during the first half of the nineteenth century, who were driven out by the failure of the post-Napoleonic upheavals. During the twentieth century we received emigrés from the Bolshevik revolution, the victims of Fascism, and now, the dissenters from the Castro regime, of whom there were said to be fifty thousand in New York City in the early sixties.[7]

There were also other factors which caused people to break their old ties—sudden collapse of fortune, ruined farms or business (as in the case of Henry Morgenthau's father), pressing debts, (the reason for Johann August Sutter's hurried departure from Europe), the snapping of ties through death, the threat of disgrace, or of an impending prison sentence. Even in the second half of the nineteenth century, we find the Russian novelist Dostoevsky suggesting through another character that the murderer Raskolnikov be shipped to America, in order to make a new start in life. However, the greatest number of immigrants were humble but honest folk, and a not inconsiderable number had the advantages of superior education and background.

It stirs the imagination to reflect on the continuous hegira of people fleeing misfortune or hampering circumstances from all corners of Europe—from the British Isles to Armenia and from Scandinavia to the southernmost points in Italy, setting out westward for what they believed was the "Golden Land," where dignity and prosperity awaited all who were willing to come. There is something of the pathetic in such extravagant expectations, something of the child's faith in magic. To Morris Raphael Cohen* his parents were "that heroic generation," who, in coming here, undertook "a journey from the mediaeval to the modern age." To O. E. Rolvaag, who became a novelist and teacher after receiving an education in America, the Scandinavians who took up homesteads in the Northwest, were "Giants in the Earth." Heroic they were, all who attempted to make a life for themselves "amid the alien corn," as Ruth did in the land of the Israelites, for the road that led to a respected place in our society represented not only a physical odyssey, but a spiritual one as well, with the danger of shipwreck in a symbolic sense ever present.

---

*Morris Raphael Cohen, *A Dreamer's Journey* (Boston, 1949) .

3

The Effect of the New World

From the very beginning of the American experience there was a compulsion to write about it. It grew out of the effect of a strange and hostile environment on people whose way of life had been totally different, and it must be judged as an attempt to come to terms with it, to reduce its strangeness, so that it could be more easily accepted. In this category belongs the very first account of the new world written in English, Captain John Smith's *A True Relation of Such Occurrences and Events as Hath Happened in the Founding of Virginia,* published in England in 1608. Despite its promotional cast, it is also the first autobiographical statement of the difficulties encountered by settlers in the new world. Governor William Bradford, second governor of the Plymouth Colony, established in 1620, and Governor John Winthrop, first governor of the Massachusetts Bay Colony, established in 1630, were also moved by the autobiographical impulse. Bradford's *Of Plymouth Plantation* and Winthrop's *Journal* are considered historical source-books, but they are autobiographical documents at the same time, for the personalities of the authors emerge from both books as clearly as if they had intended to offer portraits of themselves. Though the motive may not have been aggrandizement of the self, they undoubtedly meant to place themselves at the center of an experience for which there was no precedent.

Visitors and travelers were similarly affected by what they saw in this country. Since they were aware of the interest in eyewitness reports about America, many either offered their observations for publication or published them at their own expense. This proved in many cases a most worthwhile investment. Some of these early reports were so widely read that they were considered responsible not only for increasing the flow of immigration, but for directing settlers to specific places. Such seminal books were Ole Rynning's *True Account of America,* published in Christiania in 1838, and Gottfried Duden's *A Report of a Journey to the Western States of North America,* published in

Germany in 1839 and republished in three consecutive editions. To Duden, who was a physician, overcrowding was the root of all evils. After buying a tract of land in Missouri and building a house thereon, he remained there three years. His praise for the state of Missouri as an "El Dorado" sent caravans of Germans to Missouri with their pianofortes and other bulky musical instruments, as well as the appropriate musical scores. Many were painfully shocked by the near-wilderness and the insalubrious climate. Some writings were enthusiastic, as were Morris Birkbeck's *Notes on a Journey in America,* published in Dublin in 1818, and Frances Wright's *View of Society* and *Manners in America,* published in 1821; sometimes unfavorable to the point of invidiousness, of which Frances Trollope's *Domestic Manners of the Americans,* published in London in 1831, is an example; or scholarly, as in Alexis de Toqueville's *Democracy in America.* Among later documents is James Bryce's *American Commonwealth,* published in 1888, André Siegfried's *America Comes of Age,* which appeared in 1927, and the comparatively recent *Reflections on America* by Jacques Maritain.

The immigrant story has found many chroniclers. Frequently writers of fiction employed the privileges of their craft in reconstructing tales they had heard from members of their families, or events they had witnessed, or could imagine. Some of them are immensely effective and possess a high degree of historical accuracy.* But because the protagonists are imaginary people, though they are undoubtedly intended to represent the "Everyman" among immigrants, the poignancy that emanates from the association of a specific individual with his good or ill fortune, is diminished. These fictional accounts stress all the angles of the immigrant experience—the impact of a totally different way of life, the tendency to huddle together, to maintain their "kitchen culture,"[8] to keep their children tied to their old traditions—which was generally a losing battle. Still, these unnamed individuals remain invisible witnesses, without faces or identity. They are analogous to T. S. Eliot's "Hollow Men" of whom it may also be said: ". . . our dried voices, when/We whisper together/Are quiet and meaningless/As wind in dry grass . . ."

---

*See the trilogy of Vilhelm Moberg.

In the memoirs of immigrants individuals are identified and are given their voices. Fascinating information that illustrates the triumph of human endurance over adversity, emerges from these pages. Also, our country and its traditions are placed into a distinct perspective—that of a land, where once initial obstacles were overcome, opportunity frequently lay, like a treasure guarded by a slain dragon, open to all who would make it an instrument for their success. The information that is disclosed in these memoirs is documentary evidence, not "hear-say" repetition.

Those who succumbed to the impulse towards autobiography, offer a variety of explanations for making the facts of their lives public. George Santayana,* the American philosopher of Spanish birth, defined autobiography as "a retrospective voyage." In a former immigrant such a "voyage" undoubtedly called forth contradictory emotions. As Emma Goldman† says: "It meant reliving my long forgotten past, the resurrection of memories I did not wish to dig out from the deeps of my consciousness." Sartre offers the explanation that autobiographers recollect their past passions in order to be able to "inter them in a calm cemetery";⁹ another is contained in the admission by David Cornel de Jong:‡ "I felt the need for a little unwinding to help me understand what it was all about"; a third comes from another immigrant writer, Anzia Yezierska,§ the "Sweatshop Cinderella," who said she hoped that if she wrote about her experiences, they would stop hurting. For some it must have been, as it was for Ludwig Lewisohn,‖ an "artistic outlet." For many the incentive was undoubtedly the same as for Benjamin Franklin, John Adams, and Charles Darwin, to mention only a few—namely to preserve the evidence for posterity. But for the immigrant autobiographer there were still other spurs: to crow a bit—in Whitman's phrase—to "celebrate" themselves; to prove that success was possible; to universalize an experience many shared—in the words of one of them#—to tell not a story of "the

*George Santayana, *Persons and Places* (New York, 1944); *The Middle Span* (New York, 1945).

†Emma Goldman, *Living My Life* (New York, 1931).

‡David Cornel de Jong, *With a Dutch Accent* (New York, 1944).

§Anzia Yezierska, *Red Ribbon on a White Horse* (New York, 1950).

‖Ludwig Lewisohn, *Up-Stream* (New York, 1922); *Mid-Channel* (New York, 1929).

#Abraham Rihbany, *A Far Journey* (Boston, 1913).

self," but of "a type"; to register their sentiments about America; perhaps, as Thomas Mann* suggests, to satisfy "educational tendencies" which he sees as inherent in the autobiographical impulse. A recent statement by an English commentator ascribes to the American autobiography a specific motive—that of spreading "the gospel of optimism applied for profit." He says: "[In the American autobiography] . . . the conquest of obstacles is a theme which has never lost its power to exert a vaguely improving influence on others. . . ."[11] This suggests a new angle —that of the foreign-born responding to environmental influences rather than to inner compulsion.

Though the initial impulse undoubtedly came from the awareness of having undergone a special kind of experience, a feeling of "inner necessity" had to be present in order to produce the incitement for dredging up one's memories. One who was often tempted to start his memoirs and went so far as to ask his secretary to take some notes, was Joseph Pulitzer.[12] But though he said: "Well, I somehow wish it could be done," he never did. Despite the assertion of Louis Adamic that his autobiography was intended to add to the rather "meager shelf" of autobiographies by immigrants, the shelf is not a "meager" one; many hundreds of such chronicles exist. An American critic of note observed: ". . . in that flood of books written by newcomers in the land who have tried to crystallize some fresh aspect of American existence, the impulse has been toward the autobiography rather than the novel."[13] Not only the intellectuals or the educated, but even those whose education was scant, or who were entirely self-taught and without intellectual leanings, reveal no little ability in organizing their material and in transmitting their ideas. This ability must be attributed to the educative effect of the American experience.

The flow of subjective writings never stopped. It rose in volume as the movement to America and the hardships immigrants suffered, increased. Those who fled their homelands during the nineteen thirties and forties have fallen into the pattern and have also come forward with their observations on American life.

There is a marked contrast in tone between earlier and later

---

* Thomas Mann, Introduction to *First Papers by Martin Gumpert* (New York, 1941).

chronicles which may be due to the difference in temperament and racial characteristics between the earlier (Northern European) and the later (Southern and Eastern European) newcomers and the conditions they encountered. Earlier chroniclers seem jejune and reportorial, even though, as in the case of Johann August Sutter,* their lives were filled with drama. Later writers are vastly more impassioned, leading one to infer that the vehemence of their response may be a reflection of the severity of their experiences. Thus, the accounts of those caught between the Scylla of unbelievably sordid living conditions and the Charybdis of unrestrained job competition are delivered with a "bang," rather than with a "whimper." These statements are more than stories of human interest. Several contain detailed observations on the progress of the Civil War; others bring back notable personalities in the political and industrial worlds as well as in the arts and letters. A reality is imparted to strikes, the effects of financial panic and depression, that no mere listing of events can. The conquest of the wilderness through the building of railroads by gangs of immigrants—"the stitching of the earth," as one called it,† is reenacted. In this interrelationship between individuals and their time, history comes poignantly alive.

---

*Johann August Sutter, *The Diary of Johann August Sutter* (San Francisco, 1932).

†Stoyan Christowe, *This is My Country* (New York, 1938).

4

"Go West, folks!"

The history of American immigration runs parallel to the development of urban life and the expansion of the frontier. While the constant influx of aliens helped to hasten the metamorphosis of the young nation into an urban civilization which Thomas Jefferson had tried to avert, newcomers also helped to settle the West. In many of the territories foreign stocks contributed towards meeting the population requirements for statehood.

Before 1862 foreigners as well as natives could secure homesteads only through purchase of land. Until the national domain was thrown open to settlers in 1862, the purchase price per acre fluctuated. While native Americans were apt to consider the price of $2.50 per acre high and constantly agitated for free land, to many Europeans such a price seemed a great bargain. This is revealed in the memoirs of a woman* born in Switzerland, who tells that when the family received a letter from an uncle in America, saying: "You cannot do better than to come to America immediately. . . . With us, land is practically given away" (at $2.50 an acre), they sold their property and in 1854 set out for America. It was the enactment of the Homestead Law in 1862 that granted one hundred sixty acres of government land to any settler, native or foreign, who, declaring his intention of becoming a citizen, undertook to live on the land for five years and to make the necessary improvements. Impecunious immigrants, however, could not become settlers, because, though the land was free, a certain amount of money was needed for fees, railroad fare, and such essentials as lumber, agricultural implements, and food until such a time as a crop could be raised. It is frequently forgotten that many of the earlier immigrants brought money with them, which they had realized through the sale of family property, or might have inherited, or might have been given to help them in making a more advantageous start.

---

*Elise Isely, *Sunbonnet Days* (Caldwell, Idaho, 1935).

Money brought from Europe proved a considerable asset to the young nation.

Among the immigrant groups who became settlers in the Middle West were the Germans, the Norwegians, the Swedes, and some Dutch and Swiss. There had been Germans in the colonies since 1683, when William Penn's advertisements induced "Krefelders" to join the newly formed colony of Pennsylvania. A new upswing in German emigration started as the aftermath of the unsuccessful uprisings of 1830 and was swelled by the failure of 1848. The first group became known as *Die Dreissiger,* the second as the "Forty-Eighters." The percentage of intellectuals among these groups was high and included people in all professions—physicians, journalists, writers, teachers, and lawyers. Hatred of slavery caused them to prefer the North, although some chose the South, especially the state of Texas, and fought in the Civil War on the side of the Confederacy. However, the number of German volunteers who fought in the Union armies exceeded by far the number of those who cast their lot with the Confederacy. The tendency of the Germans was to purchase farms already under cultivation in order to assure themselves of immediate subsistence. They were *die Lateinische Bauern,* —Latinists, who, in the words of Crevecoeur, became "cultivators of the soil." Unlike the Scandinavians, the Germans were generally not fit for pioneering. Johann August Roebling,* who settled on a farm in Pennsylvania before he became a pioneer in the construction of suspension bridges, explains: ". . . only poor Americans wander on the frontier accustomed to a wild forest life; these must first clear the path more for the Germans."[14] The number of Germans who arrived here between 1830 and 1900 is held to be about five million.[15] Till the 1850s, the Germans furnished half of our immigration, and thirty-five percent until the late 1880's. Thereafter the German exodus began to drop to about twenty-five thousand annually, due to the fact that Bismarck's reforms removed some of the most conspicuous motives for emigration. Whole regions were turned into German-speaking communities, so that in the 1850s Henry Villard† observed: "While at my uncle's in Belleville [Illinois], I hardly ever heard a word of English, for there was not a single American there."[16]

---

*Johann August Roebling, *Diary of My Journey* (Trenton, 1931).
†Henry Villard, *The Memoirs of Henry Villard* (Boston, 1916).

Sängerfeste, picnics, athletic meets, dramatic and literary clubs, concerts, remained an integral part of their lives. These newly arrived Germans insured the defeat of Senator Douglas, whose concept of "Popular Sovereignty" they detested, and helped to elect Lincoln by campaigning actively for him. (Even earlier, in 1828, the Irish were said to have helped elect Jackson.) The Germans, it was believed, "probably" kept the state of Missouri from going over to the Confederacy.[17] They saw no conflict between their loyalty to German traditions and the German tongue, which they insisted on keeping alive in their children and grandchildren, and the claims of their adopted country.

After the Civil War the favorable legislation under the Homestead Act proved particularly attractive to the Scandinavians. But like all other immigrant groups, many of them, too, chose to remain in the cities. Chicago, for instance, is said to have "more people of Swedish descent than any city except Stockholm."[18] Shiploads of immigrants were conducted to the prairie states by their own countrymen, who went back and forth to shepherd new arrivals across the ocean and in immigrant trains to the West. They were "the farmers without soil who came to a land with soil but no farmers."[19] An agent for the Cunard Line who was responsible for bringing thousands of Norwegians to America, expressed his awareness of the contribution of these hardy agriculturists in these words:

> The Scandinavian American feels a certain sense of ownership in the glorious heritage of American soil . . . and he feels that the blessings he enjoys are not his by favor or sufferance, but by right. . . . For he took possession of the wilderness, endured the hardships of the pioneer, contributed his full share to the grand result accomplished.[20]

These pioneers were escaping from stony crofts that had been subdivided for generations and had become so small that enough food for subsistence could not be raised on them. Their desire for enough land to make them self-sufficient is movingly described by O. E. Rolvaag:

> "Go West! . . . Go West, folks! . . . The farther West, the better the land—. . . Men beheld in feverish dreams the endless plains, teeming with fruitfulness . . . here on the trackless plains, the thousand-year-old hunger of the poor after human happiness had been unloosed.[21]

5

Immigrants in the Cities

At the same time many immigrants went no farther than the city where they disembarked. Conspicuous among them were the Irish, who had been a rural people in England. In America they concentrated in the cities, living in a kind of squalor that shocked native Americans. They became longshoremen, laborers on the canals, the railroads, and riverboats. Later in the century the Jews and the Italians swelled the population of our urban centers to the bursting point. In the cities the Jews found "the shears, the iron and the treadle of the sewing machine,"[22] and the Italians the "pick and shuvvle gangs." It is considered the unique contribution of the "Russian Jew . . . [to have turned] the average American girl into a tailor-made girl."[23]

The cities of the nineteenth century were unprepared for the heavy influx of population which was caused by mounting immigration as well as by the movement of rural elements to the cities. To cite an example, between 1830 and 1850, the years of the heaviest influx from Ireland, New York more than doubled in population, twenty six percent of whom were of Irish birth."[24] The consequence was that our prominent cities, which had been pronounced "beautiful" by foreign visitors, including the acidulous Frances Trollope, early in the century, became increasingly defaced by slums. For instance, in 1831, Roebling considered Philadelphia "the most beautiful city in the world" and asserted that "Berlin, e.g., offers no comparison and seems to be a city of poor oppressed people."[25] At the end of the century John Cournos* was so repelled by conditions in Philadelphia that even after he had removed himself to London, he and the native Philadelphian poet, Hilda Doolittle, amused themselves by jeering at "The City of Brotherly Love." Carl Schurz was charmed with Boston, whereas Chicago with its plank sidewalks, an army of rats scurrying underneath, evoked disgust. Thomas Jefferson's prediction: "Whenever we get piled up on one another in cities, we shall become as corrupt as in Europe and go on eating one

---

*John Cournos, *Autobiography* (New York, 1935).

another as they do there," proved prophetic. But Jefferson could not foresee the extent to which it would become true. According to Jacob A. Riis,* overcrowding in the slum sections of New York's East Side reached three hundred and thirty thousand per square mile, whereas "the densest crowding of Old London . . . never got beyond a hundred and seventy five thousand." In block after block, back-to-back tenements reared their bulk, shutting out air and sunlight. Sinks were in the hallway and the "squeaking pump was the lullaby of tenement house babies." Public bathing facilities were unavailable. Remedial legislation followed the organization of the Board of Health in 1866 and the passage of the "Tenement House Act of 1867."† Tenement landlords made improvements only when compelled to do so and consequently "the packing-box" tenement was still in evidence at the end of the century. By then public bath houses had made their appearance. Jacob A. Riis, who sometimes reveals a startling acerbity in discussing the various immigrant stocks, admits that the "great unwashed" were not so from choice. Immigrants were compelled to pay exorbitant rents for the most delapidated housing—"always one-fourth of the family income, often more."‡

The working conditions were equally wretched. Even in the last quarter of the nineteenth century, a working-day of twelve hours was not unusual. One commentator states: "Ninety hours a week was not uncommon, and in many cases they averaged well over one hundred."[26] This is corroborated by an immigrant in the following description:

> Then come the days when one went to work, when one was farmed out to an employer in a ramshackle building on Attorney Street. This was home and factory. There in three dark, miserable rooms, lived the employer and his wife, with three children, and three machines for making children's shoes. And foul-smelling leather and the dirt and grime and sweat of yesterday's work. Here one worked and one received $1.50 as pay for six days each week. Days which began at seven in the morning. Days which seldom ended before ten at night. Days in a room where meals were cooked and clothing was washed and dried. And children screamed. . . .

*Jacob A. Riis, *How the Other Half Lives* (New York, 1890).
†*Ibid.*, p. 15.
‡Jacob A. Riis, *Battle with the Slum* (New York, 1902) .

If they worked in lofts, they were not better off. Factories were generally unheated during the winter, hot beyond anything Europeans had known during the summer, lit by flaring gas jets all day and filthy and hazardous. The noon-day meal, which was apt to have been brought from home wrapped in newspaper, was eaten at the machine, or on work-tables amidst the cuttings, the shavings, the unfinished work, if not on the floor or on the pavement. From there they returned to their dark and cheerless holes that were freezing in the winter, steamy in the summer, where rats attacked sleeping infants, and inflicted bites that caused scars for life.[27] Whole families, from the oldest to those old enough, the healthy, the infirm, the consumptive, attempted to eke out the family income by working at home, at such jobs as making artificial flowers, wrapping candy, or fashioning trimmings of all kinds. Immigrants did not bring their slums with them; they were forced to live in them. The reality of Chicago's Halsted Street, New York's East Side, Boston's North End, stunned them. One autobiographer stresses the anguish he felt when he visited a relative for the first time, and realized how low he had fallen.* Edward Corsi† tells of his mother's despair when she discovered their East Harlem tenement home from which one could view a patch of sky only from one window. Michael Gold,‡ the son of immigrants, painted a grim picture of slum life. No matter how hard his mother scrubbed, she could not eliminate bedbugs. Awakened at night, he would go into paroxysms of weeping.

In addition there was the feeling that they were let loose in a ruthless, heartless, predatory society. No one cared; no protection was available. One had to accept reality if one wished to survive. People who lacked specific technical skills, and very few possessed those, found out very quickly that only brawn had market value, or that only "strength was appreciated."[28] James Baldwin's statement that he had known too many college-educated handymen applies equally to immigrants, because educated and non-educated alike could find subsistence in manual labor only. The view of a cannibalistic society shows clearly in Michael Gold's statement: "America is so rich and

---

*Marcus E. Ravage, *An American in the Making* (New York, 1917).

†Edward Corsi, *op. cit.*

‡Michael Gold, *Jews Without Money* (New York, 1930).

fat, because it has eaten the tragedy of millions of immigrants."
Similarly, Louis Adamic* quoted a returned Slovenian as saying
that immigrants were considered "dung" in America, the "fertilizer feeding . . . America's . . . greatness." The lament: "Why
did we leave home to come to this?" was not infrequent. Some
did return, sometimes with savings, sometimes more defeated
than ever, but most remained, for the reason that they had nothing to return to. Among the millions who scrambled for a toehold, many continued to live without a shred of hope, getting
more bowed, more misshapen from back-breaking labors, having
accepted that even in America one could expect no more than to
be permitted to draw breath and to keep on laboring for the
minimum necessities with which to sustain life until death ended
the misery. For some the struggle ended with unexpected suddenness. Pascal D'Angelo,† who was familiar with a pick and shovel,
turned this bit of realism into a poem:

> Like a dream that dies in crushed splendor under the weight
>   of awakening,
> He lay, limbs spread in abandon, at the bottom of a smooth
>   hollow of glistening coal.
> We were leaning about on our shovels and sweating,
> Red-faced in the lantern-light,
> Still warm from our frenzied digging and hardly feeling the
>   cold midnight wind.
> He had been a handsome quiet fellow, a family man with
>   whom I had often talked
> Of the petty joys and troubles of our little dark world; in
>   the saloon on Saturday night.
> And there he was now, huge man, an extinguished sun still
>   followed by unseen faithful planets,
> Dawning on dead worlds in an eclipse across myriad stars—
> Vanished like a bubble down the stream of eternity,
> Heedlessly shattered on the majestic falls of some unknown
>   shores,
> And we turned slowly toward home, shivering, straggling
>   sombre—
> Save one youngster who was trying to fool himself and his
>   insistent thoughts,

---

*Louis Adamic, *Laughing in the Jungle* (New York, 1932).
†Pascal d'Angelo, *Pascal D'Angelo Son of Italy* (New York, 1924).

With a carefree joke about the dead man.
Snow began to fall like a white dream through the rude sleep
   of the winter night,
And a wild eyed woman came running out of the darkness.

As dwelling places, Chicago, where refuse from the packing
plants flowed in open sewers, and New York (in this order)
received the most scathing denunciations. The other big cities
were not exempt. It cannot be an accident that immigrants who
were acquainted with New York and Chicago, remembered Chicago as the very embodiment of superhuman malevolence and
iniquity. After the "Haymarket Tragedy" of 1886, Chicago became to many, ipso facto, a symbol of evil. Even people who
were not tainted by radicalism, disliked Chicago. The notorious
Police Captain Bonfield, who played an important role in the
Haymarket trial, was one "whose prowess as a skull-cracker was
fully recognized."[30] In the description of Chicago by Carl Sandburg, the son of Swedish immigrants, as "stormy, husky, brawl-
ing," there is a hint of its repellent characteristics. The Japanese,
Yone Noguchi, who spent some time on the ranch of Joaquin
Miller, the "Byron of Oregon," remarked: "Chicago is as cold
as a jail" and "the God of the Chicagoans is a devil."[31] To Edward
Steiner,* Chicago was a place to inspire "a distinct feeling of
fear, so forbiddingly pitiless it seemed." Even after he had
found security, he said, he breathed easier on his departure from
Chicago. Though Stoyan Chistowe† was fascinated by the vitality
of Chicago, he described it as having "a pump for a heart and
to be stuck-up and gaudy and studded with diamonds." Even the
Swedish novelist, Vilhelm Moberg, writing in the 1950s of the
settlement of Minnesota by the Swedes one hundred years
earlier, says through one of his fictional characters: "This town
was the only place in North America he detested."[32] But in
none of the large cities did immigrants avoid, at least at first,
a desperate struggle with insufficient wages, overwork, hunger,
cold, and worry about unemployment, for all were aware of the
fate that awaited them if their rent went unpaid. His belongings,
as Michael Gold so graphically describes, were put into the
street and neighbors went begging for the destitute family among
one another.

*Edward Steiner, *From Alien to Citizen* (New York, 1914).
†Stoyan Christowe, *op. cit.*

6

The Panaceas of Labor Organization, Socialism, and Anarchism

The natural corollary of the miseries to which the immigrant urban worker was subjected, was to search for amelioration through the labor movement. Early workers had been fortunate, for the problem then had been to secure an adequate work force, not to keep labor in check. But this advantageous position had begun to change even before the Revolution.

The history of American labor is closely linked to the cycle of panic, economic depression, and economic recovery. It was characteristic for combinations of workers to be formed during periods of brisk business activity, to make some gains, which would be wiped out during the business recessions that followed, approximately every twenty years, and oftener. When the economy returned to normal conditions, labor started the uphill fight again.

Though the first broadly based labor organizations—the National Labor Union formed in 1866 and the Noble Order of the Knights of Labor, formed in 1869, had been founded and directed by native labor leaders, foreign-born organizers had begun to enter the labor area since before mid-century. Many of them were Germans who had been trained by Socialist leaders. They were more radical than the British, Scotch, and Welsh workers who aspired to leadership. One of them, the Welsh ironworker, James J. Davis* rose to prominence in his union by advocating restraint in dealing with employers rather than applying pressure. He acquired such admiration for the capitalist system and the panache that surrounded prominent industrialists, that during the Harding administration he found himself rewarded by being appointed Secretary of Labor. Nevertheless, he claims that he considered this honor secondary to being an "educator." He had established through the backing of the Loyal Order of the Moose a resident school in Mooseheart, Indiana, where fatherless chil-

---

*James J. Davis, *Iron Puddler* (New York, 1922).

dren of working men were educated (according to the ideas of Mr. Davis) and widowed mothers and aged workers were taken care of. It was this achievement of which he was proudest.

Unlike Mr. Davis, most labor leaders strove to secure tangible improvements in the lives of laboring people, not to imitate the suavity of employers. Most immigrants, with the exception of the "factory English," and those Germans who had been exposed to trade unionism, had only the haziest notions, if any, of what the functions of a trade union were. Misery, adversity, joblessness proved effective teachers. Many of the early unions considered immigrants, who were largely unskilled workers, unorganizable. Those immigrants who were permitted to join unions, more often than not gave them passionate attachment. People who lived in perpetual dread of unemployment and were wretchedly underpaid, were easy to convince that the union was their only friend, since the government was evidently totally indifferent to their fate; that the union was the only place where a worker counted as a human being. For instance, an official of the cloakmakers union was looked upon by the membership as a "Moses sent to lead the enslaved cloakmakers out of Egypt."[33]

Among labor organizations whose cast was more foreign than native, the cigarmakers, the ladies garment workers and the men's clothing workers unions were in the vanguard. The men's clothing workers forged their strength in one of the most significant strikes in America's labor history—the strike against Hart, Schaeffner & Marx factories in Chicago in 1910. It was led by a recent newcomer—Sidney Hillman and a co-worker whom he was about to marry, Bessie Abramowitz.[34] The International Ladies Garment Workers Union, which embodied the hopes of thousands of the most sweated immigrant workers, also gained a significant victory at that time—when Louis D. Brandeis (to be nominated for the Supreme Court in 1916), helped to negotiate "The Protocols of Peace" between employers and workers, thus making it possible for the union to develop into one of the most forward-looking labor organizations in the trade union movement.

The most important role in the labor movement was reserved for an immigrant from England, Samuel Gompers.* He and his associate, Adolf Strasser, brought several craft unions together in 1881 and in 1886 formed The American Federation of Labor.

---

*Samuel Gompers, *Seventy Years of Life and Labor* (New York, 1925).

Though it was considered "a coffin society" by the more radical I.W.W. (the "Wobblies"), it proved itself the first viable labor organization in America. Gompers held the office of president until his death in 1924, except for one year—1895.

Women workers, too, began to enroll enthusiastically in the trade union movement. They were aided and abetted by the Women's Trade Union League of Chicago,[35] an organization of prominent women who were not necessarly manual workers. Two of their presidents were Jane Addams and Marry McDowell. The spur to union activity was not only the desire to improve wages and working conditions; but also the realization that in union membership they would find social and cultural outlets. A foreign-born woman who rose to unbelievable heights of achievement was the Swedish-born Mary Anderson.* Beginning as a domestic worker, she became a stitcher on shoes and joined the United Boot and Shoe Workers Union, ending her career as Director of the Women's Bureau in the Department of Labor.

Most workers wished only to gain a larger slice of the benefits of the captitalist system, not to destroy it. On the contrary, the hope of being able some day to escape into the entrepreneurial classes animated many who had before them the examples of the frequency with which such metamorphoses were taking place, inspiring them to superhuman efforts. As one remarked, who had risen from printer's devil to becoming the owner of a large printing establishment: "The laborer may become a city contractor; the waiter may some day own a string of hotels— who knows?"[36] Consequently, such hopes died hard.

But there were also those who had become convinced that capitalism was inimical to the welfare of the common man. For them the remedy lay in far-reaching social and economic reforms, which would eliminate a system permitting some to become multi-millionaires and dooming the rest to remaining wage slaves.

These were the people who were drawn to the ideological movements—principally Socialism and Anarchism. Both began to attract disciples at the end of the nineteenth century, the decades of the greatest exploitation and the most severe labor troubles in the history of our nation. Of these, Socialism, estab-

---

*Mary Anderson, *Woman at Work* (Minneapolis, 1951).

lished, as Morris Hillquit tells us, in the 1870's as the Socialist Labor Party,[37] drew the greatest number. Many among them were recently arrived Jewish immigrants to whom Socialism became a religion, one that was entirely consonant with the principles of Judaism. One commentator's opinion is that ". . . for most Jewish Socialists, although often unaware of it, Socialism was Judaism secularized."[38] But Socialism attracted natives as well, who became known as "Yankeefied" Socialists. Among the best known were Edward Bellamy, author of the widely read *Looking Backward*, Eugene V. Debs, son of an Alsatian immigrant, and Norman Thomas, a Presbyterian minister, whose convictions caused him to abandon the ministry for the Socialist lectern. Bellamy and his followers founded the Nationalist Party, which advocated a new social and economic order. Debs became converted to Socialism while serving a prison sentence for his role in the Pullman Strike of 1894. Upon his release he committed himself to Socialism, becoming its standard-bearer. Norman Thomas took over Debs's mantle after his death in 1926. Prominent names among native Socialists included: Henry Demarest Lloyd, a minister's son, who embraced Socialism as an expression of democracy, without becoming a party member; the writers Floyd Dell, Max Eastman, Jack London, and Upton Sinclair. However, much of the strength of the Socialist movement came from the foreign-born and most of the leadership seems to have been supplied by the foreign-born intelligentsia in New York. Among them may be counted: Morris Hillquit,* Daniel de Leon, Oscar Ameringer,† Meyer London, Joseph Barondess, Abraham Cahan, and many others. Abraham Cahan, it is said, considered Socialism as representing "the poetry of the oppressed miserable workman."[39]

Socialism reached its high-water mark in 1912, when close to one million votes were polled and thousands of public offices throughout the nation were captured by Socialist candidates.[40] By 1919 the effectiveness of the Socialist Party had dwindled, partly because of its opposition to World War I, which was viewed as an "imperialist" war, and partly because it had become infiltrated by more radical elements. When the Socialists purged the radicals from their midst, a severe reduction in membership

---

*Morris Hillquit, *Loose Leaves from a Busy Life* (New York, 1934).
†Oscar Ameringer, *If You Don't Weaken* (New York, 1940).

The New Americans

resulted that rendered them impotent. But since many of the Socialist planks were adopted during the twentieth century (with the support of both major parties), Socialist teachings cannot be held to have been without far-reaching effect on the economic and political thinking of America.

The most radical and the most negative of all protest movements was Anarchism, described by a recent commentator as "the last revolt against organization and the last refuge of innocence."[41] In this movement, too, the foreign-born played a large part. Like socialism, anarchism in America began in the 1870's. Its strongest impetus came from the execution of the Haymarket victims. By 1920 the movement was seriously deflated, though terrorist acts continued into the 1920's when the Sacco-Vanzetti trial dominated the news. One of the targets was the home of Judge Thayer, the presiding judge in the trial, and another, the home of a juror. This justifies the conclusion that these violent occurrences were a specific reaction to this particular event. It was Anarchism's dying gasp. Though dynamitings continued to occur during the decades after World War I, they have been attributed to labor saboteurs.

Josiah Warren and Henry David Thoreau, both of old American background, are considered the first American ancestors of the non-violent variety of Anarchism. Josiah Warren was born in Boston in 1799 and lived through three-quarters of the nineteenth century. A disciple of Robert Owen,[42] he attempted several times during his life to implement two distinct Anarchist features: he opened "time stores," where people received credit for what they brought in on the basis of the amount of time spent on producing the article; he also started several "equity villages," where people erected their own homes and lived as they pleased without interference. Thoreau, who was born later—1817—and died earlier—1862—, expressed one of the most basic anarchist principles when he asserted in his essay "Civil Disobedience" (1849): " 'that government is best which governs not at all; and when men are prepared for it, that will be the kind of government they will have." But Anarchism advocating "direct action"—acts of assassination and terrorism—must be considered a foreign bloom. Sponsored by Mikhail Bakunin (and other European revolutionaries), this gospel of violence was exported all over the civilized world. An anarchist in this tradition was Johann Most, who came to Amer-

ica in 1882. A romantic and truculent German, he suffered from
a pronounced inferiority complex, due to his illegitimate birth
and a dislocated jaw which deformed his face. Emma Goldman*
speculated that if not for his disfigurement, he might have turned
to the stage, for which he seemed to have had a conspicuous
talent. There is no clear-cut evidence that Most favored assassination, unless the fact that he published formulae for home-made
bombs may be held as reasonable proof. He specifically dis-
avowed Alexander Berkman's attack on Henry Clay Frick in
1892, thus arousing Berkman, then in prison, to impotent fury.
Like so many European Anarchists, Most was a book-binder†
by profession, and had also been a member of the German
Reichstag. After losing his seat, he betook himself to England,
asylum for many European revolutionaries. He had served prison
sentences in Germany and in Austria and was to serve one in
England before he transferred his activities to America. Here, he
continued to publish his paper—*Freiheit*—and began to make
converts among disillusioned proletarians and radical intellectuals. One reader whom he converted was the youthful Emma
Goldman, then living in Rochester and earning a weekly wage
of $2.50. Despite the violent strikes and the economic upheavals
of the post-Civil War era, the membership remained small. Even
during the hey-day of anarchist influence the membership is said
to have numbered only some "seven thousand . . . in eighty
localities."[43] Not only Anarchists, but conservatives as well, were
horrified at the execution of the Haymarket anarchists and inter-
terpreted it as "judicial murder." For instance, William Dean
Howells remarked in a letter, dated 1887: "The historical perspective is that this free Republic has killed five men for their
opinions."[44]

The two most notorious Anarchists in America were Emma
Goldman ("Red Emma")‡ and Alexander Berkman.§ All Anarchists were not hostile to the American way of life. This is revealed
in the account of a woman, a self-confessed philosophical
Anarchist, who admits to "a reverent, first generation American

---

*Emma Goldman, *Living My Life* (New York, 1931).

†It is interesting to note that in Henry James's novel of anarchist activity
in England—*The Princess Casamassima*—the power behind the movement
is a book-binder.

‡Goldman, *op. cit.*

§Alexander Berkman, *Prison Memoirs of an Anarchist* (New York, 1912).

soul."[45] When her husband expected her to return with him to Russia to show their support for the revolution, she refused because of "my passion for America."

To give frustration and disillusionment as the reasons why some chose to affiliate with a cause that was so futile and offered so little in the way of fruitful results, seems an inadequate explanation. Temperament seems to have been a very important factor. Those who were practical and realistic rejected the futility of the anarchist movement and shrank from the lawlessness inherent in it; those who were unbridled individualists and excessively idealistic to boot, embraced the phantom of an idyllic world without coercion which Anarchism promised.

To Edward Corsi, Commissioner of Immigration under President Hoover, who understood the feelings of immigrants by virtue of his own background, it was the combination of economic *and* intellectual deprivation that drove immigrants into radical movements. He says:

> We come here upon the secrets of the power of radicals in our lives. . . . To the submerged worker at their gatherings this movement is so thrilling, not only because it prophesies this changed social order of equal rights for all in the living present, but also because it gives intellectual and cultural opportunities that are not to be despised.[46]

The American tradition caused Americans to be particularly hostile to the Anarchist credo. Americans were outraged at the implication that our system, considered to be so flexible and adaptable to peaceful change, should be considered so vile ("and by foreigners, at that!") as to require violent overthrow. That the Anarchist group was small, is proved by the fact that the notorious Palmer raids (under President Woodrow Wilson) yielded only two hundred forty-nine radicals who could be deported. Only fifty-nine of them were acknowledged Anarchists.[47] In December of 1919, on the eve of Christmas, these two hundred and forty-nine men and women were ejected from American soil. They were shipped off on the S.S. Buford—the very opposite of a luxury liner—so hurriedly that they were not enabled to bid goodbye to their nearest relatives and friends. They were dumped within walking distance of the Russian border, where they were received with appropriate fanfare.

Almost immediately thereafter the returned Anarchists encountered a shockingly different attitude.[48] A little more than a year after their departure, in April of 1920, the Sacco-Vanzetti case burst upon the public. Liberals and intellectuals flocked to their aid, because it was assumed that the political views of the accused were sufficient to prejudice judicial attitudes against them. This contention has remained a debatable issue to this day.

7

Paths to Success

Inevitably, success came to many. Some grasped it within a surprisingly short period of time; others became "victors on the installment plan."[49] Many had to content themselves with the success of their children. André Maurois recognized this when he wrote: "The wishes that the poor immigrant made for his children . . . have been more or less fulfilled.[50] Immigrant children who watched their parents bear the brutal hardships of immigrant life, were apt to be notoriously lavish with their parents even before they reached a state of affluence. For instance, when the pianist Samuel Chotzinoff* found a coveted summer job as a pianist in a summer hotel, he sent his parents and his younger sister to "the country," so that they too would escape the heat. Michael Gold's angushed cry: "Mother! Momma! . . . I cannot forget you . . ." echoed in the hearts of many children of immigrants. Those who met with financial success found special satisfaction in showering their parents with luxuries they had never dreamt of, endowing institutions and charitable projects in their names. The striving for betterment was as characteristic of immigrants as their toiling for subsistence. To Michael Harrington, who made a study of poverty in mid-twentieth century, the reason that immigrants "were not defeated by their environment" was that they possessed "internal vitality, a will . . . aspiration." He recognized that though they found themselves compelled to live in slums, "they were not slum dwellers." The slums, he declared, were for them, "a way station, a goad to talent."[51]

To say that those who succeeded, did so because of hard work and the opportunities they found in America, is to state the most obvious truths. For those who possessed special mechanical or industrial experience the path was easy. Jobs as shop superintendents and foremen were waiting for them. Andrew Carnegie's

---

*Samuel Chotzinoff, *The Day's at the Morn* (New York, 1963).

autobiography* reveals that throughout the nineteenth century immigrants were no more restricted in reaching the millionaire class than natives. People with technical skills found themselves as welcome as atomic physicists today. Those who had vision to realize that the natural resources were waiting, as it were, to be exploited, or who were able to introduce new processes or new products, found that the climb to "millionairedom" was quicker than anyone could have imagined. Examples are: Charles Fleischmann, Eberhard Faber, Joseph Bulova, H. J. Heinz, Michael Cudahy, August Spreckels, and many others.

Even among the unskilled phenomenal success was not unusual. The immigrant who perceived an opportunity and had the courage to seize it, or possessed the ingenuity to create something new and was willing to work harder than he had ever imagined himself capable of working, often found himself lavishly rewarded. What was needed was the ability to appraise an opportunity as Henry Villard† did, when in his mind's eye he envisioned the state of Oregon criss-crossed by a system of communications; or to have Henry Morgenthau's‡ vision of New York City pushing northward beyond Harlem; or Andrew Carnegie's talent for sensing what would come to be in great demand. Sometimes one needed only to be first with an idea, such as to import Oriental rugs,§ or to mass-produce an item of wearing apparel that had hitherto been made at home.‖ In order to succeed quickly, they expoited not only the people who worked for them, who were often their own countrymen, if not their own kin, but also themselves and their willing wives. "In the sweatshop," one remarked, "the hand and the boss belonged to the same class."# The boss worked no less hard than his "hands."

Though all newcomers wanted desperately to succeed, not all had visions of becoming rich. For many the greatest, the most hoped-for boon was the opportunity for education. Those who were young enough to be sent to school, "the great American

---

*Andrew Carnegie, *The Autobiography of Andrew Carnegie* (New York, 1920).

†Henry Villard, *The Memoirs of Henry Villard* (Boston, 1916).

‡Henry Morgenthau, *All in a Life-Time* (New York, 1922).

§Hagop Bogigian, *In Quest of the Soul of Civilization* (Washington, 1925).

‖Louis Borgenicht, *The Happiest Man* (New York, 1942).

#Ravage, *op. cit.*

Grist-Mill," as Hugo Münsterberg* spoke of the American public school, were assured of being accepted as Americans. But even the young were often unable to finish grammar school. Though it has been recognized that in America "youth is king," immigrant children were not carefree youngsters enjoying the benefits of childhood. Mary Antin,† who became one of the most publicized immigrants, gives a clear idea of the sacrifices that were required to keep her in school. In Mary Antin's case it was her sister, only two years older than herself, who was sent to work. As Mary Antin says: "Frieda [Mary's sister] was relied on for help and her sister [herself] for glory." An affecting story of how some immigrant children managed to finish grammar school, is told by John Cournos.‡ Though less than twelve, he rose at two A.M., even on the coldest winter nights, picked up the early newspaper edition, then sold it to people coming off the night shift before leaving for school.

All newcomers would have appreciated the existence of official channels by which to secure aid or counsel. Though it was recognized that protective legislation was desirable and President Grant requested it,[52] the laissez-faire attitude towards immigrants was never amended. They either sank or swam. But though they received no helping hand, nor any indication of paternalistic interest in their welfare, they had the enormous good fortune not to be hindered from seizing whatever advantages were open to any other residents of the United States. The greatest benefaction offered to them was the grant "of a status equal to that of the older residents."[53] This encouragement towards upward mobility was a variant of the "mudsill" theory (so beloved of President Lincoln) that no one's station in life should be permanently fixed. The fact that immigrants were not held back from reaching for anything open to any one else, proved of incalculable value in the realm of education. A European education was of little practical benefit, except as a mind-sharpener, or as preparation for further study in the United States. But an American education was an open sesame to a respected position in the American world. Consequently, many of those who were not too old or too apathetic to be stirred by

---

*Hugo Münsterberg, *The Americans* (New York, 1904).

†Mary Antin, *The Promised Land* (Boston, 1912).

‡John Cournos, *Autobiography* (New York, 1935).

dreams of self-betterment, saw unlimited possibilities opening before their eyes. The reaction of Mary Antin's father (who was bitterly disappointed about his own lack of success), that education was "the essence of American opportunity, the treasure that no thief could touch, not even misfortune or poverty," would have been understood by all foreigners. People of all nationalities and backgrounds were affected by the desire to dip into this "treasure." A Hindu student explains why the hope of a college education represented an oasis in the desert of their reality. "Colleges are far kinder than anything or any place else," he stated. "They give you knowledge without hurting you."[54]

The strongest encouragement lay in the fact that some colleges were known to provide the opportunity to work while attending school. Since the only obstacle was the accumulation of an initial sum of money, any sacrifice became worthwhile, and any job bearable. New York City preparatory schools did a "land-office" business. The foreign-born of all nationalities—Italians, Scandinavians, Syrians, Slavs, Jews—were affected by the "diploma-mania"[55] attributed to the Jews. The same authors who state that the Jews "wherever they went . . . showed a fierce passion to have their children educated and become professionals,"[56] state that the Italians repeated the pattern "on a smaller scale and a generation later."[57] How they succeeded forms an impressive saga, which demonstrates that material success was not the only aspect of the immigrant success story.

8

The Lure of Education

Though most newcomers were of "the huddled and the poor," the children of some of them had either received the beginnings of a classical education or they came from families where there was a tradition of reverence for learning. For instance, Morris Hillquit tells us that he had all but completed the course of studies at the Gymnasium of Riga when the time for the family's departure arrived. Michael Pupin, Louis Adamic, and Stoyan Christowe, among others, had been Gymnasium students before they left their natal countries. Selman Waksman,* discoverer of streptomycin, had all the preparation necessary for entering college, and since he was fortunate in having relatives to lean on, he entered Rutgers University within months of arrival. It was to be expected that people of this caliber would continue their education with all the haste possible. But even those who had had scant schooling, if any, began to dream of overcoming this handicap and of securing the much coveted advantage of education.

Foreigners residing in New York City were fortunate in having Cooper Union and the College of the City of New York. Cooper Union became a starting-point for countless immigrants in quest of self-improvement. Peter Cooper, inventor, financier, and philanthropist, had founded the institution in 1859. It proved an intellectual oasis; its effect on the foreign population cannot be overestimated. Andrew Carnegie was so impressed by the variety of functions and services which Cooper Union performed, that he recommended the endowment of similar institutions to nineteenth century millionaires who were desirous of easing their consciences. It seemed to him the best way "to return surplus wealth to the mass of their fellows in the forms best calculated to do lasting good."[58] In addition to free education in engineering and in some branches of science, the intellectual fare offered by Cooper Union consisted of lectures, debates, rallies, and mass

---

*Selman Waksman, *My Life with the Microbes* (New York, 1954).

meetings. The audiences were introduced to some of the greatest political figures of their day. Presidential aspirant Abraham Lincoln, Carl Schurz, Governor Altgeld of Illinois, Henry George, Eugene Debs, Morris Hllquit, Norman Thomas, and many others appeared on Cooper Union's rostrum. A large number of immigrants were always in the audience. To some Cooper Union represented all the intellectual stimulation they would ever get; for others it was a stepping stone to greater opportunities. For instance, Michael Pupin* inched his way towards Columbia College by attending Cooper Union at night. Louis Waldman,† labor lawyer, studied engineering at Cooper Union first before turning to the study of the law. Carl Christian Jensen,‡ social scientist, began his education by attending Cooper Union at night. Samuel Gompers, who was entirely self-educated, speaks of satisfying his "intense mental hunger" at Cooper Union. Justice Frankfurter,§ too, paid homage to this famous institution. He says he found it "exciting" to be able to read the various daily newspapers of the United States on its top floor.

Higher education was a difficult goal to achieve for natives as well as for the foreign-born, unless there was assurance of financial support. The significant point in this connection is that it was not made harder for foreigners to secure an education than for natives. The story of Samuel S. McClure‖ illustrates the difficulties that stood in the way of many young people. In order to be able to attend the newly opened high school in Valparaiso, Indiana, he had to hire himself out as a chore boy to a local family in order to be assured of his food and lodging. When his help was needed on the farm, he left school. After the death of his stepfather he felt it incumbent upon him to run the farm for his twice-widowed mother. Carl Sandburg might not have been able to go to Lombard College, if not for his enlistment in the Spanish-American War. Because young people frequently missed a secondary education, some colleges offered preparation on the secondary school level as part of the college course.

---

*Michael Pupin, *From Immigrant to Inventor* (New York, 1923).

†Louis Waldman, *Labor Lawyer* (New York, 1944).

‡Carl Christian Jensen, *An American Saga* (New York, 1927).

§Felix Frankfurter, *Felix Frankfurter Reminisces* (New York, 1960).

‖Samuel S. McClure, *My Autobiography* (New York, 1914).

The sacrifices to which young people submitted willingly in quest of education, form an impressive record. Like Samuel McClure, who lived in a state of semi-starvation throughout his student years at Knox College, many went cold and hungry for years on end. The statement that one did not possess an overcoat for years, or that, at last, it was purchased second-hand, or at a fire-sale, or that it was acquired at the local morgue, is not unusual. It was a difficult task to save the money for transportation alone. Fred Kenyon Brown,* who was born in England, tells that when he set out for the Evangelical College at Groat's Crossing in Michigan, all he owned was the sum of twenty dollars he had saved over years of labor in the mills of New Bedford. He spent most of it on fare and when he presented himself at the college, he was told it was not unusual for a student to possess no money—that someone had arrived in possession of four cents.

Sometimes impecunious students traveled on cattle trains in charge of cattle. For Edward Steiner it proved calamitous, for professional cattle tenders threw him off the train, crippling him, and stole all his money.

Free tuition at the College of the City of New York proved an inestimable advantage to ambitious young New Yorkers. Numerous of the foreign-born received their education there and went forth to gather laurels for themselves and their alma mater in teaching, medicine, the sciences, the law, and in other branches of the humanistic professions.

The heroes and heroines of the foreign-born were their teachers. They taught the language, lent books, coached in speech as well as manners, and protected young aliens from taunts and jeers. One of the reasons why Mary Antin became such an enthusiastic American so quickly and why she became known as a talented immigrant, was because of the encouragement she received from her teachers, who sent her poems and patriotic effusions to the newspapers and helped her in every way. Angelo Pellegrini,† an Italian immigrant boy in the state of Washington, was another who admits he was groomed by his teachers and encouraged to go on to college and graduate school. In addition to being helpful, teachers were usually tactful. Stoyan Christowe, a native

*Fred Kenyon Brown, *Through the Mill* (Boston, 1911); *Through the School* (Boston, 1912).
†Angelo Pellegrini, *Immigrant's Return* (New York, 1953).

of the Balkans, who admits to a conspicuous accent, mentions
that the president of Valparaiso University was the first person
who did not embarrass him by making his first question an
inquiry where he came from. Maurice Hindus,* describing his
reception by Dr. Rollins, principal of Stuyvesant High School
in New York City, says of him: "He might have been an uncle
whom I was seeing for the first time." Michael Shadid† mentions
that "one of my teachers . . . took a particular interest in me,
encouraging me in my determination to study medicine." At
the medical school of George Washington University in St. Louis,
he says, his instructor in anatomy was one "to whom I felt I
could go with any problem." Selman Waksman appreciated his
relationship with one of his teachers so much that he named his
son after him. Max Thorek,‡ a Chicagoan, found in the dean
of medical students at Rush Medical College "my greatest
mentor . . . whose interest in me was more than perfunctory."
Teachers advanced money or made loans possible. For instance,
a young man who graduated from the University of Wisconsin
and went on to become a journalist, tells that one of his teachers,
a woman, countersigned a note so that his family would be
protected during a workless winter.[59] The absence of discrimination in American schools and the sympathetic attitude of American teachers during what Ludwig Lewisohn calls "the years of
the primitive Republic" (at the turn of the century), were of
primary influence in redirecting the lives of those who were able
to avail themselves of higher education in American schools. The
picture changed during the early decades of the twentieth
century. Indivious nativist propaganda by the Immigration Restriction League and other groups and individuals, which stressed
the inferiority of certain racial stocks, succeeded in erecting bars
to the ambitions of those they stamped as "undesirable." A
recent study states that in 1922, President Lowell of Harvard
openly proposed a Jewish quota and that in 1945, President
Hopkins of Dartmouth openly defended a quota policy, but
that these objections have now declined.[60]

---

*Maurice Hindus, *Green Worlds* (New York, 1938).
†Michael Shadid, *Doctor for the People* (New York, 1939).
‡Max Thorek, *A Surgeon's World* (Philadelphia, 1943).

9

The Attitude of Immigrants

While all the professions claimed their share of votaries among the foreign-born, the choice of occupation seems in no small degree to have been influenced by the immigrant experience. Fervent declarations of gratitude for the opportunities that had opened the doors to achievement and respectable positions, encourage the belief that the guiding motive in deciding one's sphere of work was often the desire to serve less fortunate fellow immigrants, and in that way one's community and country.

The dedication that some of the foreign-born felt to their own people is expressed in the words of a physician Max Thorek. When he was ready to "hang up his shingle," his choice of neighborhood, he says, was dictated by "my heart." In his words:

> I know what it means to be a stranger in a strange land, hearing a strange tongue, eating strange food, bewildered by strange customs. I had a fellow feeling for those dwellers in the multiple ghettoes of Chicago. My place was in their midst.

Another confirmation of this premise that the immigrant experience often influenced the choice of vocation, may be found in the career of Jacob A. Riis.* He states unequivocally that he turned to journalism because he felt that as a journalist he could crusade against slums and anti-social tendencies to which he had been exposed during his immigrant days. Though the foreign-born themselves were less prone to criminality than their American-born children, moral disintegration was a serious threat to the first as well as to the second generation. It was possible, Morris Raphael Cohen stated, "for the same family to produce saints and sinners, philosophers and gunmen." Social betterment was a banner under which "uplifters"—physicians, labor lawyers, teachers, crusading journalists, labor leaders, and others could rally.

*Jacob A. Riis, *The Making of an American* (New York, 1947).

No group indicates more clearly than ministers and social workers that people of immigrant background were drawn to this work by the awareness of how urgently their help and guidance were needed. To immigrants in the grip of misfortune the social worker who knew of such situations only from hear-say, was apt to seem too scientific, detached, even heartless. Foreign-born social workers and settlement directors, to whom such difficulties were not unknown, could be expected to respond with understanding and empathy. The immigrant experience was responsible for directing many people into the ministry and sometimes even for redirecting them to other faiths.[61] While the effect of America on some people was to loosen the bonds of orthodoxy, others became more dependent on the solace of religion. From the immigrant communities came many who were sincerely committed to work for social betterment, not only among their own people, but among all underprivileged groups. A very good example is Edward Corsi, who acted as Director of Relief in New York during the days of the Depression.

Though one encounters more praise than criticism for the American way of life, the amount of indictment is not negligible. There are indictments on intellectual grounds, but criticism is most frequently directed against the miseries of daily life—exploitation at work, fear of unemployment, the drabness of life in filthy and congested quarters, and the fact that immigrants were without any protection whatever. "Why is the government so indifferent to the miserable life of those who produce the wealth of this country?" was the cry of one, "Is this country free only for capitalism?"[62] George Engels, one of the eight found guilty of having precipitated the explosion at Haymarket in Chicago, put it more strongly. He said: "Can anyone feel any respect for a government that accords rights only to the privileged classes and none to the workers?"[63]

The most serious attackers happen to be writers and journalists. Among them is a Filipino poet* who makes a moving attack on race prejudice on the West Coast and a West Indian† who was bitterly opposed to the principle that the Negro who wants to live in America must accept a position of inferiority. One who assailed

---

*Carlos Bulosan, *America is in the Heart* (New York, 1943).

†Claude McKay, *A Long Way From Home* (New York, 1937).

51

discrimination on religious grounds was Ludwig Lewisohn. His indictment also includes insincerity, philistinism, intellectual shallowness, and repressive Puritanism. Though Lewisohn lived in voluntary exile·for many years, he professed nostalgia for and attachment to the physical America. Louis Adamic* is another critic, one who condemned the Darwinian aspect of the American system, while claiming affection for other character-istics of American life. His view of America during the early decades of the twentieth century, as a place in which an indi-vidual could not flourish without possessing some of the defensive mechanisms of jungle inhabitants, is shared by John Cournos.† Though more gentle than Adamic, Cournos made a bitter and telling attack on "Big Business" and its "supposed function of running the Universe." Other complaints mention brutal treat-ment by the police and by immigration officials, personal dis-honesty and sharp dealings, the tendency to resort to violence, and above all, the lack of concern in their welfare.

A subject which is rarely overlooked by intelligent Europeans is the intense race consciousness of Americans. The repulsion pre-Civil War settlers felt for such spectacles as slave auctions and corporal punishment administered to slaves, has given way to the recognition that the integration of the Negro is America's most serious unsolved problem. The Negro problem has not only caught the attention of such distinguished minds as Albert Einstein's and Jacques Maritain's, but many of the educated refugees have commented on it as a conspicuously American concern.

However, fervent declarations of gratitude and a passionate concern that the meaning of Americanism be properly appreci-ated in the world, are more prevalent than criticism. As for visitors, the tendency to recognize the idealism of Americans, to praise their regard for the individual and for freedom under democracy, has become markedly more generous. Also, it is generally recognized that Americans are inclined to be tolerant and understanding of foreigners. Jacques Maritain (and others, as well) sees this tolerance for foreigners as being due to "the perpetual arrival of a new first-generation of immigrants." His fellow Frenchman, André Maurois, puts it this way: "America

---

*Adamic, *op. cit.*
†Cournos, *op. cit.*

is not and never will be something that is finished but (in Joyce's words)—a work in progress."[64]

One charge that has been hurled at Americans since the beginning of the national establishment, is that of materialism. In the eighteen-twenties Frances Trollope remarked with what undoubtedly was intended to be withering sarcasm:

> . . . could they once be thoroughly persuaded that any point of the ocean had a hoard of dollars beneath it, I have not the slightest doubt that in about eighteen months we should see a snug-covered railroad leading direct to the spot.[65]

An interesting reaction to America's materialism as compared to materialism in other places was Robert Frost's, whose lineage goes back to a period before Mrs. Trollope's presence graced the frontier town of Cincinnati. While Frost said: "I never deny that we are a materialistic nation," he declared Sao Paulo to be "the most materialistic city in the entire Western hemisphere.[66] Having been sent as a cultural emissary, his status was that of a visitor. Could we deduce therefrom that visitors to foreign lands share a tendency to develop "blind spots" toward the host country, as well as "fresh, significant insights," which is Jacques Maritian's claim? This suggestion is supported by the fact that those who have been exposed to the American climate for a reasonably long period, vehemently deny that America is materialistic. From Roebling on, many people of foreign birth have asserted that Europeans are much more materialistic than Americans. Edward Bok* stamped the Dutch as being much more in the clutches of materialism than Americans, and Angelo Pellegrini† was appalled at the materialistic spirit exhibited in Italy during the years following World War II. As for the French, no one can deny that Balzac's presentations of the French character clearly establish the French as being thoroughly in the grip of Mammon. We also have an ardent defender (in this respect) in Hugo Münsterberg, who sees in the fact that American men scorn dowries a refutation of the spirit of materialism. Jacques Maritain goes furthest in upholding America as "the least materialistic among the modern peoples which have attained the industrial age."[67]

---

*Edward W. Bok, *The Americanization of Edward Bok* (New York, 1922).
†Pellegrini, *op cit.*

To claim that newcomers have made enormous contributions to the physical growth and the economic as well as the intellectual development of our nation, requires no emphasis. Also it would be supererogatory to do more than offer a reminder that immigrants changed America no less than they were made over by America. The purpose of this attempt is not to pile proof where proof is not required, but rather to jog the memory in regard 'to some aspects of our national experience that have become dim because they have been so thoroughly accepted. There are among America's immigrants many whose role in our society has made them legendary figures. However, there are many more, who are less well known, or not known at all, who deserve to be better known. This is one of the reasons why they are being summoned to repeat their messages in the pages that follow.

The number of people who appear in this volume is an infinitesimal percentage of the multitudes who came to America to make homes for themselves and their progeny, and those whom curiosity and other reasons (some of them materialistic) brought here for limited periods. Many of the foreign-born who deserve to be considered among the "builders of our nation" left no record of their lives and are therefore not represented here, because in order to include them, it would have been necessary to depend on other people's interpretations of what they thought of and did for America.

Though not all who appear in these pages are autobiographers, every statement credited to an individual has been made by him, not by others about him. The reason for including comments by visitors is that they often represent the response of an outsider to a new situation. More objectivity may be expected of them than of those who had made their "beds here and had to lie in them." The mirror that is held up by strangers is not a mirror we are accustomed to using. Sometimes it reflects an image flattering to ourselves and at other times it returns what may strike us as distortions of the national picture. We should recognize ourselves despite the distortions. What unites all is that they speak in their own voices.

Since many hundreds of such records exist, choice had to be exercised. It was dictated by the following aims: to assemble only the most meaningful statements and to omit those that seem trivial, insincere, or unworthy of the subject; to underline the specific contributions some individuals were enabled to make through the catalytic action of the American system; to show how unsuspected abilities and talents were brought to the surface by the compound of adversity and opportunity, both of which were abundantly supplied by the American environment. The salient points should be implicit, if not always explicit.

And now let us summon the witnesses.

NOTES

1. Philip Rahv, *Literature in America* (New York, 1957), p. 12.
2. David Felix, *Protest* (Bloomington, 1965).
3. Eric F. Goldman, *Crucial Decade* (New York, 1956), p. 128.
4. Edward N. Saveth, *American Historians and European Immigrants* (New York, 1948).
5. Edward Corsi, *In the Shadow of Liberty* (New York, 1935).
6. Eva Lips, *Rebirth in Liberty* (New York, 1942).
7. Nathan Glazer and Daniel Patrick Moynihan, *Beyond the Melting Pot* (Cambridge, 1963).
8. Helene S. Zahler, *The American Paradox* (New York, 1964). This phrase means the difference between customs among immigrants.
9. Quoted by Roy Pascal, *Design and Truth in Autobiography* (Cambridge, 1960).
10. Thomas Mann, Introduction to *First Papers by Martin Gumpert*, New York, 1941.
11. "The Reflecting Mirror," *The American Imagination, A Critical Survey of the Arts from the Times Literary Supplement* (New York, 1960), p. 54.
12. Alleyne Ireland, *Joseph Pulitzer* (New York, 1914).
13. Constance Rourke, *American Humor* (New York, 1953), p. 221.
14. Johann August Roebling, *Diary Of My Journey* (Trenton, 1931).
15. Francis J. Brown and Joseph S. Roucek, *One America* (New York, 1952), p. 111.
16. Henry Villard, *The Memoirs of Henry Villard* (Boston, 1916), p. 391.
17. George M. Stephenson, *History of American Immigration* (Boston, 1926), p. 134.
18. Albert Q. Maisel, *They All Chose America* (New York, 1951).
19. The phrase is used by Vilhelm Moberg in *The Last Letter Home* (New York, 1961).
20. Hans Mattson, *The Story of an Emigrant* (St. Paul, 1891).
21. O. E. Rolvaag, *Giants in the Earth* (New York, 1927).
22. Oscar and Mary F. Handlin, *A Century of Jewish Immigration to the United States* (Philadelphia, 1949), p. 18.
23. Abraham Cahan, *The Rise of David Levinsky* (New York, 1917).

55

24. William V. Shannon, *The American Irish* (New York, 1963), p. 38.
25. Roebling, *op. cit.*
26. Henry David, *The History of the Haymarket Affair* (New York, 1936), p. 160.
27. Max Thorek, *A Surgeon's World* (Philadelphia, 1943).
28. Theodore Saloutos, *They Remember America* (Berkeley, 1956).
29. Michael Gold, *Jews Without Money* (New York, 1930).
30. David, *op. cit.*, p. 192.
31. Yone Noguchi, *The Story of Yone Noguchi* (London, 1914).
32. Vilhelm Moberg, *Unto a Good Land* (New York, 1954), p. 13.
33. Abraham Rosenberg, unpublished MS *"Memoirs of a Cloakmaker"* translated from the Yiddish by Yetta Jay.
34. Mary Anderson, *Woman at Work* (Minneapolis, 1951).
35. *Ibid.*
36. Gregory Weinstein, *The Ardent Eighties and After* (New York, 1947).
37. Morris Hillquit, *Loose Leaves from a Busy Life* (New York, 1935), p. 324.
38. Moses Rischin, *The Promised City* (Boston, 1962), p. 166.
39. *Ibid.*
40. Joseph G. Rayback, *A History of American Labor* (New York, 1959).
41. Ihab Hassan, *Radical Innocence* (Princeton, 1961), p. 68.
42. James Joll, *The Anarchists* (Boston, 1964).
43. Harvey Goldberg, ed., *American Radicals* (New York, 1957), p. 244.
44. Quoted by Van Wyck Brooks, *New England: Indian Summer* (New York, 1949), p. 38.
45. Lucy Robins Lang, *Tomorrow is Beautiful* (New York, 1948).
46. Corsi, *op. cit.*
47. Sidney Fine, "Anarchism and the Assassination of McKinley," *The American Historical Review*, X, No. 4 (July, 1955), 777-799.
48. Emma Goldman, *Living My Life* (New York, 1931).
49. The phrase is used by David Felix, *op. cit.*, in referring to immigrants and workers.
50. André Maurois, *From the New Freedom to the New Frontier* (New York, 1963), p. 345.
51. Michael Harrington, *The Other America* (New York, 1962), p. 10.
52. Stephenson, *op. cit.*, p. 253.
53. Oscar Handlin, *The Uprooted* (Boston, 1951), p. 5.
54. Dhan Gopal Mukerji, *Caste and Outcast* (New York, 1923).
55. Will Herberg, *Protestant, Catholic And Jew* (New York, 1955).
56. Glazer & Moynihan, *op. cit.*, p. 143.
57. *Ibid.*, p. 206.
58. Andrew Carnegie, "Wealth," *North American Review*, CXLVIII (June, 1889), 253-264, *passim*.
59. Elias Tobenkin, "What America Did For Me," *Success*, IX, No. 3 (March, 1925), 18-19, 90, 108-109.
60. Glazer & Moynihan, *op. cit.*, p. 158.
61. Examples are: Constantine Panunzio, *The Soul of an Immigrant* (New York, 1921); born a Catholic, he was ordained a Protestant minister. Edward Steiner, *From Alien to Citizen* (New York, 1914); born a Jew, he became a Protestant minister. Max Wertheimer, *From Rabbinism*

to Christ (Ada, Ohio, 1934); a rabbi, he became a Baptist minister. Abraham Rihbany, *A Far Journey* (Boston, 1913); born of Greek Orthodox parents, he became a Protestant minister.

62. Elizabeth Hasanovitz, *One of Them* (Boston, 1918).
63. Henry David, *The History of the Haymarket Affair* (New York, 1936).
64. Maurois, *op. cit.*
65. Frances Trollope, *The Domestic Manners of the Americans* (London, 1831).
66. Louis Mertins, *Frost: Talks Awalking* (Norman, Oklahoma, 1965), p. 335.
67. Jacques Maritain, *Reflections on America* (New York, 1958).

PART TWO

IN THE BEGINNING

From 1607 to the 1830's

... "yea, I say the Action being well followed ...
will tend to the everlasting renowne of our Nation, and to the exceeding good and benefit of our
Weale publicke in generall, whose Counsells, labours, godly and industrious endeavours, I be-
seech the mighty Jehovah to blesse, prosper, and
further, with his heavenly ayde, and holy assistance ..."

Captain John Smith

10

A New World Beckons

> ". . . no friends to wellcome them, nor inns to
> entertaine or refresh their weatherbeaten bodys,
> no houses or much less townes to repaire too, to
> seeke for succoure . . ."
>
> William Bradford
> *History of Plymouth Plantation*

The American experiment was begun by clusters of intrepid people traveling in groups of about one hundred. Some were adventurers—soldiers of fortune—others sought to establish the Kingdom of God on earth, where their religious beliefs would not be interfered with. They formed enclaves that were tiny, vulnerable dots in a wilderness stretching along the shore of the Atlantic. During the "seasoning" process, at least a half died. Those who survived, suffered from starvation, illness, fear. In this way they built their first homes, raised their food, dealt with the Indians and shipped back furs, fish, tobacco and other products of a virgin country, which they exchanged for commodities they needed for survival, or which went towards the reduction of their indebtedness to the backers who had made their emigration possible.

The growth of the American experiment was dynamic; the increase in population continuous and greater than in Europe. Accurate figures are lacking until 1790, but it is held that the population of the colonies doubled approximately every twenty-five years. By 1700 the population is estimated at about 250,000; in 1725 at about 500,000; in 1740 one million; in 1760 one and a half million. This high rate of accretion is attributable not only to immigration, but also to longevity and a high birth rate due to early marriages. From the seaboard, settlement fanned out into the interior, filling the backcountry of Pennsylvania, Maryland, Virginia, and the Carolinas.

Among the early immigrants were not only the English-speaking peoples (English, Irish, Scotch-Irish, and Welsh), but also the Dutch, Germans from the Rhine valley, Swiss, and

Huguenots. While the bulk were agriculturists, some were craftsmen, or turned to trade. Among the Scotch-Irish many showed an interest in politics and education. They are responsible for establishing the first academies and log colleges.

By the time of the Revolution all the earlier stocks—the English, the Scotch-Irish, the Dutch, the Swedes in Delaware, had been thoroughly assimilated, with, perhaps, the exception of the "Pennsylvania Dutch," who have retained some of their characteristics to this day. Between the Revolution and 1815, the influx of aliens was comparatively light—about one quarter of a million; after 1820 immigration increased sharply. But among the newcomers at the turn of the century were individuals who enriched the young nation enormously by their skills, energies, and prestige. Among them were: Joseph Priestley, from England, discoverer of oxygen, who had suffered persecution in England due to his attitude of favoring the French Revolution; Samuel Slater, also from England, who carried in his head the model of the spinning machine and thus laid the foundation for the manufacture of textiles in America; Albert Gallatin from Switzerland, who became Jefferson's secretary of the treasury; John Jacob Astor from Germany, who started the American Fur Company and became the country's richest man before the Civil War; the journalists Mathew Carey and William Cobbett from Ireland and England respectively, whose running war of words about issues of their day, roiled the tempers of many Philadelphians.

Through the eyes of people who were accustomed to riper civilizations, we perceive the pattern of our society's growth. Though the outline may be faint, the thread of progress is clearly discernible.

11

Comment from 1607 to the 1830's

John Smith
Soldier, Adventurer, Colonizer, Explorer
1580-1631

> . . . the action [is] most honorable, and the end
> to the high glory of God, to the erecting of true
> religion among Infidells, to the overthrow of
> superstition and Idolatrie, to the winning of many
> thousands of wandring sheepe, unto Christs fold,
> who now, and till now, have strayed in the un-
> knowne paths of Paganism, Idolatrie and super-
> stition.

These pious considerations are given by John Smith as the
motives for English colonization on the North American continent. As one of the leaders in the planting of the first colony
which survived—Jamestown—founded in 1607, he occupies a
unique place in the history of the development of North America. He was the first to describe that part of the new world
claimed by Great Britain in *A True Relation*, published in
1608. His is also the distinction of being the first to mention
Pocahontas, who is supposed to have rescued him from decapi-
tation at the court of her father, Powhatan.

As a soldier of fortune he had served the French, Dutch, and
Transylvanian armies (against the Turks) since the age of fifteen. After his return to England, a new and exciting opportunity
awaited him, that of joining a group of colonists sailing for
Virginia. Twenty-seven years of age, he proved himself to be
a dauntless, resourceful leader, who displayed unusual ability
in dealing with the Indians and in procuring food for his
starving colony. He showed less aptitude for harmonious relations with the other members of the council for the colony.
Twice he was faced with death at the hands of his rivals and

was saved only by miraculous intervention. In 1609 he suffered
a gunshot wound and had to return to England.

There charges of maladministration awaited him and though
he managed to have them dismissed, the Virginia Company,
which had financed the Jamestown expedition, refused to employ him again. Undaunted, he undertook to explore for different employers the northern parts of the continent, to which
he gave the name of New England. The hope was that he would
bring back gold. But the cargo of fish and furs with which he
returned was a disappointment to the backers and he received
the empty honor of being called "Admiral of New England."
Other explorations in New England proved unsuccessful. His
offers to guide Puritan groups to New England were rejected.

Settling in London, he turned to writing. The intention may
have been to promote colonization, but for a man who had
always sought adventure, it was undoubtedly also a means of
feeding the ego. In 1624 he produced *The Generall Historie
of Virginia* in which he described the first significant Indian
uprising in Virginia, reproduced herein. He had not witnessed it.

FROM *A True Relation**

. . . I can say nothing more then is here written . . . that
the Country is excellent and pleasant, the clime temperate
and health full, the ground fertill and good, the commodities
to be expected (if well followed) many, for our people, the
worst being already past, these former having indured the
heate of the day, whereby those that shall succeede, may at
ease labour for their profit in the most sweete, coole and
temperate shade. . . .

. . . You shall understand that after many crosses in the
downes by tempests, we arrived safely upon the Southwest
part of the great Canaries; within foure or five daies we set
saile for Dominica . . .; the first land we made, wee fell with
Cape Henry, the very mouth of the Bay of Chissiapiacke . . .
the end of June, leaving supplies for thirteen or fourteen weeks

[Having arrived late in April the captain sailed back for
England the end of June, leaving supplies for thirteen or
fourteen weeks] Our provisions being now within twentie

---

*John Smith, *A True Relation* ("Narratives of Early Virginia," Lyon
Gardiner Tyler, ed. [New York: Charles Scribner's Sons, 1930]).

dayes spent, the Indians brought us great store both of Corne and bread ready made: and also there came such an aboundance of Fowles into the Rivers, as greatly refreshed our weake estates, whereuppon many of our weake men were presently able to goe abroad. As yet we had no houses to cover us, our Tents were rotten and our Cabbins worse than nought: our best commoditie was Yron which we made into little chissels. The President and Captaine Martins sicknes, constrayed me to be Cape Marchant, and yet to spare no paines in making houses for the company; who notwithstanding our misery, little ceased their mallice, grudging and muttering. . . .

[A year later in 1608 after many dealings with the Indians] . . . Wee now remaining being in good health, all our men wel contented, free from mutinies, in love with one another, and as we hope in continuall peace with the Indians, where we doubt not but by Gods gracious assistance, and the adventures [backers] willing minds and speedie furtherance to so honorable an action, in after times to see our Nation to enjoy a Country, not onely exceeding pleasant for habitation, but also very profitable for comerce in generall; no doubt pleasing to almightie God, honourable to our gracious Soveraigne, and commodious generally to the whole Kingdome.

FROM *The Generall Historie of Virginia*[*]

. . . such was the treachery of those people [Indians] when they had contrived our destruction, even but two daies before the massacre, they guided our men with much kindnesse thorow the woods and one Browne that lived among them to learne the language they sent home to his Master. Yea, they borrowed our Boats to transport themselves over the River, to consult on the devillish murder that insued, and of our utter extirpation, which God of his mercy (by the meanes of one of themselves converted to Christianitie) prevented; and as well on the Friday morning that fatall day, being the two and twentieth of March, as also in the evening before, as at other times, they came unarmed into our houses, with

---

[*]John Smith, *The Generall Historie of Virginia* ("Narratives of Early Virginia," Lyon Gardiner Tyler ed. [New York: Charles Scribner's Sons, 1930]).

Deers, Turkies, Fish, Fruits and other provisions to sell us; yea in some places sat downe at breakfast with our people, whom immediatly with their owne tooles they slew most barbarously, not sparing either age or sex, man woman or childe; so sudden in their execution, that few or none discerned the weapon or blow that brought them to destruction. In which manner also they slew many of our people at severall works in the fields, well knowing in what places and quarters each of our men were, . . . and by this meanes fell that fatall morning under the bloudy and barbarous hands of that perfidious and inhumane people, three hundred forty-seven men, women and children; mostly by their own weapons. . . .

William Bradford
Builder of Plymouth Colony
1589-1657

. . . Our fathers were Englishmen which came over this great ocean and were ready to perish in this willderness, but they cried unto the Lord, and he heard their voyce, and looked on their adversities, etc. Let them therefore praise the Lord, because he is good and his mercies endure for ever.

As he gazed on the bleak shore of Cape Cod in November of 1620, William Bradford imagined what future generations would think, and he bade them not to forget the mercies of Divine Providence that had preserved their forefathers. These biblical phrases convey the strength of the faith that had sustained these emigrants in their perilous search for a haven in the New World. They were the "Pilgrims"; their avowed intention was to live by the word of God. In consequence, they created what was to be known as a "Bible Commonwealth."

William Bradford had been a religious dissenter since his middle teens. In 1609 he had fled with the congregation of William Brewster to Holland and in 1620 he left on the Mayflower with part of that group for the New World. Whereas the "Puritans" who were to follow ten years later professed to aim only at purification of the Church of England, to the Pilgrims, who were Separatists, it was beyond redemption. Before leaving the Mayflower, these Pilgrims bound themselves through a compact into a "civill body politic." What awaited them was starvation, sickness, death, and ever present danger—from Indians, from exposure, from wild animals.

Their first governor, John Carver, died during the first year and Bradford was elected in his place. He was reelected every year until 1656, except for four separate years when he begged off. Bradford guided the colony, legislated, and sank the iron of his moral force deep into the lives of the people. Seven years after they had come to New England, Bradford and several of the original settlers assumed the debt of eighteen hundred pounds that bound them to the merchant adventurers who had financed their emigration and distributed the land as well as the cattle equally among the original group. The growth of Plymouth was slow; they prospered modestly and in 1691 Plymouth was merged with the much more prosperous Massachusetts Bay Colony.

Ten years after his coming to New England, Bradford began his monumental source book—*The History of Plymouth Plantation,* covering events until 1646. What emerges are not only the difficulties which beset these people, but the thoughts and fears by which they were possessed. The medieval quality of his thinking is visible, particularly in suggesting that "Satane" may have more power in "heathen lands." The manuscript had a mysterious history. It disappeared during the Revolution after having been perused by several colonial historians. In 1855 it was discovered in the library of the Bishop of London at Fulham. It is not known how it found its way there. Through reference to the book, it was recognized as the long lost manuscript of Bradford. At first the Massachusetts Historical Society was given only a copy, but in 1897 the original was returned.

FROM *The History of Plymouth Plantation**

So they lefte that goodly and pleasante citie [Leyden], which had been ther resting place near 12. years; but they knew they were pilgrimes, and looked not much on those

---

*William Bradford, *History of Plymouth Plantation* ("Original Narratives of Early American History" [New York: Charles Scribner's Sons, 1908]).

things but lift up their eyes to the heavens, their dearest cuntree, and quieted their spirits. . . . The next day, the wind being faire, they went aborde, and their friends with them, where truly dollful was the sight of the sade and mournfull parting; to see what sighs and sobbs and praires did sound amongst them, what tears did gush from every eye and pithy speeches peirst each harte; that sundry of the Dutch strangers that stood on the key as spectators could not refraine from tears. . . .

Being thus arived in a good harbor [Cape Cod] and brought safe to land, they fell upon their knees and blessed the God of heaven who had brought them over the vast and furious ocean, and delivered them from all the periles and miseries thereof, againe to set their feete on the firm and stable earth, their proper elemente. . . . And for the season it was winter, and they that know the winters of that cuntree know them to be sharp and violent, and subjecte to cruell and feirce stormes, deangerous to travill to known places, much more to serch an unknown coast. Besids, what could they see but a hidious and desolate wilderness, full of wild beasts and willd men? and what multituds there might be of them they knew not. Nether could they, as it were, goe up to the tope of Pisgah to vew from this willdernes a more goodly cuntree to feed their hops; for which way soever they turnd their eys (safe upward to the heavens) they could have little solace or content in respecte of any outward objects. For summer being done, all things stand upon them with a wetherbeaten face, and the whole cuntree, full of woods and thickets, represented a wild and savage heiw. . . .

In these harde and difficulte beginnings they found some discontents and murmurings arise against some, and mutinous speeches and carriags in other; but they were soone quelled and overcome by the wisdome patience and just and equall carrage of things by the Govr and better part, which clave faithfully togeather in the maine. But that which was most sadd and lamentable was that in 2. or 3. moneths time halfe of their company dyed, espetially in Jan: and February, being the depth of winter, and wanting houses and other comforts; being infected with the scurvie and other diseases, which this long vioage and their inacomodate condition had brought upon them; so as ther dyed sometimes 2. or 3. of a day, in the foresaid time; that of 100. and odd persons scarce 50. remained. . . .

All this while the Indians came skulking about them, and and would sometimes show themselves aloofe of, but when any approached near them, they would rune away. . . . But about the 16. of March a certaine Indian came bouldly amongst them and spoke to them in broken English, which they could well understand, but marvelled at it . . . His name was Samaset; he tould them also of another Indian whose name was Squanto, a native of this place, who had been in England and could speake better English then him selfe. Being, after some time of entertainmente and gifts, dismist, a while after he came againe, . . . and made way for the coming of their great sachem, called Massasoyt; who, about 4. or 5. days after, came with the cheefe of his freinds and other attaendance, with the aforesaid Squanto. With whom, after frendly entertainments, and some gifts given him, they made a peace with him (which hath now continued this 24. years). . . .

[In 1623] All this whille no supply was heard of, neither knew they when they might expecte any. So they begane to thinke how they might raise as much corne as they could, and obtaine a better crope then they had done, that they might not still thus languish in miserie. . . . And so assigned to every family a parcell of land, according to the proportion of their number for that end, only for the present use (but made no devission for inheritance), and ranged all boys and youth under some familie. This had very good success; . . . the women now wente willingly into the feild, and tooke their little-ons with them to set corne, which before would aledg weaknes, and inabilitie, whom to have compelled would have bene thought great tiranie and oppression. . . .

This spring also, those Indians that lived aboute their trading house there fell sick of the small poxe and dyed most miserably; for a sorer disease cannot befall them; they fear it more than the plague; . . . But thos of the English house, (though at first they were afraid of infection,) yet seeing their woefull and sadd condition, and hearing their pitifull cries and lamentations, they had compastion of them, and dayly fetched them wood and water, and made them fires, gott them victuals whilst they lived, and buried them when they dyed. . . But by the marvelous goodness and providens of God not one of the English was so much as sicke, or in the least measure tainted with this disease, though they dayly did these offices for them and for many weeks togeather . . .

Marvilous it may be to see and consider how some kind of wickedness did grow and breake forth here, in a land wher the same was so severly punished when it was knowne; . . . But . . . one reason may be, that Devill may carrie a greater spite against the churches of Christ and the gospell hear, by how much the more they indeaour to preserve holyness and puritie amongst them, and strictly punisheth the contrary when it ariseth either in church or comone wealth; that he might cast a blemish and staine up on them in the eyes of [the] world who use to be rash in judgmente. I would rather think thus, then that Satane hath more power in these heathen lands, as some have thought, then in more Christian actions, espetially over Gods servants in them.

John Winthrop
Governor of Massachusetts Bay Colony
1588-1649

> God Almightie in his most holy and wise provi-
> dence hath soe disposed of the Condicion of man-
> kinde, as in all times some must be rich some
> poore, some highe and eminent in power and
> dignitie; others meane and in subieccion.

One of the most revered names in the history of American settlement is that of John Winthrop. He was elected governor of what was to be the Massachusetts Bay Colony before the departure of the group from England in 1630. Seven ships set sail with the "Arabella" in the lead. This group of emigrants were Puritans. Rev. Higginson, who preached the farewell sermon when they reached Land's End, expressed the difference between the Puritans and the Pilgrims in these words: "We will not say as the Separatists [Pilgrims] were wont to say at their leaving of England, Farewell Babylon, farewell Rome! but we will say, farewell dear England! farewell the church of God in England, and all our Christian friends there! We do not go to New England as Separatists from the Church of England, though we cannot but separate from the corruptions in it, but we go to practice the positive part of church reformation and propagate the gospel in America." The Puritans professed to want only to "purify" the Church of England, not to separate from it. But in New England they completely embraced the Calvinist faith, and even persecuted Anglicans. Their government was based on a covenant with God; their fundamental law was the Bible.

John Winthrop, forty-two years old when he emigrated, was a member of an upper-class family. He had been a student at Cambridge, known as a stronghold of religious dissension. He had received some legal training which shows in his legalistic interpretations of the secular and religious laws of the colony. Of the nineteen years of his life in Massachusetts, he was governor for nine years and deputy governor for ten. A man of massive convictions, he concurred in the banishment of Roger Williams and Anne Hutchinson for heresy. He lived to see the colony thrive, for unlike Plymouth Plantation, the Massachusetts Bay Colony grew in prosperity as well as in population like the proverbial Green Bay Tree. To the Puritans it was an indication of God's special favor.

John Winthrop left an invaluable record of life in America—his *Journal*—which was written in the "plain style" characteristic of Puritan writing. If, as Increase Mather, one of the most influential New England divines, asserted: "God's altar needs not our pollishings," the prose of Governor Winthrop did not call for literary embellishment. Of the three original notebooks, one seemed to be lost, until discovered in 1816 in the tower of the historic Old South Church in Boston. Of greater interest than his *Journal* is his statement—"A Modell of Christian Charity"— composed on board the ship that carried the group to New England. It clearly indicates the depth of his religious convictions and his views on how the colonists should conduct themselves in order to succeed in building the "New Jerusalem."

71

A Modell of Christian Charity.*

Written·
On Boarde the Arrabella,
On the Attlantick Ocean.
By the Honorable JOHN WINTHROP Esquire.

In His passage, (with the great Company of Religious people, of which Christian Tribes he was the Brave Leader, and famous Governor;) from the Island of Great Brittaine, to New-England in the North America. Anno 1630.

Now the onely way to avoyde this shipwracke and to provide for our posterity is to followe the Counsell of Micah, to doe Justly, to loue mercy, to walke humbly with our God, for this end, wee must be knitt together in this worke as one man, wee must entertaine each other in brotherly Affeccion, wee must be willing to abridge our selues of our super-fluities, for the supply of others necessities, wee must vphold a familiar Commerce together in all meekenes, gentlenes, patience and liberallity, wee must delight in eache other, make others Condicions our owne reioyce together, mourne together, labour, and suffer together, allwayes haueing before our eyes our Commission and Community in the worke, our Community as members of the same body, soe shall wee keepe the vnitie of the spirit in the bond of peace, the Lord will be our God and delight to dwell among vs, as his owne people and will commaund a blessing vpon vs in all our wayes, soe that wee shall see much more of his wisdome power goodnes and truthe then formerly wee haue beene acquainted with, wee shall finde that the God of Israell is among vs, when tenn of vs shall be able to resist a thousand of our enemies, when hee shall make vs a prayse and glory, that men shall say of succeeding plantacions: the lord make it like that of New England: for wee must Consider that wee shall be as a Citty vpon a hill, the eies of all people are vppon vs; soe that if wee shall deale falsely with our god in this worke wee haue vndertaken and soe cause him to withdrawe his present help

---

*John Winthrop, *The Winthrop Papers*, (Boston: The Massachusetts Historical Society, 1925).

from vs, wee shall be made a story and a by-word through the world, wee shall open the mouthes of enemies to speake euill of the wayes of god and all professours for Gods sake; wee shall shame the faces of many of gods worthy seruants, and cause theire prayers to be turned into Cursses vpon vs till wee be consumed out of the good land whether wee are goeing. And to shutt vpp this discourse with that exhortacion of Moses that faithfull seruant of the Lord in his last farewell to Israell Deut. 30. Beloued there is now sett before vs life, and good, deathe and euill in that wee are Commaunded this day to loue the Lord our God, and to loue one another to walke in his wayes and to keep his Commaundements and his Ordinance, and his lawes, and the Articles of our Covenant with him that wee may liue and be multiplyed, and the Lord our God may blesse vs in the land whether wee goe to possesse it: But if our heartes shall turne away soe that wee will not obey, but shall be seduced and worshipp [serue *cancelled*] other Gods our pleasures, and proffitts, and serue them; it is propounded vnto vs this day, wee shall surely perishe out of the good Land whether wee passe over this vast Sea to possesse it;

> Therefore lett vs choose life,
> that wee, and our Seede,
> may liue; by obeyeing his
> voyce, and cleaueing to him,
> for hee is our life, and
> our prosperity.

Jasper Danckaerts
Emigrant Leader
1639-1702 (or 1704)

The [Indians] were all lustily drunk, raving, striking, shouting, jumping, fighting each other and foaming at the mouth like raging wild beasts. . . . And this was caused by Christians. . . . How will they escape the horrible judgment of God; how evade the wrath and anger of the Lord and King, Jesus, whom they have so dishonored and defamed, and caused to be defamed among the heathen?

73

This outraged reaction to the debaucheries the colonists encouraged among the Indians, comes from one of the earliest diarists—a Hollander who visited the seaboard colonies in 1679. Danckaerts was a follower of the French Calvinist, Jean de Labadie, who, banished from France, started several religious establishments in Geneva and in Holland. Because the Labadists were a persecuted sect, Danckaerts and a friend were sent to the New World to find a site on which to found a Labadist colony. In New York they met the son of the owner of a large estate in Maryland, who was prevailed upon to sell a tract of land for the settlement of the group. Danchaerts and his friend traveled through Manhattan, Long Island, Delaware, Maryland, upper New York State, New Jersey, and Boston before returning to Holland. In 1683 they brought over a group of followers. The colony grew to about one hundred people, but broke up before the end of the seventeenth century.

The picture this traveler presents is that of thinly strung out settlements. Manhattan may not have been the biblical place of milk and honey, but it was laden with luscious fruit. While he found the Dutch to be hospitable to another Hollander, some of the English struck him as "cross." As a highly moral individual, he was not only sympathetic to the Indians, but also to indentured servants, who struck him as overworked and poorly fed. He was disdainful of "that vile tobacco"; "the sot-weed," as an English hudibrastic poet of the early eighteenth century referred to it. A recent writer used this as part of the title for a novel on an Englishman's experiences in Maryland during the early colonial period. Danckaerts' esteem for those who treated the Indians with consideration, led him to seek out John Eliot, "The Apostle to the Indians," who translated the Old and the New Testaments into the Indian idiom.

Curious about the "only college or would-be academy of the Protestants in all America," he investigated Harvard College, but he was not impressed by the building, the students, or its library.

His manuscript has a curious history. It was discovered in a second-hand bookstall in Amsterdam in 1864 by Henry C. Murphy, corresponding secretary of the Long Island Historical Society, who translated it into English.

FROM *The Journal of Jasper Danckaerts**

. . . As soon as you begin to approach the land [the Narrows], you see not only the woods, hills, dales, green fields and plantations, but also the houses and dwellings of the inhabitants which afford a cheerful and sweet prospect . . . . We came up to the city [Nieuw Amsterdam] about three o'clock, where our ship was quickly overrun with people who came from the shore in all sorts of craft, each one inquiring & searching after his own, and his profit. . . .

. . . As we walked along we saw in different gardens trees full of apples of various kinds, and so laden with peaches and other fruit that one might doubt whether there were more leaves or fruit on them. I have never seen in Europe, in the best seasons such an overflowing abundance.

. . . we came to a road which was entirely covered with peaches. We asked the boy why they left them lying there, and did not let the hogs eat them. He answered, We do not know what to do with them, there are so many; the hogs are satiated with them and will not eat any more. . . .

I must here remark, in passing, that the people in this city, who are almost all traders in small articles, whenever they see an Indian enter the house, who they know has any money, they immediately set about getting hold of him, giving him rum to drink, whereby he is soon caught and becomes half a fool. If he should then buy anything, he is doubly cheated, in the wares, and in the price. . . . They do not rest until they have cajoled him out of all his money, or most of it . . .

[At a Newcastle Plantation] . . . For their usual food the servants have nothing but maize bread to eat, and water to drink, which sometimes is not very good and scarcely enough for life, yet they are compelled to work hard. They are brought from England in great numbers into Maryland, Virginia and Menades and sold each one according to his condition, for a certain term of years, four, five, six, seven or more. And thus they are by hundreds of thousands compelled to spend their lives here and in Virginia and elsewhere in planting that vile

*Jasper Danckaerts, *The Journal of Jasper Danckaerts* ("Original Narratives of Early American History," eds. Bartlett Burleigh James & J. Franklin Jameson [New York: Charles Scribner's Sons, 1913]).

tobacco, which all vanishes into smoke, and is for most part miserably abused. . . .

The lives of the planters in Maryland and Virginia are very godless and profane. They listen neither to God nor his commandments, and have neither church nor cloister. Sometimes there is someone who is called a minister; . . . you hear often that these ministers are worse than anybody else, yea, are an abomination. . . .

We went accordingly, about 6 o'clock in the morning to Rocxbury . . . in order that Mr. Eliot might not be gone from home. . . . On arriving at his house, he was not there. . . . Returning to his house we spoke to him, and he received us politely, as he could speak neither Dutch nor French, and we spoke but little English, we were unable to converse very well; however, partly in Latin, partly in English we managed to understand each other. He was seventy-seven years old and had been forty-eight years in these parts. He had learned very well the language of the Indians, who lived about here. We asked him for an Indian Bible. . . . thereupon he went out and brought us one of the Old Testaments in the Indian language and also almost the whole of the New Testament, . . .

We started out to go to Cambridge. . . . The college building is the most conspicuous among (the houses). We went to it, expecting to see something unusual, as it is the only college, or would-be academy of the Protestants in all America, but we found ourselves mistaken . . . We entered and went upstairs. . . . We found there eight or ten young fellows sitting around, smoking tobacco, with the smoke of which the room was so full, that you could hardly see; and the house smelt so strong of it that when I was going upstairs I said, "It certainly must be also a tavern." . . . They knew hardly a word of Latin, not one of them, so that my comrade could not converse with them. They took us to the library where there was nothing particular. . . .

Hector St. John de Crevecoeur
Soldier, Farmer, Man of Affairs
1735-1813

I am but a feller of trees, a cultivator of land, the most honourable title an American have. I

> have no exploits, no discoveries, no inventions
> to boast of; I have cleared about three hundred
> and seventy acres of land, some for the plough,
> some for the scythe; and this has occupied many
> years of my life. I have never possessed, or wished
> to possess anything more than what could be
> earned or produced by the united industry of
> my family.

One of the most idyllic pictures of rural life to be found in literature is presented by this genial and astute Frenchman in *Letters From An American Farmer*. The inspiration came from living on a farm in New York state before the Revolution. Here a young man worked the soil, raised a family, observed natural phenomena around him—the habits of birds, bees, snakes, hornets, wasps—and at the same time pondered the meaning of Americanism.

Crevecoeur had been a member of the minor nobility. After finishing his education in England, he joined Montcalm's expedition to Canada as an engineer, taking part in the battle of Quebec, which determined that a vast territory be added to "His Majesty's Colonies across the Seas." After the failure of the military mission, he made his way to the British colonies and after some travels settled in New York state, where he married an American woman. For reasons that are not known he was recalled by his father on the eve of the Revolution, was arrested in New York as a spy, and spent some time in prison before being allowed to proceed to France in 1780.

From the tone of some of his writings it is obvious that he was torn between his loyalty to Britain and the new revolutionary spirit and that he was repelled by the excesses of the revolutionaries. When he returned to America in 1783, he found his wife dead, his farms burned and his children scattered. In his new job, that of French consul-general to the United States, he tried to promote trade between France and the United States and to organize a packet line between New York and Great Britain. In 1790 he returned to France to spend the rest of his life in the land of his birth.

His *Letters,* most of which are assumed to have been written during the tranquil years on the farm, include his reactions to slavery, which repelled him no less than it did other Europeans. His views on Indian life and the effect of the frontier on people

living away from civilization are remarkable for their understanding.

FROM *Letters from an American Farmer**

Some few towns excepted, we are tillers of the earth, from
Nova Scotia to West Florida. We are a people of cultivators,
scattered over an immense territory, communicating with each
other by means of good roads and navigable rivers, united by
the silken bands of mild government, all respecting the laws,
without dreading their power, because they are equitable.
. . . We have no princes, for whom we toil, starve, and bleed:
we are the most perfect society now existing in the world. . . .

What then is the American, this new man? He is either an
European, or the descendant of an European, hence that
strange mixture of blood, which you will find in no other
country. I could point out to you a family whose grandfather
was an Englishman, whose wife was Dutch, whose son married
a French woman, and whose present four sons have now four
wives of different nations. He is an American, who, leaving
behind him all his ancient prejudices and manners, receives
new ones from the new mode of life he has embraced, the new
government he obeys, and the new rank he holds. He becomes
an American by being received in the broad lap of our great
Alma Mater. . . .

Let us suppose you and I to be travelling; we observe that
in this house, at the right, lives a Catholic, who prays to God
as he has been taught. . . . About one mile farther on the same
road, his next neighbor may be a good honest plodding German Lutheran, who addresses himself to the same God . . . .
Next to him lives a seceder. . . . Next again lives a low Dutchman, who implicitly believes the rules laid down by the synod
of Dort. . . . Thus all sects are mixed as well as all nations;
thus religious indifference is imperceptibly disseminated from
one end of the continent to the other; which is at present one
of the strongest characteristics of the Americans. . . .

Often when I plough my low ground, I place my little boy
on a chair which screws to the beam of the plough—its motion

---

*Hector St. John de Crevecoeur, *Letters from an American Farmer*
(London, J. M. Dent & Sons. Ltd, 1912).

and that of the horses please him, he is perfectly happy and begins to chat. . . . I relieve his mother of some trouble while I have him with me, the odoriferous furrow exhilarates his spirits, and seems to do the child a great deal of good, for he looks more blooming since I have adopted that practice; can more pleasure, more dignity be added to that primary occupation? The father thus ploughing with his child, and to feed his family, is inferior only to the Emperor of China ploughing as an example to his kingdom. . . .

I must tell you, that there is something in the proximity of the woods, which is very singular. It is with men as it is with the plants and animals that grow and live in the forests; they are entirely different from those that live in the plains. . . . By living in or near the woods, their actions are regulated by the wildness of the neighbourhood. The deer often come to eat their grain, the wolves to destroy their sheep, the bears to kill their hogs, the foxes to catch their poultry. This surrounding hostility immediately puts the gun into their hands; they watch these animals, they kill some; and thus by defending their property, they soon become professed hunters; this is the progress; once hunters, farewell to the plough. . . .

While all is joy, festivity, and happiness in Charles Town [Charleston, South Carolina], would you imagine that scenes of misery over spread in the country? Their ears by habit have become deaf; their hearts are hardened; they neither see, hear nor feel for the woes of their poor slaves, from whose painful labors all their wealth proceeds. Here the horrors of slavery, the hardship of incessant toils, are unseen; and no one thinks with compassion of those showers of sweat and tears which from the bodies of Africans, daily drop, and moisten the ground they till. . . .

Let us say what we will of them [Indians], of their inferior organs, of their want of bread, etc., they are as stout and well made as the Europeans. Without temples, without priests, without kings, and without laws, they are in many instances superior to us; and the proofs of what I advance, are, that they live without care, sleep without inquietude, take life as it comes, . . . and die without any kind of apprehension for what they have done, or for what they expect to meet with hereafter. . . .

Mathew Carey
Pamphleteer, Bookseller, Publisher
1760-1839

'A prophet is seldom honored in his country'

The "prophet" in this case was Mathew Carey himself. He came to this bitter conclusion after many decades in America during which he had been a successful pamphleteer, bookseller, and publisher. The reason for his disillusionment was that he had fallen victim to a pet idea which he hoped would gain him recognition as a "political economist." But though he labored for nine years at building up a following, he failed to secure the support he needed.

His career as a pamphleteer began in Ireland, the country of his birth, when he published a defense of Irish Catholicism, which was considered subversive. To avoid punishment, he escaped to France, where he served an apprenticeship with Benjamin Franklin at Passy, and in 1784 he came to America. In Philadelphia, then the most sophisticated center of the newly formed nation, he began to print and publish books that agents loaded on wagons and then sold by going from one community to the next, much like their peddler-competitors who hawked household goods and other necessities from place to place. "Parson" Weems, the author of the earliest biography of George Washington, was one of Carey's agents and authors. Carey also published works by Cooper, Poe, Irving, and other contemporary writers.[1]

After the War of 1812, which ushered in a wave of optimism that encouraged broader interests than those that had occupied colonial minds, Mathew Carey succumbed to a vision—that American infant industries which had come to life during the Napoleonic wars, must be protected through a tariff on foreign importations. Merchandise of foreign manufacture that was again swamping the seaboard cities, was to him "trash disgorged on our shores from Europe," intended to draw "hard cash" out of the country. He attacked the laissez-faire theories of Adam Smith,

---

1. Van Wyck Brooks, *The Times of Melville and Whitman* (New York, 1947), p. 36.

frowned on the anti-tariff faction of the South, and announced that "protection of manufacturers was superior in importance to any question ever agitated here, execpt that declaration of independence and the adoption of the federal constitution [*sic*]."

By disseminating his ideas through pamphlets he called "Letters," he became one of the nation's earliest lobbyists. He bombarded manufacturers as well as Congress, but Congress ignored his propaganda and manufacturers were indifferent to his theories and refused to back him with adequate financial support. His "Letters" bristle with condemnation for the "indifference of Congress" and "the parsimony of manufacturers," and prove that during the early decades of the nineteenth century Congress was lukewarm to the interests of developing industry. His *Autobiographical Sketches* are basically an account of his failure to become accepted as a "political economist."

After nine years of effort, Mathew Carey finally gave up. The recognition that was withheld from him, came easily to his son, Henry C. Carey, who is known as our first writer on economics.

FROM *Autobiographical Sketches**

The present volume is confined wholly to the single object, the American system—its rise and progress—the course that has been pursued—the causes that have rendered its success incomplete, and the part I have acted in the contest. . . .

Whatever I have at any time engaged in, I have generally undertaken *con amore*. But throughout a life, approaching. . . . three-score and ten, I have engaged in nothing which so completely engrossed my mind and all my faculties, and for so long a period, as the protection of American Manufacturers, which I have uniformly regarded as the grand means of enabling the United States to arrive at that pinnacle of prosperity and greatness intended for them by God and nature. . . .

The unworthy treatment I received from some of the wealthy manufacturers here is scarcely credible—and tends to corroborate, indeed, greatly outruns the old proverb 'A prophet is seldom honored in his own country!'. . . . The magnificent idea, that I was pleading the cause of unborn millions, enabled me to smother my disgust; to look down on such conduct with

*Mathew Carey, *Autobiographical Sketches* (Philadelphia: J. Clarke, 1829).

scorn and indignation and to 'pursue the even tenor of my way' for so many years. . . .

Some miserable creature has asserted that I sought to make money by the manufacturers! To have spent so large a portion of the best years of my life—and disbursed, as I have done, in this cause, nearly $4000—in hopes of making money, would not be throwing sprats to catch salmons, but throwing salmons or rather whales to catch . . . sprats. . . .

The assertion may appear extravagant—but I am nevertheless persuaded it is true—that . . . the manufacturers forming nearly a fourth of the entire population of all the states from Maryland to Maine inclusive, were treated as cavalierly by the 15th Congress as those of the American provinces were by George III and lord North. . . .

These positions, absurd, futile and untenable as they are, form the basis of the *Wealth of Nations* [Adam Smith]. To a person wholly unbiassed by prejudice, it must be a matter of astonishment, how a work, resting on such gaudy and miserable foundation, could have obtained, and still more, have so long preserved its celebrity. The monstrous absurdity of these doctrines, and the facility with which they might be refuted, induced me to enter the lists against this Goliath with the sling and stone of truth. . . .

Desirous of furnishing the public with a book of reference on the all important subject of political economy, containing the result of all my researches, I collected all my essays into one large octavo of 556 pages, which I published by subscription. Profit was wholly out of the question. I distributed proposals among the most respectable and influential manufacturers of Boston, New York, Philadelphia, Wilmington and Baltimore. And having indefatigably laboured in their defence for above three years, I might have expected that they would devote a few hours to serve me . . . I was, with scarcely an exception, wholly disappointed. . . . Above one-third of the persons refused to take the books. . . . Suffice it to say, I actually lost by the edition, about three hundred dollars. . . .

Thus closed my labours in this important cause. My spirits sunk, and I could not proceed when I found myself so entirely unsupported by those whose vital interests were depending on the issue. . . .

William Cobbett
Journalist, English Reformer
1762-1835

"The times are onerous indeed
When quack to quack cries purge and bleed."

This ditty, a sample of nineteenth century journalistic attack (which was apt to be invidious), was directed at the highly esteemed Dr. Benjamin Rush and the physicians who supported his methods of curing patients by bleeding them. It earned the attacker, William Cobbett, who in America called himself "Peter Porcupine," a judgment of five thousand dollars and, in consequence, drove him back to England.[1]

William Cobbett came from humble yeoman background of which he said: ". . . if I derive no honour [from it], I derive no shame." His father, he asserted, had been pro-American during the Revolution, but in America William Cobbett appeared to be pro-English. His education in England was scant, but as a young man he enlisted in an infantry regiment stationed in Nova Scotia and there he educated himself by reading and studying grammar.

When he came to Philadelphia in 1793, he attempted to establish himself as a pamphleteer. Apparently his intention had been to become an American citizen. He submitted his first article to Mathew Carey, who had preceded him by ten years and was by then well established, but Carey turned it down, calling Cobbett "my lad," which infuriated the author. Eventually Cobbett became a bookseller and the vituperative editor of *The Porcupine Gazette,* where he attacked not only Benjamin Franklin Bache, grandson of Benjamin Franklin and editor of a rival newspaper, the equally belligerent *Aurora,* for his pro-French views, but also such well known personages as Tom Paine, Dr. Priestley, Mathew Carey, Dr. Rush, and the prominent actress and romancer, Susanna Rowson. His specific complaint about America

---

1. This information is contained in Mary Elizabeth Clarke's *Peter Porcupine in America* (Philadelphia, 1939).

was that the much vaunted principle, "liberty of the press," existed only for natives. It was based on the fact that his printed opinions aroused an especially virulent type of hostility.

After his return to England, the climate became too hot for him again and in 1817 he was back in the United States. This time, he confined himself to farming in Long Island (except for a few attacks on Morris Birkbeck, with whose colonizing schemes he disagreed). After two years he again returned to England and it was during his later years that he dedicated himsef to advocating reforms for farmers and workers.

His biographer points out that Cobbett benefited from his stay in America and that his American experience served as preparation for English politics. She states that it was during his American sojourn that he developed his abilities as a writer and that it was here he found the opportunity to try out "the various forms that became characteristic of the later Cobbett."[2]

FROM *The Life and Adventures of Peter Porcupine**

My determination to settle in the United States was formed . . . even before I quitted the army. A desire of seeing a country, so long the theatre of a war of which I had heard and read so much; the flattering pictures given of it by Raynal [Abbe Reynal who wrote about America]; and, above all, an inclination for seeing the world led me to this determination. It would look a little like coaxing for me to say, that I had imbibed principles of republicanism, and that I was ambitious to become a citizen of a free state, but this was really the case. I thought that men enjoyed here a greater degree of liberty than in England; and this, if not the principal reason, was at least one, for my coming to this country. . . .

My writings, the first pamphlet excepted, have had no other object than that of keeping alive an attachment to the Constitution of the United States and the *inestimable* man who is at the head of the government, and to paint in their true colours those who are the enemies of both; to warn the people of all ranks and descriptions, of the dangers of admitting among them the anarchical and blasphemous principles of

---

2. *Ibid.*, p. 284.

*William Cobbett, *The Life and Adventures of Peter Porcupine* (Philadelphia: William Cobbett, 1796).

the French revolutionists, principles as opposite to those of liberty as hell is to heaven. . . .

I should not have noticed the distinction between *foreigners* and *Americans*, had I not perceived that several persons, who are, generally speaking, friends to their country, seem to think that it was impertinent in me to meddle with politics here, because I was an Englishman. I would have these good people to recollect, that the laws of this country hold out, to foreigners, an offer of all that liberty of the press which Americans enjoy, and that if this liberty be abridged, by whatever means it may be done, the laws and the constitution and all together is a mere cheat; a snare to catch the credulous and enthusiastic of every other nation; a downright imposition on the world. If people who emigrate hither have not a right to make use of the liberty of the press, while the natives have, it is very ill done, to call this a country of *equal* liberty. . . . for, if none but Americans have access to the press, they are the masters and foreigners are their subjects, nay their slaves. . . . The emigrants from some countries may be content with it, perhaps: I would not say that the 'Martyrs in the cause of liberty' from England, would not quietly bend beneath the yoke, as, indeed, they are duty bound to do; but for my part, who have not the ambition to aspire to the crown of martyrdom, I must and will be excused. Either the laws shall be altered, or I will continue to avail myself of the liberty that they held out to me, and that partly tempted me to this country.

Morris Birkbeck
Colonizer
1763-1825

There prevails so much good sense and useful knowledge, joined to a genuine warmth of friendly feeling, a disposition to promote the happiness of each other, that the man who is lonely among them, is not formed for society. Such are the citizens of these new states, and my unaffected and well considered wish is to spend among them the remainder of my days.

The New Americans

Morris Birkbeck was an Englishman of Quaker background and high principles who gave up his farming interests in England to start a new colony in America. In 1817, at the age of forty-six, he set out, traveling first through the South, where he was horrified by the effects of slavery, then North. After choosing a site in Illinois, he established a colony called "Albion." Finding his funds insufficient, he sent his partner back to England to raise additional funds and to induce people to join their colony. In 1818 his book appeared in which he published his impressions of the country and its people. No references are found to spitting, which shocked Frances Trollope a scant ten years later. He considered Americans "good looking," but deplored the lack of cleanliness "to a degree which is greatly revolting to an Englishman." One hundred and fifty people are supposed to have been brought over, who were sold land at very low prices. Birkbeck himself operated a dairy and farmed his land with considerable success.

In 1825, at the age of sixty-two, he drowned, but not before he had made a lasting contribution to the state of Illinois. A proslavery state convention proposed to legalize slavery; he agitated against it so strenuously by means of letters he wrote under the name of "Jonathan Freeman," that the measure was defeated. Appointed Secretary of State for Illinois, he served three months, but a pro-slavery Senate would not confirm his appointment. His death occurred shortly thereafter.

Neither Birkbeck nor his partner prospered financially. When his partner left Albion in 1849, it was with two and a half dollars in his possession. One of Birkbeck's sons went to Indiana; of his other children one went to Mexico, another to England, eventually to emigrate to Australia. Traces of the original colony have disappeared. Today he is remembered only by the Illinois Historical Society, which credits him with having prevented the possibility that Illinois might have become a member of the Confederacy.[1]

FROM *Notes on a Journey in America**

. . . Slavery ". . . that broadest, foulest blot," which still prevails over so large a portion of the United Staes, will cir-

---

1. L. E. Shoemaker, "A Biography of Morris Birkbeck," *Illinois State Historical Society Journal*, XXIII (July, 1930), p. 339.
*Morris Birkbeck, *Notes on a Journey in America* (London: Ridgway & Sons, 1818).

cumscribe my choice within still narrower limits; for, if political liberty be so precious, that to obtain it, I can forego the well-earned comforts of an English home, it must not be to degrade myself and corrupt my children by the practice of slave-keeping. . . .

In exchanging the condition of an English farmer for that of an American proprietor, I expect to suffer many inconveniences; but I am willing to make a great sacrifice of present ease, were it merely for the sake of obtaining in the decline of life an exemption from that wearisome solicitude about pecuniary affairs, from which, even the affluent find no refuge in England, and for my children, a career of enterprize, and wholesome family connections, in a society whose institutions are favourable to virtue; and at last the consolation of leaving them efficient members of a flourishing, public-spirited, energetic community, where the insolence of wealth, and the servility of pauperism, between which, in England there is scarcely an interval remaining, are alike unknown. . . .

This embryo metropolis [Washington], with its foreign decorations [marble from Italy for the Capitol], should have set a better example to the young republic, by surrounding itself first with good roads and substantial bridges, in lieu of those inconvenient wooden structures and dangerous roads, over which the legislators must now pass to their duty. . . .

But what is most at variance with English notions of the American people, is the urbanity and civilization that prevail in situations remote from large cities. In our journey from Norfolk, on the coast of Virginia, to this place, in the heart of the Allegheny mountains, we have not for a moment lost sight of the manners of polished life. Refinement is unquestionably far more rare than in our nation and highly cultivated state of society; but so is extreme vulgarity. In every department of common life, we here see employed persons superior in habits and education to the same class in England. . . .

Here, whatever their original, whether English, Scotch, Irish, German, or French, all are Americans; and of all the imputations on the American character, jealousy of strangers is surely the most absurd and groundless. The Americans are sufficiently alive to their own interest, but they wish well to strangers; and are not always satisfied with wishing, if they can promote their success by active services. . . .

Let a stranger make his way through England, in a course

remote from the great roads, and going to no inns, take such entertainment only as he might find in the cottages of labourers, he would have as much cause to complain of the rudeness of the people, and far more of their drunkenness and profligacy than in these backwoods. . . .

Frances Trollope
Writer
1780-1863

> I speak . . . of the population generally, as seen in town and country, among the rich and the poor, in the slave states, and the free states. I do not like them. I do not like their principles, I do not like their manners. I do not like their opinions.

This outspoken statement comes from one of the most pungent commentators on the American scene during the first part of the nineteenth century. Frances Trollope was an Englishwoman and the mother of Anthony Trollope, whose *Barchester Towers* became one of the classics of English literature. When she sailed for America in 1827 at the age of forty-seven, it was with the intention of starting a dry goods emporium in order to shore up a much depleted family fortune. But her plan failed dismally and three years and nine months later she was back in England.

Mrs. Trollope embarked for New Orleans in the company of her friend, the reformer Frances Wright, who was returning to America for the third time. Three of Mrs. Trollope's five children accompanied her. Frances Wright had toured America between 1818 and 1820 and had published a glowing account of the new country. On a later trip she had founded the Nashoba Community in Tennessee as an experimental project for the education of Negroes. It was to Nashoba that Mrs. Trollope proceeded. But instead of experiencing a favorable reaction, the primitive conditions at Nashoba and the climate so disappointed Mrs. Trollope that she hastily betook herself to Cincinnati—after first securing a loan of three hundred dollars from the trustees of Nashoba.[1]

---

1. Frances Trollope, *Domestic Manners of the Americans* (New York, 1960). p. xvii.

Founded in 1789, Cincinnati, the seventh American city in 1830, was recognized on one hand, as "the Queen of the West," and on the other, as "Porkopolis."[2] Mrs. Trollope began to implement her plans for a bazaar that would make her rich and would elevate the taste of Cincinnatians, by building a fantastic edifice distinguished for its Greek, Roman, and Moorish features. (After its abandonment it became known as "Trollope's Folly.") Before she could open for business, she succumbed to a severe attack of malaria. By the time she had recovered, her investment had evaporated; the goods her husband had sent from England to be sold over the counters, were seized to satisfy the debts she had incurred. She attempted several schemes to put the building to some other use, but failed. The only possibility that remained, was to write a book on America. Consequently when she left Cincinnati it was to visit other parts of America in order to gather material. She decided to go south to Baltimore and Washington first, then east to Philadelphia and New York and north to Niagara Falls, the Mecca of European travelers. When she returned to England in 1831, she had an almost completed manuscript, for within less than one month after her return it was ready for submission to a publisher. The book was destined to repair the family fortune handsomely (She was said to have made between one hundred thirty thousand and one hundred and forty thousand dollars.)[3] and to make her famous in Europe and infamous in America. It was also to launch her on a lucrative career as a travel writer and novelist and to assure her a luxurious and prestigious existence for the rest of a long life.

Considered ill-humored, invidious and unjust, the book caused a furore in America. It was Mrs. Trollope who declared "spitting" and tobacco-chewing the national habit and thus opened the sluice-gates to comments on the uncouth manners of Americans. The "incessant and remorseless spitting," which she asserts she encountered everywhere, in the halls of Congress as well as in genteel Philadelphia, filled her with loathing. She was repelled no less by the tendency of American males to sit in their shirtsleeves, their heads covered, surrounded by odors of onion and fumes of whiskey, their legs raised above their heads. That spitters with an amazing aim were not uncommon even later in

---

2. Robert E. Riegel, *America Moves West* (New York, 1957), p. 253.
3. Frances Trollope, *op. cit.*, p. ix.

the century, is borne out by many witnesses. Mrs. Trollope is easier on the women. She is one of the first of a long line of European observers, both male and female, to remark about the good looks of American women. However, she found them to be of "lamentable insignificance" and "lacking in grace and intelligence," which she links to the tendency to keep the sexes separated and to "excessive" church attendance on the part of women.

A more serious and no less infuriating criticism than spitting, was her insistence on the dichotomy between the boast of Americans that all men are equal and the reality which disproved it. She asserted flatly that all Americans are "not equal," basing it not only on the treatment of Negroes and Indians, but also on clearly discernible class distinctions. The assertion "I'm as good as you" acted on her like the proverbial red rag on a bull. It induced a virulent anti-Jeffersonian bias which led her to refer pointedly to the canard that Jefferson was the father of a Negro progeny, who were his slaves, and to assert: "His hot-headed democracy has done a fearful injury to his country."

Other derogatory remarks included the statement that moral standards in America were lower than in Europe, that Americans were coarse and showed no familiarity with the classics, newspapers being "the principal vehicles of wisdom." In her distaste for revival meetings, she echoes the rejection of other Europeans who pronounced the behavior at revivals an "unholy spectacle." She informed Britons who believed that greater democratic privileges awaited them in the United States, that if they could pass a few years in the United States, they would realize how much better off Britons are, and advised them to emigrate to Canada.

She was not wholly ungenerous. She was very favorably impressed with Baltimore and she liked Washington. The sight of the Capitol drew this remark: "None of us, I believe, expected to see so imposing a structure on that side of the Atlantic." She liked Philadelphia and pronounced New York "a lovely and noble city . . . one of the finest cities I ever saw." But it was the sight of Niagara Falls which moved her to raptures. Of that spectacle she said: "I wept with a strange mixture of pleasure and pain," but, she "fancied" American tourists were "but little observant of the wonders around them."

The consensus of opinion today is that she was neither untruthful, nor particularly harsh. If there is truth in the remark of one of the twentieth century refugees[4] that the period before the Civil War corresponds to the Middle Ages of America, then the eighteen-twenties might be considered the "Dark Ages." Some of her observations were extremely shrewd and to the point. Today the main value of her criticism might be taken to lie in the proof of the tremendous changes that have taken place in the manners and social customs of Americans.

FROM *Domestic Manners of the Americans**

I hardly know any annoyance so deeply repugnant to English feelings as the incessant, remorseless spitting of Americans. . . . It is possible that in this phrase 'Americans,' I may be too general. The United States form a continent of almost distinct nations, and I must now, and always, be understood to speak only of that portion of them which I have seen. . . .

In truth the pigs are constantly seen doing Herculean service in this way through every quarter of the city; and though it is not very agreeable to live surrounded by herds of these unsavoury animals, it is well they are so numerous and so active in their capacity as scavengers, for without them the streets would soon be choked up with all sorts of substances in every stage of decomposition. . . .

I will not draw any comparisons between a good dinner party in the countries [America and England]; . . . but in speaking of general manners, I may observe, that it is rarely they [men] dine in society, except in taverns and boarding houses. Then they eat with the greatest possible rapidity, and in total silence; I have heard it said by American ladies, that the hours of greatest enjoyment to the gentlemen were those in which a glass of gin cock-tail, or eggnog, receives its highest relish from the absence of all restraint whatever; and when there were no ladies to trouble them. . . .

The greatest difficulty in organising a family establishment in Ohio, is getting servants, or, as it is there called 'getting help,' for it is more than petty treason to the Republic, to call a free citizen a *servant*. The whole class of young women,

---

4. Martin Gumpert, *First Papers* (New York, 1941), p. 85.
*Frances Trollope, *Domestic Manners of the Americans* (New York: Vintage Books, Inc., 1960).

whose bread depends upon their labour, are taught to believe that the most abject poverty is preferable to domestic service. Hundreds of half-naked girls work in the paper-mills, or in any other manufactory, for less than half the wages they would receive in service; but they think their equality is compromised by the latter, and nothing but the wish to obtain some particular article of finery, will ever induce them to submit to it. . . .

To me, the dreary coldness and want of enthusiasm in American manners is one of their greatest defects, and I therefore hailed the demonstrations of general feeling which this day elicits with real pleasure. On the fourth of July the hearts of the people seem to awaken from a three hundred and sixty-four days' sleep; they appear high-spirited, gay, animated, social, generous, or at least liberal in expense; and would they but refrain from spitting on that hallowed day, I should say, that on the fourth of July, at least, they appeared to be an amiable people. . . .

Any man's son may become the equal of any other man's son, and the consciousness of this is certainly a spur to exertion; on the other hand, it is also a spur to that coarse familiarity, untempered by any shadow of respect, which is assumed by the grossest and the lowest in their intercourse with the highest and most refined. This is a positive evil, and, I think, more than balances its advantages. . . .

In America, with the exception of dancing, which is almost wholly confined to the unmarried of both sexes, all the enjoyments of the men are found in the absence of the women. They dine, they play cards, they have musical evenings, they have suppers, all in large parties, but all without women. . . .

[At a revival meeting] . . . above a hundred persons, nearly all females, came forward, uttered howlings and groans, so terrible, that I shall never cease to shudder when I recall them. They appeared to drag each other forward, and on the word being given, 'let us pray,' they all fell on their knees; but this posture was soon changed for others that permitted greater scope for the convulsive movements of their limbs; and they were soon lying on the ground in an undescribable confusion of heads and legs. . . . Hysterical sobbings, convulsive groans, shrieks and screams the most appalling, burst forth on all sides. I felt sick with horror. . . .

If the American character may be judged by their conduct

in this matter [the Indians], they are most lamentable deficient in every feeling of honour and integrity. . . . Had I, during my residence in the United States, observed any single feature in their national character that could justify their eternal boasts of liberality and the love of freedom, I might have respected them, however much my taste might have been offended by what was peculiar in their manners and customs. But it is impossbile for any mind of common honesty not to be revolted by the contradictions in their principles and practice. . . .

. . . The extreme beauty of the chamber [Congress] was itself a reason for going again and again. It was, however, really mortifying to see this splendid hall, fitted up in so stately and sumptuous a manner, filled with men, sitting in the most unseemly attitudes, a large majority with their hats on, and nearly all, spitting to an excess that decency forbids me to describe. . . .

The effect produced upon English people by the sight of slavery in every direction is very new, and not very agreeable, and it is not the less painfully felt from hearing upon every breeze the mocking words, 'All men are born free and equal.' . . . Among the poorer class of landholders, who are often as profoundly ignorant as the negroes they own, the effect of this plenary power over males and females is most demoralising; and the kind of coarse, not to say brutal, authority which is exercised, furnishes the most disgusting moral spectacle I ever witnessed. . . .

All the enthusiasm of America is concentrated to the one point of her emancipation and independence; on this point nothing can exceed the warmth of her feelings. She may, I think, be compared to a young bride . . . the independence is to her as a newly-won bridegroom; for him alone she has eyes, ears or heart;—the honeymoon is not over yet;—when it is, America will, perhaps, learn more coquetry, and know better how to *faire l'amiable* to other nations.

Johann August Roebling
Bridge Builder
1806-1869

Every American, even when he is poor and must

serve others, feels his innate rights as a man. What a contrast to the oppressed German population.

Among the many immigrants whose education and skills became available to the new nation, Johann August Roebling occupies front rank. Educated as an engineer in Berlin, he emigrated with a group of friends at the age of twenty-four, arriving in Philadelphia in 1831. Starting as a pioneer farmer in the vicinity of Pittsburgh, he became within eight years engineer on the State Canal and surveyor for a proposed railroad system. In 1845 he built the first suspension bridge over the Monongahela in Pittsburgh.

The most significant contribution to his adopted country came in 1867 when he made the plans for the bridge over the East River, known as the Brooklyn Bridge. He lost his life just after construction had begun, as the result of an accident while directing operations. His American-born son, Washington Augustus Roebling, who had contributed his engineering skills to the Union Army during the Civil War, completed the bridge.

FROM *Diary of My Journey**

Today we journeyed from Muehlhausen, took leave of our friends, relatives and acquaintances, and said farewell to our native plain, in the hope of establishing a new home, a new Fatherland which will treat us indeed as a father, in the western continent, beyond the Atlantic Ocean. . . . We are not going with exaggerated views or extravagant hopes. To what extent America corresponds with our moderate expectations and affords us what we seek, the future must teach. . . .

The impression, which the populace has made on me, has turned out more favourably than I had expected. . . . The outward demeanor of the people or of the townsfolk, and their public conduct is more modest here and at the same time more free and unconstrained than I have noticed in any important city in Germany. . . . Nowhere does one see a person in rags; all, even the common workmen go very cleanly and neatly dressed. . . .

We have altered our previous opinion regarding the Southern

---

*Johann August Roebling, *Diary of My Jounrey* (Trenton, N.J.: The Roebling, Press, 1931).

States. In consequence of this we have made our decision to settle in a free State. Here one is universally prejudiced against the slaveholding States and that with right.

The Northern states criticize the Southern ones very much, and it is neither lying nor dissembling, and in this all reasonable Americans agree, to say that slavery is the greatest cancerous affliction from which the United States are suffering. Slavery contrasts too greatly with the rest of their political and civic institutions. The republic is branded by it and the entire folk with its *idealistic* and altogether purely *reasonable* Constitution, stands branded by it before the eyes of the civilized world. Grounds enough for us not to go into any slaveholding State, even if Nature had created a Paradise there! . . .

Let one inquire about the gigantic construction of the New York Canal, the Ohio Canal, the multitude of smaller canals, roads and railways, and the German wonders how all this could have been accomplished without first having had an army of governmental counsellors, ministers and other functionaries deliberate about it for ten years, make numerous expensive journeys by post, and write so many reports about it that for the amount expended for all this, reckoning compound interest for ten years, the work could have been completed.

Gustav Koerner
Lawyer, Public Servant, Informal Historian
1809-1896

> The domestic life of the German families of culture in the Fatherland, the emigrants' trials and struggles in the primeval forests of the far West; the struggles of the young lawyer to make a precarious living at a time when judges and preachers rode the circuit, must be interesting to the careful student of the history and growth of a young nation.

Spare, dignified, prematurely gray, as later contemporaries described the successful lawyer and citizen, Gustav Koerner was, in the words of Oswald Garrison Villard, "a fiery revolutionist."

He belongs to the group of Germans whom the political upheavals of the early eighteen-thirties had driven from their
homeland. Like so many Germans, he had intended to settle
in Missouri. But slavery frightened him and his group and
they settled in Ohio instead.

Unlike many of his friends, Koerner did not become one of
die Lateinische Bauern, tillers of the soil—who purchased farms
with money brought from Germany. Having received a Doctor
of Laws degree in Germany, he decided on law as his career.
After immersing himself first in *Blackstone's Commentaries* and
then in American constitutional history, he departed for Transyl-
vania University in Kentucky to study law, not in someone's
office, but in the continental fashion, through formal, prescribed
study. Within two years he passed the bar and settled down
to the practice of law.

Like many of the foreign-born who were repelled by the
nativist tendencies of the Whigs, Koerner turned to the Democratic Party. His political career began when he was chosen
one of the electoral messengers to carry the Illinois vote to
Washington in 1840—when such a trip consumed several weeks.
After serving in the Illinois legislature and as judge of the
Supreme Court of Illinois, he was elected Lieutenant Governor
of the state. "The inborn hostility to the institution of slavery,"
which is recognized as characteristic of the Germans, made him
desert the Democratic party and Senator Douglas, when Douglas
sponsored the concept of "Popular Sovereignty." Joining the
Republican Party, Koerner acted as chairman of the convention
of 1856 and was active during the Lincoln-Douglas debates and
during the campaign of 1860 as an anti-slavery speaker. When
the Civil War broke out, he organized volunteer regiments in
Belleville and St. Louis and served as aide-de-camp to General
Fremont, whom, like most Germans, he liked. After the resignation of Carl Schurz as minister to Spain, President Lincoln
appointed him to that post. At Lincoln's funeral, Koerner was
one of the pall bearers.

Koerner's participation in politics was sporadic, possibly because political jobs meant loss of income, which, he says, he
could not afford. Instead he became, in the words of Henry
Villard, "one of the best known lawyers in Southern Illinois."

His contribution to American life was two-fold: as a representative of the best German traditions to the American community;

and to those whose roots were German, as publisher of a book, *The German Element,* in which he gathered together the individual contributions of the Germans to American life. The memoirs, intended originally for family use only, are a valuable eye-witness account of the events and the people of his time by a man whose trained intelligence made him a keen and accurate observer.

FROM *The Memoirs of Gustav Koerner**

. . . Passing the court house, we saw colored men, women and children sold at auction. We were also shown a sort of prison, where refractory slaves were confined at the request of their masters or were whipped at their masters' cost, by men regularly appointed for that purpose. . . . From the second story of our residence we could see into the yard of a neighboring house, where we once saw what appeared to be an American lady, lashing a young slave girl with a cowhide. Had there still been a lingering disposition in the Engelmann or Abend family to settle in Missouri, these scenes would have quenched it forever. . . .

In January Henry Clay died, following the great statesman Calhoun in less than two years. The regret at his loss was general and sincere. Indeed, I know of no man who represented the American character in its best features as well as in its foibles more truly than Henry Clay. If Webster can be said to have loved his country, it was love springing from reason; Clay loved it from his heart. . . .

. . . I must say that I left my old party not without many pangs and that it cost me much to burn my bridges. . . .I always hated slavery, and while constitutionally I saw no way of abolishing it, I could not prevail on myself to favor it in any way whatever, or to extend it into any Territory heretofore declared to be free. . . .

It is doubtful to my mind whether anyone but Lincoln could have carried the Union through the raging war of the rebellion. It required just such a complex and anomalous character. His success in saving the Union without overstepping the Constitution to a total extent, has made him the

---

*Gustav Koerner, *Memoirs of Gustav Koerner* (Cedar Rapids, Iowa: The Torch Press, 1909).

idol of the people. Perhaps for his fame in the world's history his death when it happened was most fortunate. . . .

. . . I knew him [Lincoln] well enough to detect certain weaknesses and defects in his character. The great and good, however, largely preponderated. Mr. Seward has said of Mr. Lincoln that he was the best man he ever knew. I should rather say he was the justest man I ever knew. . . .

Early in 1880 my book, "The German Element," was published. As far as the reviews in the public press both in the United States and Germany were concerned, it met with great favor; and many private letters of competent persons expressed a highly favorable opinion of it. Nevertheless, the sale of the book proceeded slowly. There were several reasons for this. . . . But perhaps the principal reason, (nowhere assigned, however) was that the book but half pleased many of those who had been forward in claiming for the later immigration after 1850, all the influence that the German element had ever exercised. . . .

I am again and again overcome with the thought that in writing these memoirs I may be guilty of egotism, or if you please, of vanity. But I do not see how any autobiographist can escape this charge. There may have been authors like Rousseau, for instance, who have laid bare even their meanest thoughts and actions; but it is questionable whether in doing this they did not also show an overweaning vanity.

Johann August Sutter
Planter of Civilization in the Wilderness
1802-1880

> . . . but for me it has turned out a folly, then without having discovered the Gold, I would have become the richest wealthiest man on the Pacific Shore.

The story of Johann August Sutter, a German-born immigrant of Swiss descent, is one of the most fantastic in the annals of those who abandoned their European homes to start anew in the Western world. He was thirty-one and a bankrupt when he was forced to flee his creditors in 1834. Drawn to the far West, he reached Monterey, California, after five years of adventure and travel and there received a large grant of land from the governor of Mexico. Within ten years he acquired a princely domain which became known as "New Helvetia." It contained a fort built with the aid of Indians, whom he had turned into soldiers by drilling them himself. He planted grain and grapes from which he distilled a brandy, acquired an immense herd of cattle, minted his own tin money, built a flour mill, a bakery, and a tannery. He erected a hospital, placed a physician in attendance, and dispensed hospitality as well as medical care to American emigrants and travelers. He was thus the first to introduce civilization to the region which became American territory after the war with Mexico.

It was on his property that gold was discovered; it initiated the Gold Rush of 1849. A sawmill was in the process of being completed when a partner in this enterprise, one Marshall Wilson from New Jersey, brought him some yellow flakes he had found on the site. A quick test disclosed that they were twenty-three carat gold. Sutter begged those who knew about it to keep it a secret; but the news leaked out. A fever seized his employees, white and Indian. Abandoning their assigned tasks, they ran off to dig for gold. Fortune seekers trampled his crops and stole his cattle. Squatters seized his property. His enterprises were ruined.

Having accepted Mexican citizenship, Sutter switched to American citizenship when California became American territory. After the loss of his property the only recourse he had was to appeal to the United States Land Commission. In 1856, in order to enable his lawyers to fight for his rights, he made a record of his experiences, tactfully avoiding to blame United States officials too harshly for their unwillingness to confirm him as the owner of all the property he claimed had been granted to him by two governors of Mexico. Instead he vented his bitterness on the people who "did a Wholesale business in Stealing." Though he finally accepted a pension of two hundred and fifty dollars a month from the state of California and removed to a Moravian settlement in Lititz, Pennsylvania, he never forgot his grievance against the United States government. Haunting the Capitol and buttonholing the lawmakers, he pleaded in vain for recognition of his "rights." He died in a Washington boarding house in 1880 and was buried in Lititz, Pennsylvania.

FROM *The Diary of Johann August Sutter**

I left the state of Missouri . . . and travelled with the party
of Men under Capt. Tripps of the Amer. fur Compy, to their
Rendezvous in the Rocky Mountains . . . from there I travelled
with 6 brave men to Oregon, as I considered myself not strong
enough to cross the Sierra Nevada and go direct to California
(which was my intention from my first Start on having got
some informations from a Gent'n in New Mexico, who has
been in Cal.) . . .

In Monterey I arranged my affairs with the Custom House,
and presented myself to Govr Alvorado, and told him my
intention to settle here in the Country. . . . I got a General
passport for my small Colony and permission to select a
Territory wherever I could find it convenient, and to come
in one Years time again to Monterey to get my Citizenship and
the title of the Land, which I have done so. . . .

The Indians was first troublesome, and came frequently, and
would it not have been for the Cannons they would have
Killed us for sake of my property, which they liked very much,
and this intention they had very often, how they have confessed to me afterwards, when on good terms. . . .

. . . Capt. Fremont was nearly all the time engaged in the
lower Country and made himself Governor, until Genl. Kearney
arrived, when an other Revolution took place. And Fremont
for disobeying Orders was made prissoner by Genl. Kearney,
who took him afterwards with him to U. States to Land across
the Mountains. After the War I was anxious that Business
should go on like before. . . .

Marshall arrived in the evening, it was raining very heavy,
but he told me to come on important business. After we
was alone in a private Room he showed me the first Specimens
of Gold, that is he was not certain if it was Gold or not, but
he thought it might be; Immediately I made the proof and
found that it was Gold. I told him most of all is 23 Carat
Gold. . . .

. . . I had a talk with my employed people all at the Sawmill. I told them that as they do know now that this Metal is

---

*Johann August Sutter, *The Diary of Johann August Sutter* (San Francisco: The Grabhorn Press, 1932).

Gold, I wished that they would do me the great favor and keep it secret only 6 weeks, because my large Flour Mill at Brighton would have been in Operation in such a time, which undertaking would have been a fortune to me, and unfortunately the people would not keep it secret, and so I lost on this Mill at the lowest calculation about $25.000. . . .

. . . One thing is certain that the pepole looked on my property as their own, and in the winter of 1849 to 1850, a great Number of horses has been stolen from me. . . . Nearly my whole stock of Cattle has been Killed, several thousands, and left me a very small Quantity. . . . I had not an Idea that people could be so mean, and that they would do a Wholesale business in Stealing. . . .

. . . I did not speculate, only occupied my land, in the hope that it would be before long decided and in my favor by the U.S. Land Commission, but now already 3 years & 2 months have elapsed, and I am now waiting very anxiously for the Decission, which will revive or bring me to the untimely grave. . . .

I think now from all this you can form some facts, and that you can mention how thousands and thousands made their fortunes, from this Gold Discovery produced through my industry and energy (some wise merchants and others in San Fr. called the building of this Sawmill, another of Sutter's folly) and this folly saved not only the Mercantile World from Bankruptcy, but even our General Gov't, but for me it has turned out a folly. . . .

Ole Rynning
Emigrant Leader
1809-1838

Many go to America with such unreasonable expectations that they necessarily must find themselves disappointed. . . . The person who neither can nor will work must never expect that riches and luxurious living will be open to him. No, in America one gets nothing without work; but it is true that by work one can expect some day to achieve better circumstances.

101

The New Americans

This sage counsel was offered by a young Norwegian to those of his countrymen who were contemplating emigration. He wrote it from America, while he was so severely ill that people doubted he would survive. His thirty-nine page pamphlet was so widely read that the increase in immigration of Norwegians which began in the 1840s, is attributed to its influence.

Ole Rynning was twenty-eight when he undertook to lead a group of Norwegians to America. He was a graduate of the University of Christiania, where he had prepared for the ministry. But when he graduated he rejected the ministry. The fact that he spoke English made him a valuable addition to a party of emigrants.

Sailing with eighty-four members, the group arrived in June after a journey of two months. In New York they took a steamer to Albany, then to Buffalo and by Lake Erie to Detroit. From there they went to Illinois, where they were persuaded to purchase a tract of land, seventy miles south of Chicago, known as "Beaver Creek."

It was an unfortunate decision, because it was swampland, as they discovered later. Attacked by sickness, the colony fared badly. Ole Rynning is said to have exerted great influence on his discouraged countrymen and to have shown unusual personal courage. He recovered from one illness, during the course of which he composed his observations on America, only to succumb shortly thereafter to the ague. His judgment was so sound that in speaking of slavery he predicted the Civil War in these words: ". . . there will in all likelihood come either a separation between the northern and southern states, or else bloody civil disputes." He was buried on the prairie. The remaining members of the colony abandoned the site and moved elsewhere.

FROM *A True Account of America for the Information and Help of Peasant and Commoner**

. . . The most important country in all America with respect to population as well as to freedom and happy form of government is the "United States" in North America. Usually, there-

---

*Ole Rynning, *A True Account of America for the Information and Help of Peasant and Commoner* (Christiania, 1838). Translated by Theodore C. Blegen as "Ole Rynning's True Account of America," *Minnesota Historical Bulletin,* II, No. 4 (1917), 221-269.

fore, this country is meant when you hear someone speak of America in an indefinite way. It is to this land your country-men have emigrated; it is this land which I shall now describe. . . .

The immigrants of different nations are not equally well received by the Americans. From Ireland there comes yearly a great rabble, who, because of their tendency to drunkenness, their fighting and their knavery, make themselves commonly hated. A respectable Irishman hardly dares acknowledge his nationality. The Norwegians generally have thus far a good reputation for their industry, trustworthiness and readiness with which the more well to do have helped poor people through the country. . . .

For the comfort of the faint-hearted, I can, therefore, de-clare with truth that in America, as in Norway, there are laws, government and authorities. But everything is designed to maintain the natural freedom and equality of men. In regard to the former, everyone is free to engage in whatever honorable occupation he wishes, and go wherever he wishes. . . . Only the real criminal is threatened with punishment by the law. . . .

In writings, the sole purpose which seems to be to find something in America which can be criticized, I had read that the American is faithless, deceitful and so forth. I will not deny that such folk are to be found in America, as well as in other places, and that the stranger can never be too careful; but it has been my experience that the American as a general rule is easier to get along with than the Norwegian, more accommodating, more obliging, more reliable in all things. . . . Since it is so easy to support oneself in an honorable way, thieving and burglary are almost unknown.

PART THREE

ACCELERATION

From the 1830's to 1880

"Each national stock is the bearer of some mental or spiritual gift which is unique, and which we cannot afford to lose. . . . The fusion of these many cultures will result in each of them shedding whatever is undesirable or unadaptable to the American environment; and, at last, in the merging of them all into a distinctively American civilization which shall transcend them all.

Horace Bridges
On Becoming an American

12

Hunger, Revolution, and the Search for Opportunity

> "In this great American asylum, the poor of Europe have by some means met together, and in consequence of various causes; to what purpose should they ask one another what countrymen they are? . . . Everything has tended to regenerate them; new laws, a new mode of living, a new social system; here they become men: . . . ."
>
> Hector St. John de Crevecoeur
> *Letters from an American Farmer*

The early nineteenth century was a time of great optimism in America. It was easy to believe that on the new continent waited "the best of all possible worlds." This optimism found expression in extravagant nationalism, in the development of the "West," in diplomatic triumphs and in great expectations. America flexed its muscles and in the confidence of coming greatness accepted the recommendation Thomas Paine had made that an "asylum" be prepared for the less fortunate peoples of Europe.

Drawn by the vast, empty continent and by the feeling that a new society could use both brawn and brain, immigration increased in geometric ratio throughout the nineteenth century. While the dominant groups were the Irish and the Germans, the same ethnic elements that had composed our population since the beginning of the American experiment continued to find a welcome.

Five million newcomers were added between 1815 and 1865, a number "greater . . . than the entire population of the United States at time of the census in 1790"[1] Of these the Irish formed the largest bloc. Famines that had occurred intermittently during the early part of the nineteenth century, reached their peak in 1846 and 1847 when the entire potato crop was destroyed for two years. "The Great Hunger" drove two million to this country,

---

1. Maldwyn Allen Jones, *American Immigration* (Chicago, 1960), p. 94.

the largest number flooding the cities. The influx fell off after the 1850s, but Irish immigration continued throughout the century, though in greatly diminshed numbers. In spite of the fact that the Irish suffered severely, which in other immigrant groups called forth much subjective comment, the autobiographical writings of Irish immigrants are few, possibly because so many of them were conspicuous for a low degree of literacy. Most of the chroniclers of Irish immigrant life in America are second and third generation descendants of the original newcomers who employ fictional means in reconstructing the experiences of their forbears.

The German exodus was also of tremendous proportion—one and a half million between the beginning of the nineteenth century and the Civil War. Though the percentage of educated people among them was high, the bulk consisted of agriculturists, small tradesmen, mechanics, and common laborers. The exodus diminished after the Civil War, reaching its lowest point after the 1880s when the benefits from Bismarck's reforms began to make themselves felt. The Germans were eager memoirists who left many valuable documents relating to their experiences in America, which attest to the fact that the Germans made contributions of great significance to every phase of American life.

A third large group to be included among the "Old Immigrants" are the Scandinavians—the Swedes, Norwegians, and Danes. In establishing the New Sweden colony on the Delaware, the Swedes were among the earliest colonists, but they became absorbed when the Dutch took the colony over, and again when the English conquered the Dutch colony of New Amsterdam in 1664. Immigration from Sweden began to increase significantly after 1840, reaching its crest in the 1880s. Norwegian immigration ran a similar course, reaching a peak in the 1840s and the highpoint in the 1880s. The Danes were the last and the fewest. While some of the Scandinavians remained in the cities, the bulk were driven by land-hunger. They settled the mid-western states of Illinois, Minnesota, Iowa, Nebraska, and the Dakotas. From the Scandinavians have come extremely moving accounts of immigrant life—autobiographies as well as fiction. Among the fiction writers are O. E. Rolvaag and Johann Bojer who wrote of Norwegians, Vilhelm Moberg, who wrote of the Swedes, and many second and third generation descendants of the original settlers.

13

Comment from the 1830's to 1880

Andrew Carnegie
Industrialist, Philanthropist, Author
1835-1919

> A word, a look, an accent may affect the destiny
> not only of individuals, but of nations. He is a
> bold man who calls everything a trifle. . . . The
> young should remember that upon trifles the best
> gifts of the gods often hang.

One of the most important personalities of the nineteenth century was Andrew Carnegie. His spectacular success was due as much to a combination of personal talents nurtured on the "Protestant ethic," as to the enormous industrial expansion of post-Civil War America. The age he lived in, and dominated, was the age of the great American millionaires, variously referred to as "The Age of the Dinosaurs,"[1] the age of "The Robber Barons,"[2] and "The Great Barbecue."[3] His qualifications were shrewdness, initiative, the capacity for untiring effort, and an uncanny awareness of the future needs of the nation. For his age he was a constructive thinker. For instance, he believed in a strong central government, and advocated control of corporations, supervision of railroads, and other restrictive measures which were anathema to the captains of finance. But many of his ideas, especially his economic philosophy, "The Gospel of Wealth," of which he was author and exponent, have a typical flavor of the nineteenth century.

The Carnegie family was driven out of Scotland by the effects of the Industrial Revolution. After seven weeks at sea and an inland journey of three weeks by way of the Erie Canal and the

1. James Truslow Adams.
2. Matthew Josephson.
3. Vernon Louis Parrington.

Ohio River, they arrived in Allegheny City in 1848. He was thirteen and the education he had received in Scotland was to be augmented only by one winter's night-schooling in America. Nevertheless, unlike many native millionaires, he was an avid reader and was well acquainted with Burns and Shakespeare. His first job as a bobbin boy paid one dollar and twenty cents a week; in his second job he earned two dollars and was given the opportunity to make out bills and to keep books in single entry. When he heard that the big firms used double entry bookkeeping, he went to night school to learn it. A job as messenger in the telegraph office was to him a huge step up the ladder of success. There he taught himself telegraphy by practising on the instrument in the absence of the operator, then, his imagination racing ahead, he proceeded to take messages by sound, considered an "extraordinary feat." From there he went as clerk and telegraph operator to the office of the superintendent of the Pittsburgh division of the Pennsylvania Railroad, and at the outbreak of the Civil War he rose to become superintendent of the division. He served the government briefly in the running of military trains and telegraphs, then returned to his job with the Pennsylvania Railroad, quitting railroad service in 1865.

By then he had become involved in several outside enterprises. While in the employ of the Pennsylvania, he was offered an eighth interest in the manufacture of sleeping cars in appreciation of an order he had helped the inventor, T. R. Woodruff, to secure from the Pennsylvania Railroad. Later he was instrumental in merging Woodruff's company with the plant of George Pullman, in whom he saw another business genius. In 1862 he acquired an interest in a bridge-building concern; in 1864 he started the manufacturing of iron rails with a boyhood friend, Thomas Miller; in 1866 he went into the manufacturing of locomotives. He knew instinctively when "iron was destined to give place to steel," and in the depression years following the Panic of 1873, he backed the manufacturing of steel rails with all his resources. Acquiring iron mines, coke plants, railroads, and other means of transportation, the Carnegie Steel Works grew fantastically, yielding an annual profit of forty million. It became a nursery for many millionaires who started as mechanics, foremen, and superintendents. In 1901 the Carnegie Steel Works were sold for $492,000,000 and became the U.S. Steel Corporation.

Though he planned as early as 1868 to give the "surplus"

above fifty thousand dollars a year to worthy charities, he gloried in his "millionairedom." He was firmly convinced that "the millionaire has a legal right to his millions" and that "million-airedom . . . was only a rightful reward" for hard work, initiative and responsibility. In this respect he was completely of the nineteenth century. But he also believed that wealth carried with it definite obligations to use it for the "benefit of the many" and to be a "trustee for the poor." His economic philosophy set forth in "The Gospel of Wealth" offered the prescription that the wealthy must look after the less privileged, not by increasing wages to the extent warranted by profits, but by providing "the ladders upon which the aspiring can rise." The man he most admired for providing such a "ladder" was Peter Cooper, founder of Cooper Union.

Andrew Carnegie's autobiography remains to this day the Bible of the aspiring businessman. Such aphorisms as "Anything in life worth having is worth working for"; "The surest founda-tion of a manufacturing concern is quality"; "Put all good eggs into one basket and watch that basket"; are reminiscent of Benjamin Franklin's *Poor Richard's Almanac,* of whose moraliz-ing he and the tycoons of the nineteenth century thoroughly approved.

It was the Homestead Strike that made the Carnegie name infamous among supporters of labor. This bloody strike, during which workers fought Pinkerton agents and which cost the lives of many on both sides, took place while Andrew Carnegie sum-mered at his castle (Skibo) in Scotland. The blame was con-veniently attached to one of the partners, Henry Clay Frick. But Matthew Josephson[4] quotes several telegrams from Carnegie to Frick, indicating Carnegie's approval. A most recent writer raises the question why Carnegie chose to stay away while the strike lasted. (Henry Phipps, a partner, explained later that it was the wish of the other Carnegie partners that he stay away, because they knew of his disposition "to grant the demands of labor, however unreasonable.") The conclusion of this new book is: "He was—or appeared to be—the hypocrite supreme."[5] An-drew Carnegie gave away close to $325,000,000. One bequest went to the Carnegie Endowment for International Peace;

---

4. Matthew Josephson, *The Robber Barons* (New York, 1934), pp. 368-372, *passim*.
5. Leon Wolff, *Lockout* (New York, 1965).

another, to the Peace Temple at the Hague. A commentator pointed out that after having made millions selling steel for the construction of battleships, he promoted peace.

FROM *The Autobiography of Andrew Carnegie**

. . . He asked how soon I could come, and I said I could stay now if wanted. And, looking back over the circumstance, I think that answer might well be pondered by young men. It is a great mistake not to seize the opportunity. The position was offered to me; something might occur, some other boy might be sent for. Having got myself in I proposed to stay there if I could. . . .

And that is how in 1850 I got my first real start in life. [as a telegraph messenger] . . . I was lifted into paradise, yes, heaven, as it seemed to me, with newspapers, pens, pencils and sunshine about me. There was scarcely a minute in which I could not learn something or find out how much there was to learn and how little I knew. I felt that my foot was upon the ladder and that I was bound to climb. . . .

. . . Looking back to-day one cannot help regretting so high a price as the Civil War had to be paid to free our land from the curse, but it was not slavery alone that needed abolition. The loose Federal system with State rights so prominent would inevitably have prevented, or at least long delayed, the formation of one solid, all-powerful, central government. . . . Uniformity in many fields must be secured. Marriage, divorce, bankruptcy, railroad supervision, control of corporations, and some other departments should in some measure be brought under one head. . . .

. . . If you want a contract, be on the spot when it is let. A smashed lamp-post or something equally unthought of may secure the prize if the bidder be on hand. And if possible stay on hand until you can take the written contract home in your pocket. . . .

. . . It would be safe to wager that a thousand Americans in a new land would organize themselves, establish schools, churches, newspapers, and brass bands—in short, provide themselves with all the appliances of civilization—and go ahead

---

*Andrew Carnegie, *The Autobiography of Andrew Carnegie* (Boston: Houghton Mifflin Company, 1920). By permission of the publishers.

developing their country before an equal number of British would have discovered who among them was the highest in hereditary rank and had the best claims to leadership owing to his grandfather. There is but one rule among Americans—the tools to those who can use them. . . .

I have never bought or sold a share of stock speculatively in my life, except one small lot of Pennsylvania Railroad shares that I bought early in life for investment . . . I have adhered to the rule never to purchase what I did not pay for, and never to sell what I did not own. In those early days, however, I had several interests that were taken over in the course of business. They included some stocks and securities that were quoted on the New York Stock Exchange, and I found that when I opened my paper in the morning I was tempted to look first at the quotations on the stock market. As I had determined to sell all my interest in every outside concern and concentrate my attention upon our manufacturing concerns in Pittsburgh, I further resolved not even to own any stock that was bought and sold upon any stock exchange. . . .

I believe the true road to preeminent success in any line is to make yourself master in that line. I have no faith in the policy of scattering one's resources, and in my experience I have rarely if ever met a man who achieved preeminence in money-making—certainly never one in manufacturing—who was interested in many concerns. The men who have succeeded are men who have chosen one line and stuck to it. . . .

I quote what I once laid down in writing as our rule: 'My idea is that the Company should be known as determined to let the man at any works stop work; that it will confer freely with them and wait patiently until they decide to return to work, never thinking of trying new men— never!'

Carl Schurz
Reformer, Statesman, Journalist
1829-1906

I felt an irresistible impulse not only to find for myself a well regulated activity, but also to do something really and truly valuable for the general

> good. . . . "To America," I said to myself. "The
> ideals of which I have dreamed and for which
> I have fought I shall find there. . . ."

The decision to go to America came to Carl Schurz suddenly while he was sitting on a bench in Hyde Park, London, where he had fled after some "cops-and-robbers" adventures connected with the uprisings of 1848. The year was 1852; he was twenty-three, a university graduate. Possessing an unusual dose of that "moral heroism" that he later remarked was most needed in a republic, he was destined to become the most honored of all the foreign-born and to play an historic part in the political and intellectual developments of America.

He settled in Wisconsin, where one could become a voter after one year's residence, and was immediately drawn to the Republican Party because of its attitude to slavery. He participated actively in the first Republican election of 1856; in 1860 his impassioned eloquence swung the foreign vote behind Lincoln. Appointed minister to Spain, he resigned his safe position in Madrid in order to volunteer for combat duty. As a brigadier general he and his troops participated in the battles of Chancellorsville and Gettysburg.

Though Schurz served three Presidents—Lincoln, Andrew Johnson, for whom he undertook a survey of the defeated South, and Rutherford B. Hayes, whose Secretary of the Interior he became, —he asserts it was his election to the Senate during the Grant administration that brought him the greatest personal satisfaction. This event elicited the pledge "that there would be no personal sacrifice too great for my devotion to the Republic." Consequently he opposed Grant on several occasions, though the President personally solicited his cooperation.

After serving as Secretary of the Interior, he devoted himself to newspaper work and to civil service reform, succeeding George William Curtis as president of the Civil Service Reform League. He spoke out against the Spanish-American War and the acquisition of the Philippines. At the same time he supported the cause of the Negro and the Indian in his newspaper and magazine writings.

In the words of Oswald Garrison Villard[1] "His is the distinction of having held higher positions under the Republic than

---

1. Oswald Garrison Villard, *Fighting Years* (New York, 1939) p. 36.

any other foreign-born citizen." Schurz listed as his two greatest endeavors: the abolition of slavery and the reform of the civil service system. The recognition of Schurz by a twentieth century newcomer as "that fully distinguished patriot, that *anima naturaliter Americana*,"[2] is one that neither native nor foreign-born would have disputed.

FROM *The Reminiscences of Carl Schurz**

My young wife and myself sailed from Portsmouth in August 1852 and landed in the harbor of New York on a bright September morning. With the buoyant hopefulness of young hearts, we saluted the new world. . . .

[After a visit to Congress] I saw the decisive contest rapidly approaching, and I felt an irresistible impulse to prepare myself for usefulness, however modest, in the impending crisis and to that end I pursued with increasing assiduity my studies of political history and the social conditions of the Republic, and of the theory and practical workings of its institutions. To the same end I thought it necessary to see more of the country and to get a larger experience of the character of the people. Especially did I long to breathe the fresh air of that part of the Union, which I imagined to be the 'real America,' the great West, where new states were growing up and where I would have an opportunity for observing the formative process of new political committees working themselves out of the raw. . . .

[Following his appointment as minister to Spain] In the course of our conversation I opened my heart to Mr. Lincoln about my troubles of conscience. I told him that since recent events had made a warlike conflict with the seceding states certain, it was much against my feelings to go to Spain as Minister and to spend my days in the ease and luxury of a diplomatic position, while the young men of the North were exposing their lives in the field, in defense of the life of the Republic; that, having helped as a public speaker, to bring about the present condition of things, I thought I would rather bear my share of the consequences; . . . and that I

---

2. Horace Bridges, *On Becoming an American* (Boston, 1918). p. x.

*Carl Schurz, *The Reminiscences of Carl Schurz* (New York: The McClure Co., 1907).

should be glad to resign my mission to Spain and at once join the volunteer army. . . .

President Johnson obviously wished to suppress my testimony as to the·condition of things in the South. [after he had returned from his survey of the South] I resolved not to let him do so. I had conscientiously endeavored to see Southern conditions as they were. I had not permitted any political considerations or any preconceived opinions on my part, to obscure my perception and discernment in the slightest degree. I had told the truth as I had learned it and understood it with the severest accuracy and I thought it due to the country that the truth should be known. . . .

I remember vividly the feeling which almost oppressed me as I first sat down in my chair in the Senate chamber. I had actually reached the most exalted public position to which my boldest dreams of ambition had hardly dared to aspire. I was still a young man, just forty. Little more than sixteen years had elapsed since I had landed on these shores a homeless waif saved from the wreck of a revolutionary movement. There I was enfolded in the generous hospitality of the American people opening to me, as freely as to its own children, the great opportunities of the new world. And here I was now, a member of the highest law-making body of the greatest of republics. Should I ever be able fully to pay my debt of gratitude to this country, and justify the honors that had been headed upon me? . . . I recorded a vow in my heart that I would at least honestly endeavor to fulfill that duty . . . that I would never be a sycophant of power nor a flatterer of multitude; that if need be, I would stand up alone for my conviction of truth and right; and that there could be no personal sacrifice too great for my devotion to the Republic.

Henry Villard
Journalist, International Financier, Empire Builder
1835-1900

No American citizen of foreign birth could have had a higher appreciation of the privileges of American citizenship. . . . He never forgot that he was himself a living illustration of the benefits

of these conditions and never failed to acknowledge his indebtedness to them. Yet, with all his
faithfulness and gratitude to his adopted country,
. . . he always remained and was proud to be a
true German.

This statement made in the third person by Henry Villard, is
the frankest admission of dual loyalty to be encountered in the
memoirs of any of America's foreign-born. Born Heinrich Hilgard,
"he soon changed his name to Henry Villard to thwart any
attempts by his father to trace him."[1] His career was one of the
most fabulous and turbulent any immigrant hewed out for himself. While he followed the path of journalism (from his early
twenties until he was thirty-one), he covered the Civil War
as correspondent on several of its fronts and there his son,
Oswald Garrison Villard,[2] tells us, he came close to being blown
up. Later he turned to the study of "public and corporate
financeering" and this led to his acquiring a fortune not only
once, but twice, and turned him into one of the most prominent
financial figures in America and in Germany.

As an eighteen-year old university student who ran away to
America in 1853, because he resented his father's attempt to
impose a distateful career on him, he went through a difficult
time at first. While clerking, teaching in a Pennsylvania Dutch
country school, and selling books by subscription, he attempted
to secure a toehold in journalism. The event that marked the
beginnings of a full-fledged journalistic career was an assignment
he suggested to the editors of the *Staatszeitung*, that he cover the
Lincoln-Douglas debates. It was there he formed an unfavorable
impression of Lincoln, which he never entirely overcame, though
he later accepted President Lincoln as "one of the great leaders
of mankind in adversity." After Lincoln's election, Villard was
detailed to remain with the President-elect in Springfield and
to accompany him to Washington for his inauguration. As war
correspondent until 1863, he left a record of more than four
hundred pages which contains his estimate of the military
maneuvers as well as of the men who executed them.

After his marriage to the daughter of William Lloyd Garrison,

---

1. Quoted by Michael Wreszyn, *Oswald Garrison Villard* (Bloomington, 1965), p. 7.
2. Oswald Garrison Villard, *Fighting Years* (New York, 1939).

he found the leisure to study "corporate financeering," and soon thereafter found the opportunity to put his new knowledge to use. During a visit to Germany, he was approached by a group of German bondholders to investigate the Oregon Railroad, which had defaulted on interest payments. The road was controlled by Ben Holladay, whose name is associated with the first overland stage lines to California. Villard took the trip to Oregon and was so impressed with the future of Oregon that, when the road defaulted again, he suggested to the German bondholders to let him take over the management of the road as well as of some steamship lines controlling the river traffic of the region. In building a communication system in the Northwest, he made in the words of his son: "A great empire . . . accessible. No longer would the grain of North Pacific slopes have to be taken around Cape Horn to Liverpool in sailing ships, a matter of months."[3] In Matthew Josephson's words he became "a prodigious captain of fortune and one of the robber barons."[4]

However, a miscalculation of about fifteen million dollars in the cost of extending the railroad, led to bankruptcy, which in Josephson's words "produced a scandal as sensational as anything Jay Gould could have evoked."[5] The uproar and, specifically, the accusations of the press, so outraged Villard's tender sensibilities that he took himself and his family to Germany to live.

After two years he returned as representative of some German banks to make his second fortune. As he says: "Once more, in 1890 Mr. Villard was the possessor of wealth." The presidency of the Northern Pacific Railroad was offered to him again and again he became involved in proxy fights, stockholders' meetings, and machinations by James J. Hill and his followers. It was during this second cycle of prosperity that he organized and became president of the Edison General Electric Company in 1889, bringing into it German capital. But when the company decided to merge with the Thomas-Houston Electric Company to become the General Electric Company, he disapproved and stepped down as president.

---

3. *Ibid.*, p. 47.
4. Matthew Josephson, *The Robber Barons*, (New York, 1934), p. 240-241.
5. *Ibid.*, p. 247.

It was also during this period that he bought the *Evening Post* and *The Nation* and installed Lawrence Godkin as editor of both. It was there that his German-born son, Oswald Garrison Villard, achieved his distinction as a fighting liberal and pacifist.

FROM *The Memoirs of Henry Villard**

My landing upon American soil took place under anything but auspicious circumstances. I was utterly destitute of money . . . and I literally did not know a single person . . . to whom I could apply for help and counsel. To crown all, I could not speak a word of English. . . .

In the course of the winter [in Belleville, Illinois where he had relatives] I had my first insight into American domestic life and society as it then existed in a comparatively new Western town. . . . I saw for the first time, the neatness, order, comfort, peace and quiet that, as a rule characterize the American home; and made the observation . . . that American women of any social position have not their equals in any other country for brightness, tact and true womanhood, and that they are as intelligent as American men and superior to them in all other respects—except, of course, knowledge of practical life. . . .

The first joint debate . . . between Douglas and Lincoln which I attended, took place on the afternoon of August 21st, 1858 at Ottawa, Illinois. . . . As far as all external conditions were concerned, there was nothing in favor of Lincoln. He had a lean, lank, indescribably gawky figure, and an odd-featured, wrinkled, inexpressive, and altogether uncomely face. . . . He was inordinately fond of jokes, anecdotes and stories. He loved to hear them, and still more to tell them himself out of the inexhaustible supply provided by his good memory and his fertile fancy. There would have been no harm in this but for the fact that, the coarser the joke, the lower the anecdote, and the more risky the story, the more he enjoyed them, especially when they were of his own invention. . . .

In one respect the Convention proved a great disappointment to me. I was enthusiastically for the nomination of William H. Seward . . . I therefore shared fully the intense

---

*Henry Villard, *The Memoirs of Henry Villard* (Boston: Houghton Mifflin Company, 1916). By permission of the publishers.

chagrin of the New York and other States delegations when, on the third ballot, Abraham Lincoln received a larger vote than Seward . . . I had not got over the prejudice against Lincoln with which my personal contact with him in 1858 imbued me. . . .

[Speaking in the third person] His faith in the future of western Oregon was so great . . . that he fully believed in the possibility of a satisfactory solution of the difficult problem he had set for himself. . . . The vast region drained by the Columbia and its tributaries formed a very empire in its extent. Its material development was entirely dependent upon the present and future transportation facilities within its limits. Mr. Villard's rule over these and, through them, over the whole future of that promising part of the country was rendered all but absolute by his personal success. . . .

Thus, in a little over two years from the birth of the Oregon Railway and Navigation Company, Mr. Villard had assumed the burden of forging a new rail chain across the continent, twenty-seven hundred miles long, by connecting the existing links. . . .

He was told [by his auditors] that he was practically insolvent, and that the Oregon & Transcontinental Company was on the verge of bankruptcy. . . . His fate was certainly tragic. Within a few years, he had risen from entire obscurity to the enviable position of one of the leaders of the material progress of our age. . . . But his fall from might to helplessness, from wealth to poverty, from public admiration to wide condemnation, was far more rapid than his rise. . . .

In the course of the summer, [after his return from Germany], a marvellous turn of affairs, almost stranger than fiction, occured, which with all but magic suddenness, raised him once more to his former position before the public. . . . Mr. Villard was called on for help . . . [by the] president of the Oregon and Transcontinental and of the Oregon Railway & Navigation companies and a representative of the imperilled firm. . . . They appealed strongly to his loyalty to save the two companies created by himself, and coupled with their terms an offer not only to turn over to him the management. . . . but to place in his hands, unconditionally, sufficient proxies for the next Northern Pacific election of directors to put it in his power to elect to the board of that company anyone he liked. . . . Having been a Journalist, he knew well the power of the press for good or evil, and that led him to the idealistic conception that he could render no better public service than by founding, or getting control of, a newspaper of absolute independence and outspokenness on public matters. . . . Every reader of "The Evening Post," the whole American press, and in fact the American people generally, know that the paper has ever been true to those high aims for which he was ready to make many sacrifices when he purchased its control. . . .

Although he was no longer a working participant in current affairs, it was not in his nature to be simply an indifferent observer of passing events. . . . The thought that, through his instrumentality, it was rendered possible to wage an incessant war against public abuses of every kind through the "Evening Post's" relentless championship of political reform, was a source of just pride to him . . .

Marie E. Zakrszewska
Physician
1829-1902

> I am not a great personage, either through in-
> herited qualifications or through the work that I
> have to show to the world; yet . . . I have ac-
> complished more than many women of genius
> and education would have done in my place, for
> the reason that confidence and faith in their own
> powers were wanting.

In Marie Zakrszewska we have a woman of German birth who stands with Dr. Elizabeth Blackwell as one of the foremost fighters for the acceptance of women in medicine and for making specialized treatment in infirmaries and hospitals available to women and children.

That "confidence and faith" in her own powers to which she attributes her success, was acquired through battling with men since her youth. Opposed by her father who disapproved of a career in trained midwifery and who wanted her to be married instead, she also battled with the authorities, who considered her too young at eighteen to be admitted for training. When she graduated at twenty-two, it was to receive a "diploma of highest degree." Through the influence of a sponsoring physician, she was appointed chief accoucheuse at the Charité, at Berlin, despite the violent objections and jealousies of physicians and older rivals, only to lose her position through the sudden death of her sponsor. At that crucial moment she remembered a pronouncement he had made when the first report of the Pennsylvania Female Medical College, established in 1850, reached him: "In America women will become physicians, like the men; this shows that only in a republic can it be proved that science has no sex."

His optimism was without foundation. When she arrived in America in 1853, at the age of twenty-four, it was five years after the Seneca Falls Conference, organized by Lucretia Mott and Elizabeth Cady Stanton, which was a protest against male tyranny. Though some medical schools admitted women, clinical study was closed to them. To get this needed experience, it was necessary to go to European schools.

Dr. Elizabeth Blackwell agreed to help. She and her sister, Emily, had procured a charter from the New York Legislature to establish the New York Infirmary for Indigent Women and Children, which soon had to be abandoned for lack of funds. Elizabeth Blackwell became Marie Zakrszewska's "preceptor," which was a necessary preliminary for anyone entering medical school. She also taught her English and secured her admission to the Cleveland Medical College [Western Reserve]. At the medical school the male students petitioned for the exclusion of the woman who had been admitted. The college refused, but had to promise that they would not again admit women. It was difficult to find a boarding house that would brave the criticism for accepting "doctoresses."

When she received the M.D. degree in 1856, at the age of twenty-seven, no one would rent an office to her and she was grateful when Dr. Blackwell let her have her back parlor. In 1857 the infirmary reopened under the direction of Elizabeth and Emily Blackwell and Marie Zakrszewska, all of whom worked without compensation.

Dr. Zakrszewska's next theater of operation was Boston, where she accepted the post of professor of obstetrics in the New England Female Medical College, only to relinquish it within three years because of lack of clinical facilities which she considered essential for medical training.

Her third attempt was to establish with the aid of interested patrons the New England Hospital for Women and Children. There her efforts were finally crowned with success. Bequests came in which made needed expansion possible. There a training school for nurses was begun, whose first graduate organized the Bellevue Hospital Training School, as well as those of the Massachusetts General Hospital and Boston City Hospital.

This medical pioneer had the great satisfaction of seeing women physicians admitted to membership by the Massachusetts Medical Society and in 1890 of having them accepted as medical students on equal terms with men at Johns Hopkins.

FROM *A Woman's Quest**

I had come here [America] for a purpose—to carry out the plan which a despotic government and its servile agents had prevented me from doing in my native city. I had to show to those men who had opposed me so strongly, because I was a woman that, in this land of liberty, equality and fraternity, I could maintain that position which they would not permit me at home. . . .

She [Dr. Elizabeth Blackwell] told me of her plan of founding a hospital—the long-cherished idea of my life—and said that she had opened a little dispensary . . . which was designed to be the nucleus for this hospital and she invited me to come and assist her. . . . Under these conditions, I became the student of Dr. Elizabeth Blackwell, she assuming the role of medical preceptor, as well as most patient instructor in the English language. . . .

'The Emancipated Woman!' That was the horror of the day, in social life as in the press. And woe to those women who perhaps through lack of physical beauty, or through want of taste in dress, or through a too profound seriousness, did not observe all social graces in detail. They became objects of criticism in private and in public. . . .

Indeed, even this feeling that our presence was objectionable was of use in our training, as it gave us a strong foretaste of

---

*Marie E. Zakrszewska, *A Woman's Quest* (New York: Appleton & Co., 1924). By permission of Meredith Press.

the prejudice which we were to meet in our professional lives. And it helped us in many ways to develop the courage which we were to need in meeting the offensive behavior of many physicians and students with whom we were obliged to come in contact when trying to seek fellowship in private practice, or to increase our knowledge, or to gain admittance to public institutions.

In this primitive, first true 'Woman's Hospital' in the world [Dr. Blackwell's dispensary], I moved in March, superintending all its arrangements. . . . And before a month had passed, we had our beds filled with patients and a daily attendance of thirty or more dispensary patients. Drs. Elizabeth and Emily Blackwell and myself each attended the dispensary two mornings a week, from nine to twelve, while four students from the Philadephia college came to live in the hospital, in the capacity of internes, apothecaries and pupils of nursing.

[On July 1, 1862] . . . was born the New England Hospital for Women and Children . . . a few men physicians being willing to aid us by giving us their names as consultants. . . . Other friends of women's education soon joined us and became directors. . . . Thus in the midst of the Civil War we started our work and many a soldier's family thanked us for so doing, for just then the darkest days of the struggle gave us special opportunity to advise and comfort. . . .

Drs. Blackwell, Ann Preston and myself stood no longer alone as the bearers of an idea—hundred of young women had joined us. The path had been broken, and the profession had been obliged to yield, and to acknowledge the capacity of women physicians. . . .

To-day, its condescending proposal for my examination for admission [to the Massachusetts Medical Society where she had been refused several times] has been made, and I am only a little more than fifty years old. But twenty-six and one half years of practice (that is nearly at the end of my career), my only personal interest in this affair is that I am happy that the younger women can have the benefit of an association which is very desirable for all beginners, and most desirable in assisting women to gain the position for which they strive.

I have done my part, and I feel satisfied with the results achieved. I have aided the women of this country by word and deed, by example and sacrifice, and I am willing to retire, leaving them the field in which to sow and reap where I have helped to plow, associated as I have been with the pioneer women in the medical profession.

Samuel Gompers
Cigar-Maker, Labor Leader
1850-1925

> In religion I am a working man. In politics I am a working man and in every nerve, in every fiber, in every aspiration I am on the side which will advance the interests of my fellow working men.

One of the towering giants among the foreign-born was Samuel Gompers. Like Andrew Carnegie he was thirteen when brought to America. By the time the Gompers family arrived in 1863, Andrew Carnegie was well on the way to "millionaire-dom." Though at opposite sides of the pole, Andrew Carnegie found an apologist in Samuel Gompers who accepted and disseminated the widely held opinion that the disastrous Homestead Strike would not have turned out as it did, if Andrew Carnegie had not been away from America at that time.

All but the last two decades of the nineteenth century represented to labor aspirants striving to establish a viable labor movement, a vast battlefield strewn with the wreckage of labor's hopes. All who had preceded Gompers as organizers of national labor movement, had failed. Guided by what he considered their errors, Gompers strove obstinately to steer clear of the reefs that had wrecked their efforts. Of these dangers the most obvious seemed to him to be participation by labor organizations in political and reform movements.

As a native of Great Britain, he had the inestimable advantage of not having to learn the language. With a self-assurance that is uncommon among the foreign-born, he asserted: "Never for a moment did I think of myself as an alien." Even as a child, he tells, he was aware of the misery of unemployment and of the benefits of unionism. He had started to work at the age of ten, first as an apprentice to a shoe-maker and when he found the work noisome, as an apprentice to a cigar-maker. A fact that influenced him was that cigar-makers in England had a "society" (which financed the emigration of the Gompers family), whereas the shoe-makers had none. As a mature cigar-maker in America he remarked that cigar-makers had "mind-peace." In post-Civil War America, beginning to seethe with labor unrest, he found a fertile field for his gospel of union organization and ample opportunity for the exercise of his talents.

At fourteen he joined the English-speaking local and at sixteen he represented his shop-mates in their demand for concessions, which he won. Ferdinand Laurrell, a "workman" like himself, to whom he dedicated his autobiography, and Adolf Strasser, also a trade union leader, became his "mental guides." His education had ended at ten and in New York he augmented it by attending lectures at Cooper Union. He also introduced the custom in the shops in which he worked for all to contribute to a fund for newspapers, magazines, and books, which one would read aloud while the rest worked, the reader being re-compensed by a certain number of cigars contributed by each listener. Trade union activities offered him additional opportunities for education as well as "many extension courses in the discipline of life."

Though he was a proud man of enormous personal dignity, when sent as union representative, he traveled on "immigrant trains, freight cars, cheap boats, frequently at his own expense. He was often in desperate straits, when everything had to be pawned, except his wife's gold wedding ring. She had married him when she was sixteen, and he eighteen, and she gave him unfaltering support throughout her life. His children, he reveals, frequently went to bed hungry. He lost several during their infancy and a favorite daughter, a singer, six years before his own death. He had just bought a piece of jewelry for her in Italy, a "trinket," as he disdainfully called it, when he received the news of her death in the influenza epidemic of 1918.

When a consolidation of several craft unions took place in 1881, he was elected Vice-President. By then he was a skilled labor leader who had experienced many setbacks and who had participated in power struggles with Socialist factions and with the Knights of Labor. Five years later, in 1886, this organization became the American Federation of Labor. It was decided that a full-time president was needed and this office went to Gompers at a salary of one thousand dollars a year, which was less than what he earned as a cigar-maker. He was then thirty-six years of age. Except for one year, 1895, which he calls his "sabbatical year," he remained president of the A.F.L. from 1886 until 1924. In 1895 he was unseated by James McBride of the United Mine Workers, who was supported by the Socialists.

During his presidency, Gompers built enormous prestige for his organization and for himself. He controlled policy, helped to organize new unions, counselled them, sponsored educational policies, lectures, trade schools, and battled for improvements. Fearless and outspoken, he appeared before commissions and committees to urge passage of laws and to condemn practices and legislation inimical to labor. Colleges and universities invited him to present his viewpoint. He conferred with legislators, Presidents, industrialists, and crowned heads. When offered a nomination for the Senate on the Democratic as well as the Republican tickets, and one year later, for Congress on the Republican ticket, he declined. Upon being informed that, if elected, William Jennings Bryan intended to offer him a cabinet post, he let it be known that he would not accept.

Because he considered Utopian schemes incompatible with the practical aims of unionism, he maintained a constant battle with the Socialists, who looked upon laboring people as their natural allies. On many issues Gompers allied himself with reactionary elements. He favored exclusion of Oriental immigrants, because of fear that the cigar industry would become "Chinaized." He was also in favor of curbing immigration and supported the literacy test as a method of halting undesirable immigration.

Unlike the Socialists, who withheld their support for World War I as an "imperialist war," Gompers fully endorsed the war effort. It was a great triumph for him when President Wilson appointed him a member of the Council of National Defense. By then the A.F.L. had grown from an organization occupying a one-room office into one that required a seven-story structure.

The war over, he was one of the representatives on the International Labor Commission, where he helped to draw up a declaration of labor principles. In 1918 he organized the Pan-American Federation of Labor "in the spirit of the Monroe Doctrine." Stricken during a meeting in Mexico, he was quickly transported to American soil, to die as the year 1924 was drawing to its end.

FROM *Seventy Years of Life and Labor**

There was a vast difference between those early unions and the unions of to-day. . . . There was no sustained effort to secure fair wages through collective bargaining. The employer fixed wages until he shoved them down to a point where human endurance revolted. Often the revolt started by an individual . . . who rose and declared: 'I am going on strike. All who remain at work are scabs.' Usually the workers went out with him. . . .

. . . From that industrial center [New York] came the first constructive, efficient American trade union organization, that of the cigar-makers, followed by the furniture workers, the printers, the tailors, the plasterers, and others. . . .

In 1873 began my experience with financial crises. As a New York workman in 1873, I first watched the crisis and depression of what we now call the business cycle. It is a frightful thing to watch a period of unemployment, but it is infinitely more terrible when your friends and fellow workmen are hungry and in dire need because denied the opportunity to earn a living. . . .

I saw how professions of radicalism and sensationalism concentrated all the forces of organized society against a labor movement . . . I saw that leadership in the labor movement could be safely entrusted only to those in whose hearts and minds had been woven the experience of earning their bread by daily labor. . . . I saw the danger of entangling alliances with intellectuals who did not understand that to experiment with the labor movement was to experiment with human life.

It has always been impossible for me to subordinate my manhood to any living person—whether he were boss or President of the United States. I treat everybody with respect. I never yield to anyone on account of his position. I never hold myself superior to the poorest devil in all the world. . . .

The 'nineties brought no spectacular growth for the A.F. of L. There was steady progress, but it seemed painfully slow

to my ardent hopes and boundless aspirations. I fairly yearned
for a stronger labor movement in order that greater justice and
opportunity might come into the lives of the world's workers.
. . . Though we labor men usually try to express the labor
movement in practical terms, still it is fundamentally spiritual
—a cause which inspires dedication as completely as any
religious movement. . . .

I had not the slightest idea of being again [after 1895] a
candidate for the presidency of the Federation. With the work
which I had done during the year, including newspaper and
magazine articles, my income was larger than the salary the
Federation paid its president. . . . But I was none the less, as
much as anyone, opposed to allowing compulsory arbitration
to constitute one of the tenets of the American labor movement
. . . Finally, I yielded and at the convention was elected to
the presidency over McBride who had occupied that position
one year. . . .

The 1908 [Denver] convention authorized the building of
a national labor headquarters. . . . To my mind the building
was to be of the nature of a Labor Temple, so I opposed the
customary plan of letting the ground floor for stores lest the
money-changers should filter into the temple. . . .

When we moved into our office building, I gave orders that
each morning the American flag should be raised on our flag-
pole and under it the pennant of the A.F. of L. and that at
sunset they should be lowered. The order typified my conception of the relationship of the A.F. of L. to the Stars and
Stripes. . . .

America to me is an ideal—though I could not condone
political shortcomings or economic injustice, yet I resent the
misinterpretation of the spirit of America in any council and
especially in a world-assembly. To befoul an adopted country
in order to manufacture Socialist propaganda seemed to me to
indicate something essentially immoral in Socialist policies. . . .

VOLUME II

Next to my desire to protect child life was my resentment
of unemployment, particularly unemployment in the United
States. . . . The whole situation had forced upon me a feeling

of outrage. If a blight came as an act of nature or what is termed an act of God, there could be no just cause for criticism or complaint or protest. But in a country such as ours, rich as a nation could be, when large masses of our citizenship were forced to endure hunger because unemployed, my protest knew no bounds. . . .

With the twentieth century there came a period of extraordinarily rapid growth in the A.F. of L. It was the harvest of the years of organizing work which were beginning to bear fruits. Increase in numbers took the form of affiliation of national trade organizations and the extension of the principle of organization to workers in what were then called the 'unskilled' occupations. . . .

America is the product of the daring, the genius, the idealism of those who left homes and kindred to settle in the new land. It is an ideal typifying a haven and an opportunity. In the early days, boundless and undeveloped resources made possible and expedient a policy of stimulating immigration. It was not until industrialism developed and there were evidences that the newer immigration was not being assimilated that as a nation we began to consider policies of regulation. . . . I have always opposed Chinese immigration, not only because of the effect of Chinese standards of life and work, but because of the racial problem created when Chinese and white workers were brought into close contact of living and working side by side. . . .

The Clayton Anti-Trust Law was signed by President Wilson. Oct. 15, 1914. . . . Despite all that judges have done to weaken Labor's Magna Charta, the concept that labor is not a commodity or article of commerce has had opportunity to become a part of the making of a national mind in a way that works an advance to a higher level of human justice. . . .

We American trade unionists want to work out our problems in the spirit of true Americanism—a spirit that embodies our broadest and highest ideals. If we do not succeed it will be due to no fault of ours. We have been building the A.F. of L. in conformity with what we believe to be the original intent and purpose of America. I have an abiding faith that we will succeed and with that success are involved the progress and welfare of the great mass of America's citizenship.

Henry Morgenthau
Lawyer, Financier, Diplomat
1856-1946

> Every man has his master passion: mine is for
> *democracy*. I believe that history's best efforts in
> democracy is the United States, which has rooted
> in its Constitution all that any group of its citizens
> can legitimately desire.

One of the most fortunate of immigrants was Henry Morgenthau. A "special gift for making money," to which he admitted, brought him a large share of the benefits from the golden shower that made millionaires of natives and foreign-born alike. In addition he could make the assertion that he had been enabled "to find satisfaction for every one of my ambitions."

Ten years of age when he was brought from Germany in 1866, the opportunity was his to keep pace with a growing New York and a growing nation. He began a college education at the College of the City of New York, but his father's business reverses forced him to withdraw. Working in a real estate office directed his attention to the study of the law. As a lawyer he served the newly established department stores, Abraham and Straus in Brooklyn, Macy's and Wanamaker's in New York. His shrewd business sense caused him to anticipate the spread uptown and, consequently he bought real estate in Harlem and as far uptown as 181st Street and Dykeman Heights, where the new subway was being built. He also developed 125th Street and turned it into an industrial artery. He was in his early fifties when he felt he had made enough money to be able to turn his back on "materialistic pursuits" and to devote himself to practising the pursuits of an "idealist."

His "idealistic inclinations" took him into philanthropy and in 1912 into the camp of the Democratic Party, where he served as chairman of the Finance Committee during the Wilson campaign. After the election of Woodrow Wilson he left twenty-five thousand dollars in the treasury and no unpaid bills. President Wilson appointed him ambassador to Turkey, a post which he accepted only after urgings by the President and by his friends. In Turkey he spread the "gospel of Americanism" and acted as political mentor to the Turks, while laboring at the same time "to avert the terrible fate of the Armenians and the Jews." No narrow sectarian, he admired the work of the missionaries and encouraged their efforts. That he was influential with the Turks is attested to by an Armenian refugee physician who states: "No United States official in history had been so successful with the Turks. . . . He often called on Talaat Pasha, as we all know, to intercede for some Armenian's life and liberty."[1]

During World War I he undertook a mission to Turkey—of which he speaks as "secret," but which Felix Frankfurter[2] (who was assigned to accompany him), reveals to have been intended to detach Turkey from her alliance with Germany. The mission failed and provided Frankfurter with the justification for saying of Morgenthau, "the froth was the man."[3]

Henry Morgenthau was such a dedicated American that he met the persistent wooing of Zionists with this answer: "We Jews of America have found America to be our Zion. Therefore I refuse to allow myself to be called a Zionist. I am an American."[4]

FROM *All in a Life-Time**

. . . In 1862 a tariff had been enacted by the United States which greatly increased the duty on cigars. For many years the largest part of his [the elder Morgenthau] production had been exported to the United States. . . . Unfortunately the slow freighter that carried the last and biggest shipment arrived one day too late . . . That day's delay meant the difference between profit and disaster to my father . . .

Of my life at City College I wish that I could write more because I wish I had been privileged to graduate with the Class of 1875. . . . My college career was rudely ended . . . when my father withdrew me and put me to work. His dif-

---

1. Dr. A. Nakashian, *A Man Who Found a Country* (London, 1940), p. 220.
2. Felix Frankfurter, *Felix Frankfurter Reminisces* (New York, 1960).
3. *Ibid.*, p. 146.
4. Quoted by Eric F. Goldman, *Rendezvous with Destiny* (New York, 1950) p. 184.

*Henry Morgenthau, *All in a Life-Time* (New York: Doubleday & Co., Inc., 1922).

ficulty in mastering the English language and American commercial methods were handicaps too severe for him. He lost most of his original money, and his unreinforced efforts could not support us all. . . .

In 1880, I turned my attention to Harlem where nearly all the brownstone and brick houses that had been built in the seventies were in the hands of mortgagees. . . . Nearly all of Harlem was for sale. . . . The success of my real estate operations had won me away from the exclusive devotion to the law which is so essential to rise in that profession. In figuring the profits that had been made by the various real estate syndicates that I had managed since 1891, I was surprised at the total . . . . So why not induce some leading financiers to join me in the formation of a real estate trust company, which would do for real estate what the banking institutions have done for the railroads and industrials? . . .

'Conscience doth make cowards of us all.' Not mine—mine made me a politician. At fifty-five years of age, financially independent . . . and recently released from the toils of materialism, it ceaselessly confronted me with my duty to pay back, in the form of public service, the overdraft which I had been permitted to make upon the opportunities of this country. Repayment in money alone would not suffice; I must pay in the form of personal service, for which my experience had equipped me. . . .

. . . During this period, in which I was 'finding myself,' I was attracted to the career of Woodrow Wilson. I admired the courage with which he was fighting the battle of democray at Princeton. . . . I asked him whether he was really a candidate for President of the United States . . . 'Governor,' I said, 'my object in asking you this question was to offer my unreserved moral and financial support of your candidacy.' . . . And when he went into the White House he went without obligations, expressed or implied, to any man for any money that had been contributed during the campaign. . . .

. . . Senator O'Gorman telephoned me from Washington that he had been requested by the President to offer me the Ambassadorship to Turkey. I apparently astonished him when I told him to please thank the President for me, but that I would not accept. . . . I called on the President and he said: 'I want you to take the Embassy at Constantinople. I am convinced that the two posts that demand the greatest intellectual equipment in our representatives are Turkey and China. Therefore, I am particularly concerned to have, in these two countries, men upon whom I can absolutely rely for sound judgment and knowledge of human nature. This is the reason I am asking you to take the post at Constantinople. . . .

America's true mission in Turkey, I felt, was to foster the permanent civilizing work of the Christian missions, which so gloriously exemplified the American spirit at its best. . . . As I frequently explained to Turkish government officers . . . this spirit of good will . . . overflowed our boundaries into other lands, partly because we wished to share our good fortune with others, and chiefly because it was prescribed by the Christian faith. . . .

In January 1916 I applied to the State Department for a leave of absence . . . I spent the first few days after my return to the United States with my old political friends in Washington, and I was shocked at the prevailing political atmosphere. Not one of the numerous men high in the Administration with whom I talked had the slightest hope that President Wilson could be reelected that fall. . . . I take pride in the consciousness—that my activities were one of the necessary factors that led to Mr. Wilsons's reelection in 1916.

Samuel S. McClure
Editorial Genius, Muckraker
1857-1949

> There was one fixed determination, one constant quantity in my life as a boy—the desire to get an education. That was my one steadiness . . . the one thing I really meant to do was to get an education and in that I never wavered.

The experiences of Samuel S. McClure during his student years offer a clear illustration of the sacrifices that were required of those in quest of an education, who depended solely on their own earnings. Their lives were a constant round of hunger, cold, and privation.

Like Andrew Carnegie and Samuel Gompers, he had the advantage of coming from an English-speaking country. Nine years old when brought from Ulster in 1866, he was the oldest son of a widow whose husband had lost his life in an industrial accident. His mother was a plucky woman. Working first as a servant, she took in washing in order to keep her family together. Later she married a farmer, who had need of all the help she and her boys could give him. Though Samuel had started high school, he had to give it up when his stepfather died. His conscience told him that as the oldest son it was his duty to work the farm for his mother.

From the farm he went to Knox College, where he spent seven years, acquiring a secondary as well as a college education and interrupting his studies on and off to earn money. Despite hardships that seem rigorous even for immigrants, he graduated third in his class. At college he met the girl he wanted to marry, who was the attractive and accomplished daughter of the professor of Latin. To her parents he was an unwelcome suitor.

He began his career with an apprenticeship in journalism. His first creative undertaking was to start a newspaper syndicate that would furnish fiction by the best known British and American writers to newspapers at fixed charges. The plan to establish his own magazine was a natural step forward. What multiplied his difficulties was the fact that the magazine began publication just before the onset of the Panic of 1893. Nevertheless the magazine survived and by 1896 began to forge ahead to become the most powerful instrument for economic and political reform. It became the leader of the muckraking movement and an example for the other magazines to follow.

In its pages were published such muckraking articles as Ida M. Tarbell's *History of the Standard Oil Company*, the exposures of Lincoln Steffens and Ray Stannard Baker, as well as fiction by the foremost British and American authors.

Affected by the propaganda of the Progressives, McClure himself turned "social critic" and became an ardent advocate of the commission form of government as a cure for municipal corruption. But the end of the reform movement was near; when the people began to lose interest in reform, hostile elements moved in to extinguish the flame by refusing credit and withdrawing advertising from the magazines engaged in muckraking. Among the victims was McClure. His magazine was taken over by the

West Virginia Pulp and Paper Company. McClure attributed the failure to "poor business methods." In his fifties, he had apparently exhausted his store of initiative and enthusiasm. Though he had been a power in the magazine world, he remained a "forgotten man" for the remainder of his life, a relic that had been washed ashore by the crest of a wave, which had receded forever.

FROM *My Autobiography*[*]

. . . our arrival in America was the beginning of very hard times for my mother and us boys. . . . my mother went to Valparaiso and got a place as servant in a household there. Later Doctor Everts' wife, who had probably heard of my mother's efforts to get along, came to her and told her that she would gladly let her have one of the downstairs corner rooms in the house for herself and her boys, if my mother would do the family washing. . . .

One day in September, my mother called me to her and told me that she could not see any chance for me on the farm. If I wanted more education, I must manage to get it for myself, and the best thing for me to do was to go away and try. At Valparaiso a new High School was to open that fall, and my mother thought I had better go there and see if I could work for my board and go to school. I followed her advice. . . . I had my board and lodging from Dr. Cass, but not a penny to buy clothes or books. Of course I had no overcoat. . . . When it was cold—and it was often bitterly cold —I ran. Speed was my overcoat. . . .

I had got off the train to Knox College at Galesburg, Illinois, with fifteen cents in my pocket. I had on my only suit of clothes and my mother had made them. . . . There are few feelings any deeper than those with which a country boy gazes for the first time upon the college that he feels is going to supply all the deficiencies he feels in himself, and fit him to struggle in the world. . . . I was seventeen, and it was a seven years' job that I was starting upon, with fifteen cents in my pocket. . . .

The winter began in November and was one of the coldest

---

[*]Samuel S. McClure, *My Autobiography* (New York: Frederick A. Stokes Company, 1914).

I have ever known . . . Nearly every night the pail of water in my room used to freeze solid and swell up in the center. I had a fur cap by this time, and I used always to eat my meals walking up and down the room, with my cap and woolen mittens on. I seldom had anything to eat but bread, and it froze so hard that it was full of ice and hard to chew. . . . Sometimes my food did not cost me more than eighteen cents a week. Then, again, I would get reckless, and would live high, spending as much as seventy-four cents a week. . . .

. . . But I had expected to be a very different fellow when I got through college from the fellow I had always been. When I found that I was still just the same boy a feeling of discouragement weighed me down. I had looked forward for eight years to graduating, and I had always thought that when I graduated I would be tall, that I would know a great deal, and that I would have all the plans made for my life. Here I was, no taller, no wiser, and with no plans at all. The future was an absolute blank ahead of me. . . .

When, at last, I went West to be married, Professor Hurd would allow me to call at the house only once before the actual ceremony. . . . I realized perfectly well that he had every reason to expect a better marriage for his daughter. . . .

Early in 1892 Mr. Phillips [a classmate at Knox] began to plan actively to launch a new fifteen-cent monthly. . . . I had begun to see that there was not much further growth to be hoped for in the syndicate. . . . The only practical expansion was in the direction of a magazine. . . . There was certainly never a more inopportune time to launch a new business. [Panic of 1893] . . .

Kipling once said to me: 'It takes the young man to find the young man.' And that is true. The new talent is usually discovered by the editor who faces the future without predilections and without a gallery of past successes. No man's judgment retains that openness for very many years. His successes become his limitations. . . .

. . . the origin of what was later called the 'muck-raking' movement was accidental. It came from no formulated plan to attack existing institutions, but was the result of merely taking up in the magazine some of the problems that were beginning to interest the people a little before the newspapers and other magazines took them up. . . .

As a foreign-born citizen of this country, I would like to do my part to help bring about the realization of the very noble American Ideal, which, when I was a boy, was universally believed in, here and in Europe. I believe that the dishonest administration of public affairs in our cities has come about largely through carelessness, and that the remedy is as simple, as easily understood, and as possible of attainment, as the remedy for typhoid fever. . . . This very simple remedy is the establishment in every municipality, of what, in a railroad, is called a board of directors, in a German city is called the Council, and in an American city is called the commission form of government.

Edward Bok
Editorial Genius, Reformer
1863-1930

> No man has a right to leave the world no better than he found it. He must add something to it: either he must make its people better and happier, or he must make the face of the world fairer to look at.

So spake Edward Bok in the fulness of his conviction that he had carried out his grandfather's dictum: "Make you the world a bit more beautiful and better because you have been in it."

The qualities considered essential for success during the "Gilded Age" were dormant in the seven-year-old boy when he was brought to America from the Netherlands in 1870. Unusually resourceful, ambitious and shrewd, he had carried out several business schemes by the time he quit school to go to work at the age of thirteen.

Starting as an office boy, he set out to learn stenography. It was as a stenographer in the Scribner organization that he began to climb the ladder to success. In true tycoon fashion he combined his regular job with other business interests. A church magazine he edited became, after he sold it, first *The American Magazine,* and later, *The Cosmopolitan Magazine.* Also while working for the Scribner company, he directed a service which supplied syndicated articles and a weekly literary letter to newspapers. He continued this service even after he had become a successful editor.

It was through his *Literary Leaves* that he attracted the attention of Cyrus Curtis, whose wife was the first editor of *Ladies' Home Journal*. In accepting Curtis' offer to become the editor of the magazine, Bok succeeded in raising the circulation of *Ladies Home Journal* from 440,000 to 1,750,000. At the time of his retirement the circulation reached two million and a single issue carried advertising amounting to over one million dollars.

This was accomplished by raising the literary level of the magazine, as well as by the introduction of many "firsts" in publishing history. For instance, Edward Bok was the first to use the idea of offering free education to young people for a certain number of subscriptions. He created a department in charge of a physician which offered to expectant mothers pre-natal as well as post-natal care, thus raising eighty thousand babies by mail. While he is credited with campaigning for many improvements in personal living and in matters of civic importance, he showed his mettle most clearly in his successful fight to ban patent medicines from the pages of the magazines. For this he has won a permanent place among the band of fighters who accomplished so much for American reform during the years prior to World War I.[1]

In 1919, after thirty years at the helm of the magazine he had made one of the most influential in America, Bok retired from active work and began the story of his "Americanization."

FROM *The Americanization of Edward Bok**

[Bok writing in the third person] Edward looked about and decided that the time had come for him, young as he was, to begin some sort of wage-earning. But how and where? The answer he found one afternoon when standing before the show-window of a baker in the neighborhood. . . . And Edward Bok, there and then, got his first job. He went in, found a step-ladder, and put so much Dutch energy into the cleaning of the large show-window that the baker immediately arranged

---

1. See Louis Filler, *Crusaders for American Liberalism*, (Yellow Springs, Ohio, 1961).

*Edward W. Bok, *The Americanization of Edward Bok* (New York: Charles Scribner's Sons, 1937). Reprinted by permission.

with him to clean it every Tuesday and Friday afternoon after school. The salary was to be fifty cents per week! . . .

Edward [who was now a stenographer] had now become tremendously interested in the stock game which he saw constantly played by the great financier [Jay Gould]; and having a little móney saved up, he concluded that he would follow in the wake of Mr. Gould's orders. . . . Of course the boy's buying and selling tallied precisely with the rise and fall of Western Union stock. It could scarcely have been otherwise. Jay Gould had the cards all in his hands; and as he bought and sold, Edward bought and sold. . . .

The editor is the pivot of a magazine. On him everything turns. If his gauge of the public is correct, readers will come; they cannot help coming to the man who has something to say himself, or who presents writers who have. And if the reader comes, the advertiser must come. He must go where his largest market is: where the buyers are. . . .

Another of Bok's methods in editing was to do the common thing in an uncommon way. He had the faculty of putting old wine in new bottles and the public liked it. His ideas were not new; he knew there were no new ideas, but he presented his ideas in such a way that they seemed new. . . .

[In discussing his views of America Bok speaks in the first person] As a Dutch boy, one of the cardinal truths taught me was that whatever was worth doing was worth doing well: that next to honesty came thoroughness as a factor to success. . . . I came to America to be taught exactly the opposite. The two infernal Americanisms 'That's good enough' and 'That will do' were early early taught me, together with the maxim of quantity rather than quality. . . . It was . . . impossible for the American to work with sufficient patience and care to achieve a result. . . .

In the matter of education America fell far short in what should be the strongest of all her institutions: the public school. . . . If there is one thing that I, as a foreign-born child, should have been carefully taught, it is the English language. . . . There was absolutely no indication on the part of teacher or principal of responsibility for seeing that a foreign-born boy should acquire the English language correctly. . . .

As the most vital part of my life, when I was to become an American citizen and exercise the right of suffrage, America fell entirely short. It reached out not even the suggestion of a hand . . . It must be recalled that I was only twenty-one years old, with scant education, and with no civic agency offering me the information I was seeking [political education]. . . .

However America may have failed to help my transition from a foreigner into an American, I owe to her the most priceless gift that any nation can offer and that is opportunity. . . . here a man can go as far as his abilities will carry him. . . . But into the best that the foreign-born can retain, America can graft such a wealth of inspiration, so high a national idealism, so great an opportunity for the highest endeavor, as to make him the fortunate man of the earth to-day.

Laurence Larson
Teacher, Historian
1868-1938

> For more than sixty years I have shared in the citizenship of the great Republic. I owe no allegiance, political or spiritual, to any other land; but my past is a fact and a vital fact that I cannot ignore. Between an active loyalty to a land and a system into which one has been received and an honest recognition of the values that inhere in a culture out of which one has come, there need be no conflict.

It is a proven fact that the attachment to old world values was felt acutely by the tradition-directed immigrants of the nineteenth century. They maintained their langauge and lore because they knew no other, and attempted to impose the status quo on their progeny as a means of strengthening the bonds between the generations. It was with bitterness that many watched their children grow away from them.

The drama of how to reconcile the conflicting claims between old and new traditions underlies the recollections of Laurence Larson. He was not quite two in 1870, when his parents and a group of relatives and friends severed their ties in Norway and set out for the West. Their destination was northern Iowa, on the edge of the settled area. At first they shared a "dugout" with another Norwegian family, then they progressed to their own, one-room dwelling, "part dugout, part loghouse," until, ten years later, they acquired a frame house. By then the father had been a citizen for years and the region had grown into a close-knit community, where people lived as Norwegians, "or as nearly so as conditions would permit." He learned to read and write Norwegian, not only because the parents of the region could not teach their children what they themselves did not know, but because "they surely would have taught us their language first." He admits that the "older generation never became Americans in a positive sense, though more loyal citizens never lived." They prospered; eventually he was sent to college.

Though Mr. Larson gives us a saga of the acculturation of a group of Norwegians in Iowa, there is about it the suggestion that what he describes was characteristic of other immigrant clusters in the prairie states. The picture that emerges from the novels of Vilhelm Moberg about the Swedes in Minnesota and the chronicles of O. E. Rolvaag about the Norwegians of the northwestern frontier of the United States, tallies with the auto-biographical facts disclosed by Mr. Larson. In his descriptions of the mode of life—the solitude, the violent thunderstorms, the ferocious blizzards, the lack of amenities, it is American history vivified. On the subjective side it is the account of the intellectual development of a young immigrant who felt the tug between wanting to remain a "home son"[1] on one hand, and on the other could not resist the magnet of the new influences of the American environment.

Before he left for Drake University in Des Moines, he acted as district teacher and he continued to teach after graduation. Though he was sympathetic to the Norwegian parents who wanted to perpetuate their language and their religion, he also understood why their children preferred to be taught subjects that would fit them to participate more fully in the life of America. He escaped from this problem by enrolling for further study at the University of Wisconsin, where he received the Ph.D. degree in history. Eventually he was appointed to the University of Illinois. Not until he found himself in this older American environment, did he succeed in adjusting his emotional ties so that they would not dominate his life as a American. The fact that he became President of the American Historical Asso-

---

1. The term is used by Vilhelm Moberg.

ciation, (a fact that is not divulged by the author) would seem to be an indication that he had a high reputation as an historian.

As an eye-witness of events that have passed into limbo and as chief actor in a drama that has both personal and historical significance, Mr. Larson's story serves as an illustration of a specific aspect of American history.

FROM *The Log Book of a Young Immigrant**

In many respects our community was a bit of the Old World transplanted to the richer soil of the Northwest. It was a garden almost entirely filled with plants of a foreign culture. ... This condition was not peculiar to our township or country; all through the Middlewest and the Northwest similar communities had been established or were in the process of formation. ... The details of local administration and to an extent the business of the country itself were often discussed in the alien tongue. My father was frequently called into jury service and it sometimes happened that every juror in a given case was a Norseman. In such cases the deliberations in the jury room were carried on in the language that all knew. ...

The immigrant is quite often and naturally afflicted with a sense of inferiority. As a rule the Norwegian settler came from a little hut in the old country and found his home in a humble log cabin in the new land. ... The Yankees were 'smart' and the immigrant had a lurking fear that he himself was not smart in the same way. Of course, he was handicapped all around; his ignorance of English put him at a disadvantage in all sorts of business transactions. ... Usury was a practice of which farmers complained most bitterly: in one case a helpless immigrant paid interest at a rate of fifty-five per cent. In their resentment the farmers sought out the traders and businessmen who spoke their own idiom. They felt safer with them, at least they could make them understand what they thought of men whom they suspected of dishonest dealings. ...

I do not remember the time when I began to read. A story was told in the family that, when my sister Katie was in-

*Laurence M. Larson, *The Log Book of a Young Immigrant* (Northfield, Minnesota: The Norwegian American Historical Association, 1939). Reprinted by permission.

troduced to the alphabet, I was near at hand watching the process. When she had acquired the reader's art, my parents discovered to their surprise that I, too, had mastered it. . . . The rule was that no one should be admitted to confirmation unless the priest felt satisfied that the candidate had a certain measure of knowledge of the fundamental doctrines held and taught in the Lutheran church. . . . Illiteracy, therefore, came to be almost unknown in the Norwegian kingdom. . . .

Some time in the early months of 1873 a school was opened in the Mattison house. Into the little dugout, which was hardly large enough for the family itself, the male population of the community above the age of five years came to receive instruction in the language of the land. There were, of course, other subjects taught besides English, but most of the pupils were adult immigrants and for them the important thing was to learn to speak, read and write the English language. . . . After my seventh year my school attendance was limited to a few months in the winter. . . . Still, by the time I was seventeen years old, I had somehow accumulated knowledge, sufficient to be allowed to try my own hand as a common-school teacher. . . .

It was the last day of the year 1888. . . . After having examined a number of college catalogues, all of which claimed great advantages and held out much promise, I had decided to enroll at Drake University. . . . For young persons like me the college had provided a preparatory department in which the work normally called for three years' residence. There was nothing unique about this: virtually all western colleges had the same problem and had made the same provision. . . . I was the only Norseman on the campus and one of a very small number who were known to be of European birth or of recent European descent. I had passed into a new stage of the highway to Americanization. At last I was beginning to learn something of what lay beneath the surface of American culture. . . .

When I returned home after commencement I had no prospects whatever of securing the sort of employment that I should like to have. . . . I found work with a neighbor farmer and was helping him stack his grain when a letter was brought to me which proved to contain the information that I had been appointed principal of Scandinavia Academy. . . .

I remained in charge of the academy for five years. . . . There was to be one subject that was to be dealt with in a particular way: Norwegian was 'to occupy the high seat.' . . . The difference was that the students wanted other lines of work. Norwegian was an old story—they had heard it all their lives. Now they wanted algebra, Latin, bookkeeping, history, natural science, and other subjects that were new to them. And, of course, they had their way. . . .

In Madison [the University of Wisconsin] I lived in an atmosphere that was almost entirely native American. The vast majority of the men who made up the faculty of the university, were of British blood. . . . Outside the university, too, my contacts were mainly with men and women of American stock, or such as used English as the language of daily life. Except in the church that I attended most of the time, I heard almost no Norwegian. . . . Since my thirtieth year, I have lived in an environment, physical and intellectual, the language of which was English. . . .

It was a far cry from the little Norwegian settlement in northern Iowa, where almost everything had a north European flavor, to the older community of Champaign and Urbana, where the native American element was in complete control and domination. . . . So it seemed that every influence, personal and institutional, that had held me in the old grooves had been removed. . . . But I have not forgotten my past. The knowledge of things Norwegian, new and old, which came to me in early life is a heritage that I prize most highly and should be loath to lose even in the slightest measure. . . . America herself has a European past, from the long experience of which she has drawn knowledge and wisdom and power. And the individual citizen no more than the nation itself can escape the implications of his past.

Jacob August Riis
Reporter, Reformer, Author
1849-1914

It seemed to me that a reporter's was the highest and the noblest of all callings; no one could sift right from wrong as he and punish the wrong.

> . . . The power of fact is the mightiest lever of
> this or any day. The reporter has his hand upon it,
> and it is his grievous fault if he does not use it
> well.

Of Danish birth, Jacob August Riis was twenty-one when he
reached America, a lovesick youth, whose beloved was un-
attainable to him because of the difference in social rank between them. He proceeded to Pennsylvania and upstate New
York and after some bouts with the usual difficulties encountered
by immigrants, he found himself in New York City. It was the
era before the Tenement House Commission, the Lexow In-
vestigating Committee, and Reverend Parkhurst's vice investiga-
tions. Jacob Riis had been taught carpentry, but he was a reformer by instinct. It was what he saw and experienced in
America that led him to become a crusader. The spark was
ignited when the homeless, hungry, and friendless immigrant,
who had by then lost the appearance of respectability, requested
admission to the shelter that the police maintained for vagrants
in the worst slum section of New York, called "The Bend."
According to his own story, the indignities he experienced that
night became "the mainspring" of his battle with the slums,
which did not abate until the police lodging house was abolished
and New York's worst slums had been transformed into decent
housing, schools, and play areas.

Though his first attempts to secure a job on a newspaper were
met with derision, he succeeded in entering the portals of
journalism by what he calls "the backdoor." After a few sporadic
jobs, he purchased a weekly in Brooklyn that some politicians
had started and dropped after the fall elections. There he
thundered with such intensity at political abuse that the bosses
were glad to buy the paper back for five times the amount he
had paid in order to silence him. He used the money to go back
to Denmark to marry his childhood sweetheart.

His first real opportunity at reporting came when he was put
on the *Tribune*. As a reporter at Police Headquarters he investigated not only murders and arson, but followed all suspicious clues that pointed to food poisoning, contamination of
water, overcrowding, health and fire hazards, and so forth. His
job became the arena for his reform campaign. While Theodore
Roosevelt was president of the Police Board of New York City,

he conducted him to the police lodging house, the memory of which burned brightly in his mind, and succeeded in having it closed. When he wished to prove that child-workers were below the legal age of fourteen, he went into factories and pried open the mouths of little workers to demonstrate that the child who had not cut his "dogteeth" could not be fourteen.

A flashlight camera (then a new invention) enabled him to take the pictures he needed to make his fight against the slums effective. With the aid of his pictures he enlisted the attention of the American Medical Society when a typhus epidemic was threatening. The revelations provided by his camera also furnished the means by which he became a lecturer and an author of several books[1] on poverty and slum life, which were widely read. Theodore Roosevelt, on whom Riis lavished the full force of his romantic attachment, describes him as the "highest kind of American"—a man who "had the most flaming intensity of passion for righteousness."

FROM *The Making of an American**

. . . as I looked over the rail [of the ship which had brought him to America], my hopes rose high that somewhere in this teeming hive there would be a place for me. . . I had a pair of strong hands, and stubbornness enough to do for two; also a strong belief that in a free country, free from the dominion of custom, of caste as well as of men, things would somehow come right in the end, and a man get shaken into the corner where he belonged if he took a hand in the game. . . .

It was now late in the fall. . . . The city was full of idle men. My last hope, a promise of employment . . . failed, and homeless and penniless, I joined the great army of tramps wandering about the streets in the daytime with the one aim of somehow stilling the hunger that gnawed at my vitals and fighting at night with vagrant curs or outcasts as miserable as myself for the protection of some sheltering ash-bin or doorway. I was too proud in all my misery to beg. I do not believe I ever did. . . .

---

1. *How the Other Half Lives* (1890); *The Children of the Poor* (1892); *Out of Mulberry Street* (1898); *The Battle with the Slums* (1902).

*Jacob A. Riis, *The Making of an American* (New York: The Macmillan Company, 1947). Reprinted by permission of the publishers.

In the midnight hour we [he and a dog that had attached itself to him] went into the Church Street police station and asked for lodging. The rain was still pouring in torrents. The sergeant spied the dog under my tattered coat and gruffly told me to put it out, if I wanted to sleep there. I pleaded for it in vain. . . .

My dog had been waiting, until I should come out. When it saw me in the grasp of the doorman [he was thrown out for complaining], it fell upon him . . . fastening its teeth in his leg. He let go of me with a yell of pain, seized the poor little beast by the legs, and beat its brains out against the stone steps. . . . The outrage of that night became in the providence of God, the means of putting an end to one of the foulest abuses that ever disgraced a Christian city, and a mainspring in the battle with the slums as far as my share in it is concerned. My dog did not die unavenged. . . .

I had been making several attempts to get a foothold on one of the metropolitan newspapers, but always without success. That fall I tried the "Tribune" the city editor of which, . . . was one of my neighbors, but was told with more frankness than flattery, that I was too 'green.' . . . But a few weeks after he changed his mind . . .

. . . this enterprise of ours was often the highest service to the public. When, for instance, in following up a case of destitution and illness involving a whole family, I, tracing back the origin of it, came upon a party at which ham sandwiches had been the bill of fare, and upon looking up the guests, found seventeen of the twenty-five sick with identical symptoms, it required no medical knowledge, but merely the ordinary information and training of the reporter, to diagnose trichinosis. . . .

There had been in 1879 an awakening of the public conscience on the tenement house question which I had followed with interest . . . But the awakening proved more of a sleepy yawn than real— . . . Five years later, in 1884 came the Tenement House Commission which first brought home to us the fact that the people living in the tenements were 'better than the houses.' . . . The Commission met at Police Headquarters, and I sat through all its sessions as a reporter, and heard every word of the testimony, which was more than some of the Commissioners did. . . .

. . . When typhus fever broke out in the city in the winter of 1891-92. . . . I warned them that there would be trouble with the lodging rooms, and within eleven months the prophecy came true. The typhus broke out *there*. The night after the news had come I took my camera and flashlight and made the round of the dens, photographing them with all their crowds . . . [then] knocked at the doors of the Academy of Medicine, demanding to be let in. . . . They let me in, and that night's doings gave the cause of decency a big push. . . .

The thing I had sought vainly so long came in the end by another road than I had planned. One of the editors of "Scribner's Magazine" saw my pictures and heard their story in his church . . . As a result . . . I wrote an article that appeared in the Christmas "Scribner's," in 1889, under the title 'How the Other Half Lives' and made an instant impression.

My own effort in that fight was mainly for decent schoolhouses, for playgrounds, and for a truant school to keep the boys out of jail. If I was not competent enough to argue over the curriculum with a professor of pedagogy, I could tell at least, if a school room was so jammed that to let me pass into the next room the children in the front seat had to rise and stand; or if there was light enough for them to see their slates or the blackboards. Nor did it take the wisdom of a Solomon to decide that a dark basement room, thirty by fifty feet, full of rats, was not a proper place for a thousand children to call their only 'playground.' . . .

Now that Theodore Roosevelt sat in the Health Board . . . they hesitated no longer. I put before the Board a list of the sixteen worst rear tenements in the city, outside the Bend, and while the landlords held their breath in astonishment, they were seized, condemned, and their tenants driven out. . . .

The Bend had become decent and orderly because the sunlight was let in, and shone upon children who had at last the right to play, even if the sign 'keep off the grass' was still there.

Walter Damrosch
Musician, Composer, Educator
1862-1950

> The musical field in America is certainly wonder-
> ful in its possibilities, and all my life I have
> reached out with both hands and have worked
> incessantly and enthusiastically in my calling. In
> part at least I have tried to repay what I owe to
> my compatriots for their confidence and help.

The name of Damrosch is one of the most respected among
the band of German musicians and symphony conductors who
were the shapers of musical taste in America. During the middle
of the nineteenth century, a Beethoven Sonata might find a
place on a concert program, but it would be sandwiched in
between dance music, church music, and "Yankee Doodle." By
the end of the nineteenth century, American audiences had become accustomed to the finest musical repertoires. This accomplishment is credited to the German conductors who labored
persistently to refine musical tastes in America.

The Damrosch family was a talented family. Dr. Leopold
Damrosch, the father, was the first of his family to make his
imprint on the musical life of New York. Having first founded
the New York Oratorio Society, his next step was to create the
New York Symphony. Death interrupted his career after a
successful start in presenting the first Wagner operas at the
Metropolitan Opera House, which had been founded in 1883.
The mother, a Wagnerian singer, led the soprano section of the
chorus. Her sister, who lived with the family, also sang in the
chorus. Frank Damrosch, the elder son, made his mark as
teacher and organizer rather than as a performer. Clara, the
daughter, who was a pianist, married David Mannes, leader of
the first violins in the New York Symphony, and with him
founded the David Mannes School of Music.

The one destined for the greatest influence in raising the level
of musical art in America was Walter Damrosch. Nine years
of age when brought here in 1871, he received an intensive
musical training. He sang in the chorus, directed it, played
among the second violins in the New York Symphony, accom-

panied a violinist on the piano during a tour through the South, and assisted his father in various ways. When death ended the career of his father, he was twenty-three and occupying his first professional job as conductor of the Newark Harmonic Society. The carrying out of his father's plan to take a company of one hundred and fifty members on a tour to Chicago and Boston, became his immediate responsibility. Besides inheriting the New York Oratorio Society and becoming the conductor of the New York Symphony, the Metropolitan appointed him assistant to the new director and second conductor of the orchestra.

From then on Walter Damrosch's role was that of activator of musical interest throughout the nation. When the Metropolitan discontinued the German repertory, he rented the house for certain evenings and, employing the New York Symphony, presented Wagner's music dramas "out of inner necessity." In 1895 he formed the Damrosch Opera Company and began to penetrate "the hinterland" of America. He took his company to the South, the mid-West, and as far West as California and Oregon. While managing his own company, he composed and produced the opera, *The Scarlet Letter*, based completely on the Hawthorne novel, which, he says, had always fascinated him. Another opera, *Cyrano de Bergerac*, was produced and staged at the Metropolitan while Giulio Gatti Casazza was its director. It was declared by Gatti Casazza an "interesting" production.[1]

He also took the New York Symphony to all parts of the United States and introduced symphonic music and great soloists to audiences who had never heard symphonic music before. In the summertime he and his orchestra provided outdoor concerts to audiences numbering between fifteen and twenty-five thousand. Other innovations were the Sunday afternoon concerts, the children's concerts, and the use of radio for lecturing.

As the twentieth century got under way, he succeeded in placing his orchestra under the financial responsibility of Henry H. Flagler.

Walter Damrosch became a devoted and enthusiastic American, which he assigns in part to the influence of the fact that he had married into an American family. His wife was the former

---

1. Giulio Gatti Casazza, *Memories of the Opera* (New York, 1941).

Margaret Blaine, daughter of James G. Blaine, presidential candidate during the election of 1884. Damrosch's love of America is revealed in the story of his life, which is at the same time a documentary account of the growth of musical interest in America.

FROM *My Musical Life**

In 1871 my father received an invitation through Edward Schubert, the music publisher of New York, to come to America as conductor of the Arion Society, and while this opening was small enough, it seemed to offer him an opportunity through which better and bigger things might develop. . . . He therefore determined, at forty years of age, to take the plunge and to precede his family to America in order to find out whether a living and a new career might be made possible in the New World. . . .

Thomas [Theodore Thomas, orchestra conductor] at that time [1873] really believed that America was not large enough to contain more than one orchestra, but he lived long enough to see my father surpass him at the head of a symphony orchestra, as founder of the first great music festival in New York and, above all, of opera in German at the Metropolitan. . . .

During one of those rehearsals in February 1885 (I think we were preparing the Requiem of Verdi) he suddenly complained of feeling ill. . . . Pneumonia set in and he was too worn with the gigantic struggles of the winter to withstand it. During this terrible week of illness the opera had to be kept going and I conducted 'Walküre' and 'Tannhäuser' without much difficulty. . . . Events moved with incredible and terrible swiftness. The contracts for the tour had to be met . . . There was no one to assume the responsibility of taking the company on tour, except poor me, and I accordingly set forth, together with the entire company of about one hundred fifty members. . . .

. . . In 1891, Wagner virtually disappeared from the stage of the Metropolitan Opera House . . . The winter of 1893-94 I had been asked to arrange something original in the way

---

*Walter Damrosch, *My Musical Life* (New York: Charles Scribner's Sons, 1926). Used by permission.

of an entertainment for a charity in which I was interested, and . . . I conceived the idea of giving a stage performance of Götterdämmerung at Carnegie Hall. . . .The success was so remarkable that we repeated the work several times and added 'Walküre.' This seemed to me conclusive proof that the American public were more than ready for the return of Wagner, and I called on Abbey and Grau [managers of the Metropolitan] to suggest that they include a certain number of Wagner performances in German in their repertoire. They threw up their hands in horror at the idea but . . . they suggested if I wanted to be foolish enough to give Wagner performances myself, they would gladly rent the Metropolitan Opera House to me in the spring and on easy terms. . . . [I] finally decided to make the plunge, and, in order to finance my mad scheme properly, I sold my house on West fifty-fifth Street. . . .

To re-enter the Metropolitan on such a Wagnerian wave after German opera had been so ignominiously snuffed out five years before, was a great triumph and satisfaction for me, especially because my father had laid the foundation eleven years before. . . .

Many of the communities that we visited had never heard a symphony orchestra before, and for them we did real pioneer work, as I maintained a high standard of music on my programmes. The classics were, of course, the foundation; but Wagner soon became a great drawing power, and Wagner programmes were often the most asked for. . . .

[In] William J. Bryan's home town of Lincoln, Nebraska . . . One of my double-bass players told me that he had played there thirty years before with Theodore Thomas. [He] told me that with a colleague, whose head was devoid of hair, he had stood directly below a proscenium box in which a group of cowboys were seated. While the orchestra was playing Beethoven's 'Fifth Symphony,' one of these cowboys, who was chewing tobacco violently, amused himself by spitting frequently and always aiming for the bald head of the bass player. . . .

[During World War I] I had myself decided that the New York Symphony Orchestra should not play the works of living German composers, and that the German language should not be sung at our concerts during the war. . . . But Beethoven,

Mozart, and Wagner I considered as classics, belonging to us just as much as to Germany, and their divine message had naught to do with the political leaders of Germany who had plunged the world into this horrible bath of blood. . . .

In this country we have no peasantry, and what slight remains of folk-songs and folk-dances we possess, apart from the music of the negro, have only recently been dug out of the isolated mountain fastnesses of Kentucky and Tennessee. These are generally of British origin and cannot be considered as having been part and parcel of our national life. As against the rich sub-soil of the folk-songs of Germany, Bohemia, Russia, France, and Scotland we can show but the thinnest artificial layer of music, and this has been created and carefully nurtured by a small educated class. . . .

. . . while our musicians have already accomplished miracles within the short period that music has played a part in our civilization, so much yet remains to be done that I long for at least one hundred more years of life, partly to continue my work but still more to satisfy my eager curiosity as to the musical future of our people.

George Santayana
Philosopher, Poet, Writer
1863-1952

I have been involuntarily uprooted. I accept the intellectual advantages of that position, with its social and moral disqualifications. And I refuse to be annexed, to be abolished, or to be grafted onto any plant of a different species.

This statement hints why George Santayana never became an American. Undoubtedly, the fact that his father was a Spaniard who wanted to live in Spain and that his mother, who was of Spanish background, chose to live in Boston, made him "the uneasy child of mixed cultures." Though he received an American upbringing (and an extensive American education), taught at Harvard College thirty years, liked the English language and used it with magnificent effect, and understood the American character, which he proved in his best-selling novel, *The Last*

Puritan, he chose to consider himself an "exiled Spaniard" all his life. To Robert Frost, for instance, who had been Santayana's student at Harvard (though Santayana did not remember him), he appeared "a lost soul."[1]

The fate that brought him to Boston at the age of nine was the outcome of a strange concatenation of events in his mother's life. Born in Glasgow of Spanish parents, she had lived in Virginia, then in Spain, then in Manila, where she had married an American, George Sturgis. Upon his death, she took her children to Boston to live. On a visit to Spain with her children, she married a Spaniard, Agustin Santayana, and remained there for several years. Of this union George Santayana was born. When the boy was five, she returned with the Sturgis children to Boston, leaving the young child to his father's care in Avila. However, at the age of nine, the boy was returned to his mother, because his father preferred the boy's "good" to his "pleasure." It was this transference that had caused a "terrible moral disinheritance." George Santayana has been described as an "unloved child of a later marriage," about whom it was clear that "he didn't like her [his mother] from the way he talked about her."[2]

His mother's first marriage, Santayana admitted, was an important event, "important even for me, since it set the background for my whole life." It also determined his name—George—because his elder sister and godmother, Susana Sturgis, chose her father's name for him.

George Santayana was educated at Boston Latin School and Harvard College. Though he did not visit his father at Avila frequently, Avila remained "the center of . . . [his] deepest legal and affectionate ties." Upon his graduation from Harvard, he went to Germany for graduate studies on a fellowship from Harvard, but he returned to America to take his Ph.D. at Harvard, because he found himself to be "too much enveloped in my American associations to lose myself in the German scene." Nevertheless he remained an onlooker in the American world.

In 1912 he left America for good to reside at various times in Rome, London, Paris, Spain, Cortina d'Ampezzo, and other places in Europe. He died in Rome and in the absence of written instructions, he was interred at the Tomba degli Spagnuoli, the

1. Louis Mertins, *Robert Frost* (Norman, Oklahoma, 1965), p. 354.
2. Corliss Lamont (ed.), *Dialogue on George Santayana* (New York, 1959), pp. 16, 18.

Spanish section of the Verono Cemetery in Rome. Professor Herbert Schneider, a friend and colleague, remembered that Santayana had said to him in Rome: "I can't be an American, and I can't be a Spaniard, and I haven't any interest in Spain because my socialist Spain is gone."[3] Professor Schneider's deduction was: "I think he puts on a big facade about all the Spanish on him. I don't think he's Spanish at all . . . he isn't Latin either, he's just a good American."[4] It is clear that George Santayana wanted the two strains, the Spanish and the American, to remain separate, in a sort of symbiosis, neither one to absorb the other.

FROM *Persons and Places**

Education such as I have received in Boston was steadier and my associations more regular and calmer than they would have been in Spain; but there was a terrible moral disinheritance involved, an emotional and intellectual chill, a pettiness and practicality of outlook and ambition, which I should not have encountered amid the complex passions and intrigue of a Spanish environment. From the point of view of learning, my education at the Boston Latin School and at Harvard College was not solid or thorough; it would not have been solid or thorough in Spain; yet what scraps of learning or ideas I might have gathered there would have been vital, the wind of politics and of poetry would have swelled them, and allied them with notions of honor. But then I should have become a different man; so that my father's decision was all for my good, if I was to be the person that I am now. . . .

. . . Boston was a nice place with very nice people in it; but it was an excellent point of vantage from which to start out, if you belonged there, rather than a desirable point to arrive at if you were born in some other place. It was a moral and intellectual nursery, always busy applying first principles to trifles. . . .

. . . The extreme contrast between the two centers [Avila and Boston] and the two influences became itself a blessing:

---

3. *Ibid.*, p. 58.

4. *Ibid.*, p. 103.

*George Santayana, *Persons and Places* (New York: Charles Scribner's Sons, 1944). By special permission of Charles Scribner's Sons.

it rendered flagrant the limitations and the contingency of both. Granted that I was to awake in Spain in the nineteenth century, I could have found myself in no place less degraded than Avila; and granted that I was to be educated in America and to earn my bread there, I could have fallen on no place friendlier than Harvard. . . . The dignity of Avila was too obsolete, too inopportune to do more than stimulate an imagination already awakened, and lend reality to history; while at Harvard a wealth of books and much generous intellectual sincerity went with such spiritual penury and moral confusion as to offer nothing but a lottery ticket or a chance at the grab-bag to the orphan mind. You had to bring a firm soul to this World's Fair; you had to escape from this merry-go-round, if you would make sense of anything or come to know your own mind. . . .

In the Boston of my boyhood there were two churches served by the Jesuits. The more modest one was a parish church for the German-speaking population . . . Here I used to go sometimes to an early Mass on Sundays, always alone . . . I got up before dawn on those winter mornings, and took that double walk at a great pace, perhaps over snow, in any case through deserted streets in biting weather. . . . If later I was taken to some Unitarian Church, it didn't matter. It seemed a little ridiculous, all those good people in their Sunday clothes, so demure, so conscious of one another, not needing in the least to pray or to be prayed for, nor inclined to sing, but liking to flock together once a week, as people in Spain flock to the "paseo," and glad to hear a sermon like the leading article in some superior newspaper, calculated to confirm the conviction already in them that their bourgeois virtues were quite sufficient and that perhaps in time poor backward races and nations might be led to acquire them. . . .

How about me? . . . Should I ever make a professor of philosophy? Everybody doubted it. I not only doubted it myself, but was repelled by the idea. What I wanted was to go on being a student, and especially to be a travelling student. I loved speculation for itself, as I loved poetry, not out of worldly respect or anxiety lest I should be mistaken, but for the splendor of it, like the splendor of the sea or the stars. And I know I should love living obscurely and freely in old towns, in strange countries, hearing all sorts of outlandish marvellous opinions. I could have made a bargain with Mephistopheles, not for youth, but for the appearance of youth, so that with its tastes but without its passions, I might have been a wandering student all my life, at Salamanca, at Bologna, in Oxford, in Paris, at Benares, in China, in Persia. Germany would be a beginning. . . .

FROM *The Middle Span**

There was no question any longer of a career in Spain; I was too old and too much expatriated by my English language and my American associations. On the other hand, I came to Avila with a sense of coming home and with the intention of always returning there. Official life would carry me out of Spain, as it had carried my father; but so long as he lived he would be my natural center. . . .

. . . a man who had been torn up by the roots, cannot be replanted and should never propagate his kind. In the matter of religion, for instance, I found myself in this blind alley. I was not a believer in what my religion, or any religion, teaches dogmatically, yet I wouldn't for the world have had a wife or children dead to religion. Had I lived always in Spain, even with my present philosophy, I should have found no difficulty: my family would have been Catholic like every other family; and the philosophy of religion, if ever eventually discussed among us, would have been a subsequent private speculation, with no direct social consequences. But living in a Protestant country, the free-thinking Catholic is in a socially impossible position. He cannot demand that his wife and children be Catholics, since he is not, in a controversial sense, a Catholic himself; yet he cannot bear that they should be Protestants or freethinkers, without any Catholic tradition or feelings. They would not then be his wife or children except by accident: they would not belong to his people. I know that there are some who accept this consequence, even pretend to have become Protestants and bury as deep as possible the fact that they were born Catholics or Jews. But I am not a man of that stamp. . . .

---

*George Santayana, *The Middle Span* (New York: Charles Scribner's Sons, 1945). By special permission of Charles Scribner's Sons.

Richard Bartholdt
Journalist, Member of Congress
1855-1932

> I believe the children of every race have brought
> with them something worthy of reception and
> absorption by the American people. . . . America
> cannot be made Anglo-Saxon any more than it
> can be made Irish, German, French or Italian.

The rewards Richard Bartholdt gathered in America few of
the foreign-born were privileged to attain. Chosen to the House
of Representatives from St. Louis in 1893, he was a member of
eleven Congresses until he resigned in 1915, at the end of the
Sixty-Fifth Congress. He reached the apogee of his career in his
activities in behalf of the Interparliamentary Union, an association for the preservation of peace through arbitration. After
organizing an American group, he became the president of the
organization and in 1904 succeeded in arranging a meeting of
the delegates in St. Louis. There he drew up a model arbitration treaty which was adopted. In 1907 he was proposed for the
Nobel Peace Prize, but it went to President Theodore Roosevelt.
Bartholdt's great hopes for his "world parliament in embryo"
turned into mockery when World War I broke out despite the
existence of machinery for peaceful settlement.

As the son of a supporter of the Revolution of '48, he claims
to have been raised to appreciate democracy and liberty. After
having completed the course of study at the Gymnasium, he left
the "Fatherland" in 1872 at the age of seventeen. In America he
was taught to set type on a German newspaper, then he became
a reporter in Albany, and later a newspaper man in St. Louis.
From there he was elected to Congress.

As a member of Congress he was a wholehearted supporter of
the Republican Party and its policies; he admired President Mc-
Kinley extravagantly and whitewashed him of any personal guilt
in regard to the Spanish-American War (placing it squarely on
the "Jingoes of the House"). He also admired "Czar Reed," who
"did him the honor" of placing him at the head of the Immigration Committee. Bartholdt opposed the literacy test, but fol-

lowed orders when directed by Reed to report the bill out. But he succeeding in "softening" the bill somewhat, by exempting the females altogether (owing to the scarcity of domestic help) and by merely requiring the ability to read on the part of males. Among his other achievements was the authorization by Congress that the World's Fair of 1904 be held in St. Louis in commemoration of the Louisiana Purchase.

As a proud citizen of America, he preached a fervent brand of Americanism, but he also retained a strong feeling of partisanship for the land "where his cradle had stood." He was convinced that many American customs, as well as "our conception of liberty," had originated in the German forests. Germany, he felt, was arming solely for defense to avoid "encirclement." The Germans of America who were being called "hyphenated citizens" were, to him, victims of pure prejudice.

When war broke out, Mr. Bartholdt became a frantic apologist for Germany. By then the great American of German birth, Carl Schurz, was dead. Mr. Bartholdt declared that the cataclysm was due to a "deep-laid European conspiracy against Germany," and that the Germans "have to defend their country, their firesides, their very existence as a nation." To him Germany could do no wrong. As ex-Congressman he kept urging William Jennings Bryan to undertake a peace mission abroad in order to avert America's entry into World War I.[1] After the war he directed his efforts toward influencing Presidents Harding and Coolidge in behalf of defeated Germany.

In the end Mr. Bartholdt turned against the Republican Party and endorsed Senator La Follette in 1924, because he felt that "every American of German blood owed the Wisconsin leader a lasting debt of gratitude." After the defeat of La Follette he advocated the formation of a third party, "The Liberal Party," with policies reminiscent of the Socialist platform.

FROM *Steerage to Congress**

. . . the question occurred to me: what has mere speech, the twisting of the tongue in one way or the other, to do with the loyalty of a citizen? It is not lip service a country needs, but

---

1. Lawrence W. Levine, *Defender of the Faith* (New York, 1965).

*From *Steerage to Congress* by Richard Bartholdt. Copyright 1930 by Dorrance & Company.

genuine patriotism, and the source of that is man's conscience and not his tongue . . . Why, a man can be a good and true American without even knowing English, the same as a man who is physically unable to speak at all. . . .

. . . And do we realize fully how fervently all believers in free government prayed for the success of our experiment in democracy, and how closely they watched us with the anxious question in their minds: 'Will America succeed in keeping alive the great principles promulgated by the fathers of the Republic?' To the liberals of the old world, therefore, every deviation on our part from the 'spirit of 1776' must naturally be a source of deep disappointment while an American imitation of, or a co-operation with, the unsound war policies of European governments would have the effect of strengthening rather than weakening the hold which the monarchical idea has on the people of Europe. . . .

. . . With the magic wand of liberty America has solved all the knotty problems which uninterruptedly puzzle European statesmen: difference of race and religion, prejudices of hereditary station and rank, traditions and superstitions of past centuries, and last but not least social unrest owing to unsatisfactory economic conditions. . . .

What would the country look like today if the Know-nothing party had had its way in the 'fifties and all the millions who have come to us since that time had been excluded! We would probably still be hunting the buffalo immediately West of the Alleghenies. As a matter of fact, these multitudes have been easily swallowed up by our factories, fields, forests and mines and have thus become the main factors in the expansion of our home market, the increase of our production, the growth of our industries and commerce. And at no time have they given the government any trouble. . . . in the following Congress when Speaker Reed asked my views on the question, I spoke my mind freely. Having enjoyed the privilege of coming here myself, how could I justly deny it to others? This country should not be made the dumping ground of criminals, paupers and cripples, or of diseased or weak-minded persons, but that was as far as I would go with any policy of exclusion. . . .

Again, the humiliating truth has come home to us that even after the untold sacrifices and agonies of the great World War the rulers could not bring themselves to do the obvious thing, and it is the abject failure and madness of the Versailles Treaty which 'broke the heart of the world,' not the refusal of our Senate to sanction an instrument as compared with which the much bewailed Brest-Litovsk Treaty and the dictates of the Vienna Congress were very models of righteousness. Therefore, the negative attitude of the United States Senate is to be hailed as the one ray of hope in the world's gloom. . . .

No, America is greater than any one race in it, and an attempted overlordship of one race above all others is bound to prove disastrous to our tranquillity, because contrary to the American ideal. Therefore, let us hear no more of one kind or the other kind of Americans. All of us have contributed our share to the grandeur of America, and what has been built up by Yankee grit, German industry, and Irish pluck, not to mention the valuable aid of many other nationalities and races, is the common heritage of all. . . .

. . . Yes, my mind was definitely made up on that point. I felt that every American of German blood owed the Wisconsin leader [La Follette] a lasting debt of gratitude, not only for his manly courage in stubbornly resisting a pernicious war propaganda, but also for defending almost singlehanded the honor of the German name against a program as conscienceless as it was unworthy of America. Ever since Lincoln's time the American Germans of the Middle West had been the backbone of the Republican party. . . . When they needed friends, did the Republican leaders have a kind word for them? No. The party champions even joined the chorus of villifiers and, more than that, when the millions of dollars were voted to feed the starving people of Europe, they put through an amendment expressly exempting the starving Germans from the benefits of the appropriation. No matter what others would do, for one I could not stoop to kiss the hands of the party responsible for that perfidy.

A Third Party! Or should it not more accurately be called a second party inasmuch as latter-day Republicans and Democrats are as like as two peas? Be that as it may, what should be the name and program of the new organization? . . . Well, to demonstrate that freedom is still a vital principle of our national life, the baby should be named 'The Liberal Party,'

defender of time-honored American institutions and champion
of the great principles of civil liberty.

Michael Pupin
Physicist, Metaphysician
1858-1935

> Seeing is believing; let him speak who has the
> faith, provided that he has a message to deliver.

The message of Michael Pupin is that of praise for "America's
idealism." It turns his autobiography into a paean to America, to
American opportunities, and to American scientists. Heartwarmingly appreciative of the advantages offered to him, Pupin became a worshiper of and a proselytizer for the American system.

Born in 1858 of peasant stock, he was fifteen when he arrived
in 1874, alone, with five cents in his pocket. As a herdsboy in
his native Idvor in Serbia (encircled by the Austro-Hungarian
Empire and swirling with nationalistic sentiments), he had become interested in the mystery of light and sound. In finding
the answers to his quest in America, he was to acquire world
fame as one of the outstanding contributors to the development
of electrical science.

His career followed the path typical of many immigrants,—at
first any kind of work that would provide the necessities—in his
case a short bout with farming, followed by a job in a cracker
factory in New York. There he found in the boiler-room engineer
his "first professor of engineering," and in another co-worker, a
man of superior classical education, one who tutored him for
college entrance. Starting at Cooper Union he passed his entrance examination at Columbia University within five years after
his arrival. Citizenship and a college degree were achieved
simultaneously. Continuing his studies first at Cambridge, England, he took the Ph.D. degree under Helmholtz at the Physical
Institute in Berlin on funds made available by Columbia University. When he returned in 1889, it was to join the newly
founded School of Mines.

From there issued a string of discoveries. Within two weeks
of Roentgen's discovery of the X-ray, he obtained the "first X-ray

photograph in America" on the basis of which "the first surgical operation [was] performed in America under the guidance of an X-ray picture." There he also developed the Pupin coil for telephonic transmission, which transformed the telephone systems of America as well as of Europe.

Michael Pupin's autobiography is an exciting story of the self meeting its destiny in the New World. His claims that "science on its abstract side is poetry" and that "physical phenomena are poems in prose" receive ample confirmation in its pages.

FROM *From Immigrant to Inventor**

Sound and light being associated in my young mind of fifty years ago with divine operations by means of which man communicates with man, beast with beast, stars with stars, and man with his Creator, it is obvious that I meditated much about the nature of sound and light. I still believe that these modes of communication are the fundamental operations in the physical universe and I am still meditating about their future. . . .

Presently the ship passed by Castle Garden, and I heard someone say: 'There is the gate to America. . . . We were carefully examined and cross examined and when my turn came the examining officials shook their heads and seemed to find me wanting. I confessed that I had only five cents in my pocket and had no relatives here, and that I knew of nobody in this country except Franklin, Lincoln, and Harriet Beecher Stowe, whose 'Uncle Tom's Cabin' I had read in translation. . . .

During the last week of September of that year [1879] I presented myself at Columbia for entrance examination. . . . The first two books of the Iliad, excepting the catalogue of ships, and four orations of Cicero, I knew by heart. . . . A note from the Registrar's Office informed me a few days later that I was enrolled as a student in Columbia College with freedom from all tuition fees. . . .

As I sat on the deck of the ship which was taking me to the universities of Europe . . . I said to myself: "Michael Pupin, the most valuable asset which you carried into New York harbor nine years ago was your knowledge of, and pro-

---

*Michael Pupin, *From Immigrant to Inventor* (New York: Charles Scribner's Sons, 1923). By special permission of Charles Scribner's Sons.

found respect and admiration for, the best traditions of your race. . . . The most valuable asset which you are now taking with you from New York harbor is your knowledge of, and profound respect and admiration for, the best traditions of your adopted country.' . . .

Why, then, should a scientist who started his career as a Serbian immigrant speak of the idealism in America science when there are so many native-born American scientists who know more about this subject than I do? . . . I shall only point out that there are certain psychological elements in this question which justify me in the belief that occasionally an immigrant can see things which escape the attention of the native. . . . Statements which, coming from a native American, might sound as boasts and bragging, may and often do sound different when they are made by a naturalized citizen. . . .

[Upon receiving a telegram from America in his home town] The wondering crowd assembled at the garden-gate, and the older peasants who had gone to school with me in my boyhood days asked if the telegram had really come from America. When I said yes, and that it had been sent on that very morning, they looked at each other and winked, as if signalling to each other to be on guard lest I fool them with an American yarn. . . . 'Who invented all that?' asked he impatiently. 'An American did it,' said I boastfully. 'These Americans must be very clever people,' said he and waited eagerly for my reply. 'Yes, indeed, they are very clever people,' said I. 'Much more clever than anyone in this village?' was his next question, and when I assured him that the Americans were much more clever than anybody in Idvor, he fired at me the following shot: 'How in the name of St. Michael do you manage to make a living there?' . . . My answer to the peasant's question . . . is this: 'The humble herdsmen of Idvor and the famous La Grange of Paris told me how to do it.' . . .

Ideal democracy, if attainable at all, will certainly be attainable in our country, whose traditions are gradually eliminating racial hatreds and suspicions and making them unknown human passions on this blessed continent. If I have ever contributed any thing substantial to the progress of this splendid movement, whether as an immigrant or an inventor, it has been most amply rewarded by the generous spirit of the letter on the opposite page . . . [Letter from President

The New Americans

Harding accepting Pupin's resignation as a member of the
National Advisory Committee for Aeronautics and acknowl-
edging Pupin's contribution to the development 'of one of the
great marvels of our age, the radio telephone.']

Hagop Bogigian
"The first native importer of Oriental goods in America"
1858-

> One of the experiences of cruelty by an American
> government representative was when one of the
> immigration agents said something to me, which
> I did not understand, and he slapped me in my
> face. . . . I do not wonder that many of the
> immigrants never forget their cruel treatment on
> landing.

An evaluation of the traits of Americans that is seldom encountered in the writings of the foreign-born, is given by this
Armenian who came to America in 1876 at the age of eighteen.
Though he started doing the most menial work, he became
eventually a highly respected, affluent business man. What impressed itself on the consciousness of this newcomer was the
(to him) glaring dishonesty among Americans. Exploiters, swind-
lers, and crooks constantly flitted across his path. He found that
some Americans were merely grasping; others revealed a degree
of gullibility that invited cheating by others; some were in-
sultingly snobbish; many were outright dishonest. Some assumed
as a matter of course that they were naturally more civilized
than foreigners by virtue of an inbred superiority.

This Adamic hero had received the first intimation that the
American Eden was not free of evil while still in Europe. This
hint came to him through the actions of a medical missionary,
to whom he had bound himself to become his servant in exchange for the privilege to accompany his family to America and
the promise that the doctor would help him find employment
in America. The young man was to provide for his own food
and lodging. While the doctor tarried in Europe, the young man's
funds (which he had borrowed) became exhausted, so that in
London he had to solicit the charity of his countrymen to

secure the money for his passage to America. The missionary lent him one pound and when he collected it three years later, he insisted on twelve percent interest for the three years.

After he became started in his own business, he found flagrant dishonesty among people of superior background. Harvard students refused to pay for merchandise they had bought and would assault him when he tried to remove it. A clerk who came from a prominent Boston family was a thief; some customers ordered rugs and *objets d'art* on consignment in order to beautify their homes for special occasions and returned them when the function was over; decorators wanted him to connive with them in fleecing clients. Lawyers and judges proved themselves willing to enter into corrupt dealings. A lawyer who acted as receiver for the goods Mr. Bogigian sent back from his buying trips, charged exorbitant interest rates and refused to give up the merchandise. A minister lent him money and exacted eighteen percent interest. He was shocked at judges who were prejudiced, stock manipulators who overstepped the bounds of legality, and physicians who overcharged. Even Clara Barton, director of Red Cross activities, who undertook to supervise Armenian relief at Mr. Bogigian's solicitation, comes in for severe criticism for using funds entrusted to her on personal extravagances and for her refusal after her recall to give a report on expenditures.

Mr. Bogigian's business dealings were with some of the most illustrious names in America. He pays high tribute to Longfellow, Charles Eliot Norton, Mr. Houghton [of Houghton, Mifflin], and other people of their stamp. Though he admits that he found "honesty and respectability . . . the prevailing spirit of the majority of the Americans," the gist of his criticism is that even among Americans of "high standing," honesty could not be taken for granted.

FROM *In Quest of the Soul of Civilization**

As my ambition was so great to reach America I was willing to grasp any opportunity and accept any terms. . . . [the medical missionary] wrote out an agreement to sign, binding me to him entirely, but said nothing on his part of what he

---

*Hagop Bogigian, *In Quest of the Soul of Civilization* (Washington, D.C.: John Sharp Williams, 1925).

would be willing to do. My friends, being much older than I, and experienced business men, saw at once that that would be signing a paper which I ought not to sign. However, I did sign. . . .

After hearing my story, he [an Armenian merchant in London] advised me very strongly to go back to Constantinople. . . . But he said: 'If you have positively decided to go to America, I will see that you get there.' . . . As I was leaving his office he . . . took my hand, looked straight into my eyes, and said, 'I hope you will consider the matter carefully. America is unknown to you. You don't know the language; you have no friends there, and you may have a repetition of of your experience since you left Turkey.' He referred to the actions of the doctor . . . and said, 'This man was sent by the American Christians to spread their form of Christianity; and if he has treated you so badly, what can you expect from ordinary Americans?' . . .

[One of his employers] . . . was an old-fashioned Yankee who utilized his time in making money, and utilized his help's time for the same purpose. I was required to rise early—between four-thirty and five o'clock—feed his horse and then go to the kitchen, clean the stove and make the fire, as they kept no servant. Then he would come down himself and start cooking the breakfast. . . . As soon as that was over, I harnessed the horse and we started out to go to work. As I remember, he had between one hundred and one hundred and fifty tenement houses. As the tenants moved in and out, we had to go to the empty house, paint (if necessary), paper, clean the floors, set glass in broken windows; in fact, clean it from top to bottom . . . I never received a penny for my work at this place or the other; [the previous one] all I got was my board. . . .

Then I began to send goods through the foreign connections to Turkey, Persia and Egypt. . . . In this way I was the first one to send American windmills and pumps to Egypt, and also I was the first to send the American plough to Siberia. . . . In fact the demand increased every year for all these things which I sent and I continued this business for many years. I am happy to say that I never lost a penny on my export business. I wish I could say the same of business dealings in America! . . .

After a while Professor Longfellow and his friends who knew me, and had never lost their interest in me, used to drop into my store. . . . Professor Longfellow, being my oldest friend, kept bringing other friends to meet me—including Professors Norton, Hosford, Lyon, Agassiz and several others from Cambridge; the poet, Whittier, who in winter lived not far from my place; Ralph Waldo Emerson, Alcott, Dr. Oliver Wendell Holmes, Cyrus Barthol and others. They used to tell anecdotes and made jokes upon each other. I never saw a group of distinguished literary people laugh and act like boys as this group did. . . .

. . . as to those who are selfish and tricky, I always attributed their spirit to their great advance in 'civilization.' To illustrate, I met a Congregational minister of 'high standing,' . . . who talked to me patronizingly as if he had some difficulty to bring himself down to my level. I asked why it was people of his prominence (?) considered the new-comers to this country inferior to themselves. He said, 'We consider ourselves highly educated and much more civilized than the foreigners who come here.' I rejoined, 'If that is the Christian sentiment you have, I pity the people who sit in the pews of your church. . . .'

We in America feel that because we are Americans we are far better than the people of other countries, and we always feel suspicious whenever we travel in foreign lands that the inhabitants of those lands are not as good as we are. . . . By coming into contact with ministers of the Gospels, judges, professors and leaders of the nation, I have come to this conclusion, that we have made ourselves liable as a nation to the just criticism of other nations.

Hugo Münsterberg
Teacher, Psychologist
1863-1916

The German immigrant can justly claim to be a respectable and very desirable element of the American population: he has stood always on the side of solid work and honesty; he has brought skill and energy over the ocean, and he has not forgotten his music and his joyfulness; he is not second to anyone in his devotion to the duties of a citizen in peace and in war, and without his aid many of America's industrial, commercial and technical triumphs would be unknown.

In 1881 a young German university professor was called to Harvard University to teach psychology. He was Hugo Münsterberg, twenty-eight years old. These were the years when admiration for German education, particularly at the graduate school level, was at its highest. Professor Münsterberg remained at Harvard, except for a short interruption, until the end of his life. It was remarked of him that he regarded the American world "through German eyes with Harvard astigmatism"; he himself admitted, "that I see it with German eyes is certainly true."

At the turn of the century he published five articles on American traits—three in the *Atlantic Monthly* and two in the *International Monthly*. It was a period when German diplomacy was oriented towards weaning Americans from their attachment to England. Under President Theodore Roosevelt there was hope of achieving a greater affinity between Germany and the United States, but World War I soon ended these aspirations. The five articles became a book in 1902: *American Traits from the Point of View of a German,* intended "for Americans, and for Americans only." The purpose was to "remove prejudices and misunderstandings," to "facilitate mutual benefit," "to measure critically the culture of the one country by the ideals of the other."

Two years later, in 1904, Münsterberg offered a book written for Germans only—*The Americans.* The objective was "to illuminate and defend a culture which I have learned to admire and . . . to interpret systematically the democratic ideals of America." In it he discusses the Indian and the Negro and states: "by far the most difficult is the Negro question." In its framework the book is reminiscent of James Bryce's *The American Commonwealth,* published in 1888.

Like other Germans who recognized the kinship between Americans and the English-speaking peoples, and felt slighted by this, to them, unjustified preference, a "chip on the shoulder" of Hugo Münsterberg is discernible. At the outbreak of World

War I, "whispers of suspicion" against him made themselves felt at Harvard. Before this matter could be fully determined, he died of a heart attack while teaching his Radcliffe students, for whom he had expressed such glowing admiration.[1]

Where Hugo Münsterberg's thinking differs from many naturalized Americans of German birth, is in his vigorous defense of the German Kaiser and hence of monarchical institutions, which few people of German origin would have openly espoused. Münsterberg attempted to endear the Kaiser to Americans by pointing out that "the brilliant young President of the United States [Theodore Roosevelt] resembled him [the Kaiser] most closely."

FROM *American Traits From the Point of View of a German**

. . . I think the true American is an idealist through and through. I perceive, to be sure, that his idealism is often loose and lax and ineffective, but it remains idealism nevertheless, and he deceives himself when he poses as a realist, like his English cousin. . . . The American is not greedy for money; if he were, he would not give away his wealth with such a liberal hand, and would not put aside all the un-idealistic European schemes of money-making which exclude individual initiative, as, for instance, the pursuit of dowries, or, on a lower level, the tipping system. The American runs after money primarily for the pleasure of the chase; it is the spirit of enterprise that spurs him on, the desire to make use of his energies, to realize his personality. . . .

. . . But the most amusing misunderstanding arises when the American himself thinks that he proves the purely practical character of his life by the eagerness with which he saves his time, on the ground that time is money. It strikes me that, next to the public funds, nothing is so much wasted here as time. . . . The whole scheme of American education is possible only in a country which is rich enough not to need any economy of time, and which can therefore allow itself the luxury of not asking at what age a young man begins to earn his living. The American shopkeeper opens his store

---

1. Helen Howe, *The Gentle Americans* (New York, 1965), p. 239.

*Hugo Münsterberg, *American Traits From the Point of View of a German* (Boston: Houghton Mifflin Company, 1902).

daily one hour later than the German tradesman, and the American physician opens his office three years later than his German colleague of equal education. . . .

Add to it the American's gratefulness and generosity, his elasticity and his frankness, his cleanliness and his chastity, his humor and his fairness; consider the vividness of his religous emotion, his interest in religious and metaphysical speculation, his eagerness always to realize the best result of science,—in short, look around everywhere without prejudice, and you cannot doubt that behind the terrifying mask of the selfish realist breathes the idealist, who is controlled by a belief in ethical values.

. . . We were all amazed at the pert and disrespectful children, and we were all fascinated by the American women . . . And one group always attracts our attention the most keenly,—the college bred woman. There are beautiful and brilliant and clever and energetic women the world over, but the college girl is a new type to us, and, next to the twenty-four story buildings, nothing excites our curiosity more than the woman who have their bachelor's degree. . . . The American woman is clever and ingenious and witty; she is brilliant and lively and strong; she is charming and beautiful and noble; she is generous and amiable and resolute; she is energetic and practical, yet idealistic and enthusiastic—indeed, what is she not?

The general American tendency to consider housework as a kind of necessary evil, . . . is not less even in the lower strata of the community. . . . The laborer's daughter has, of course, not such a complete theory as the banker's daughter; but that it is dull to sit in the kitchen and look after the little sister she too knows. In consequence she also rushes to the outside life as saleswoman, as industrial laborer, as office worker . . .

. . . no one can suggest that woman's education in this country ought to take any steps backward; . . . and only one practical change must come in response to the urgent needs of our period: the American man must raise his level of general culture. In short, the woman's question is in this country, as ultimately perhaps everywhere, the man's question. Reform the man, and all the difficulties disappear.

PART FOUR

IMMIGRATION IN HIGH GEAR

From 1880-1929

Wer nie sein Brot mit Tränen ass
Wer nie die kummervollen Nächte
Auf seinem Bette weinend sass
Der kennt euch nicht, ihr himmlischen Mächte
Johann Wolfgang von Goethe

14

The Circle Widens

> "What should I see? Trees with trunks of Chrys-
> olites, with all the jewels of Aladdin's cave drip-
> ping from their boughs, streets paved with gold,
> people dressed like lords? . . . Oh, the breaking
> down of dreams, the disillusionment of the de-
> luded."
>
> Fred Kenyon Brown
> *Through the Mill*

The 1880s! A decade between two severe business depressions
—1873 and 1893. The economy was in high gear again; the
railroads were expanding madly and acting in such a high-
handed fashion that the first shackles in the form of the Inter-
state Commerce Act were imposed in 1887. Immigrants were
needed as laborers in the industrial centers and on railroad
gangs. On the frontier the land was calling to be cultivated, to
be made habitable. In 1890 the frontier would be declared
ended. The steamship companies, the railroads, anxious to dispose of land given to them in the form of federal subsidies, sent
representatives to the hamlets of Austria Hungary, to Italy, to
the Balkans, to spread fantastic tales of the prosperity that
awaited all who would come.

The siren song had its effect; a mighty caravan streamed
out of Europe. By 1890 the pattern of immigration was showing
a perceptible change. More and more immigrants from Italy,
Russia, and the Balkans were pouring in, while the number of
Northern Europeans declined. Of twenty three million newcomers between the 1880s and 1920, the majority was composed
of Eastern and Southern Europeans. The balance shifted so
drastically that in the peak year of 1907 over eighty percent
represented the "new immigration and less than twenty percent
the peoples who had made up the bulk of the earlier settlers."[1]
Between 1900 and 1910 the number of Italian immigrants alone

---

1. Maldwyn Allen Jones, *American Immigration* (Chicago, 1960), p. 179.

was close to two million[2]—twenty five percent greater than that of any other national group.

These "new immigrants" bore special earmarks. In language, appearance, customs, and religion they were unlike the North Europeans to whom Americans were accustomed. There was a preponderance of males among them. Some were "birds of passage" who wanted only to earn some money to take back home; others had to earn money first with which to pay for the passage of their families, a matter that could take years. In religion they were predominantly Catholic and Jewish. Catholicism was thoroughly entrenched by then. It was the third wave of Jews to come to America. The first Jews arrived here during colonial days and in 1820 numbered about four thousand. The second wave was composed of German Jews, who were looked upon as Germans and who had assimilated rapidly. By 1880 the number of Jews had risen to two hundred and fifty thousand. After 1880 the Jews who sought admission stemmed from Russia, Poland, Roumania, and Austria-Hungary, and were driven out either by religious massacres or by dire economic necessity. From 1881 to 1914 more than two million Jews from Eastern Europe entered the United States.[3] These newer immigrants thronged the industrial centers in savage competition for unskilled jobs. It was during this period that immigrants experienced the greatest hardships.

In the wake of this huge outpouring of immigrants whom many of the older Americans considered unassimilable, prejudice and agitation for curbs on immigration mounted. In the 1890s it led to the formation of the Immigration Restriction League, composed of "Brahmin" elements among the older Americans.[4] Through the support of Henry Cabot Lodge, a bill imposing a literacy test was passed in 1896, to be vetoed by President Cleveland. This was also supported by Samuel Gompers, president of the American Federation of Labor, who admitted it was the first time he found himself on the same side of the fence with Henry Cabot Lodge. Later attempts to enact this legislation were vetoed by Presidents Taft and Wilson, until the law was finally passed in 1917 over President Wilson's veto. In 1921 came

---

2. Angelo Pellegrini, *Immigrant's Return* (New York, 1953).
3. Albert Q. Maisel, *They All Chose America* (New York, 1957), p. 157.
4. For thorough documentation see Barbara M. Solomon, *Ancestors and Immigrants* (Cambridge, 1956).

the first attempt at numerical restriction, which was tightened in 1924 and made final in 1929. The National Origins Law permitted the entrance of one hundred and fifty thousand immigrants annually, based on quotas for each national group according to the census of 1890, when the percentage of Eastern and Southern Europeans residing in America was at its lowest. The purpose was to keep their numbers down. From these people—Italians, Russians, Jews, Slavs—have come the most moving testimonials attesting to the effect of the American environment on them and to their acculturation to American life.

The wide-open gate through which millions had streamed in without hindrance, was narrowed and the influx of these "undesirables" among immigrants severely restricted.

15

Comment from 1880-1929

Emma Goldman
Anarchist, Magazine Editor, Lecturer, Writer
1869-1940

> I want freedom, the right to self-expression, every-
> body's right to beautiful, radiant things! Anar-
> chism meant that to me, and I would live it in
> spite of the whole world—prisons, persecution,
> everything.

During the fateful year of 1886, a seventeen-year-old girl
left her native Russia for Rochester and there obtained a job
sewing men's ulsters for ten and a half hours a day, at a salary
of two dollars and fifty cents a week. She was destined for a
turbulent career as the most embattled Anarchist in America,
the editor of a radical magazine and the author of articles and
book-length works of a controversial nature. Always a rebel, it
was not long before she was dissatisfied with her job. After less
than a year she married, but was disappointed in her marriage.
In her mood of disillusionment she followed the trial of those
implicated in the Haymarket Riot in the newspaper *Freiheit,*
edited by Johann Most. The conviction of these men was to
her "judicial murder." She decided to leave Rochester for New
York and there to seek out Johann Most, who was the power
behind the anarchist movement.

He became her mentor and within six months she was on the
way to becoming the formidable orator she turned out to be.
Another who sealed her commitment to anarchism was Alexander Berkman. Two years of joblessness and homelessness
before she came to New York, had turned him into a dedicated
Anarchist. They became lovers; together they plotted the assassination of Henry Clay Frick. Had there been enough money for
two railroad tickets to Pittsburgh, she would have accompanied

him and shared his fate of a long prison sentence. His sentence was for twenty-two years.

Though constantly hounded by the police and arrested on numerous occasions (she said she never knew whether she would sleep in her own bed on any given day), "Red Emma," as she came to be called, was convicted only three times. The first sentence was for one year at Blackwell's Island for attempting to make a speech in Philadelphia to organize the unemployed, which the authorities designated as "inciting a riot." The second one was for fifteen days for advocating birth control, and the third for two years at the penitentiary at Jefferson City, Missouri, for obstructing the draft.

For anarchists, prison sentences were blessings in disguise because of the opportunity to improve one's education by reading and studying. Like all of them, Emma used her time profitably in adding to her education. Furthermore, her first sentence provided her with the opportunity to alter her way of making a living. When the prison physician realized how intelligent she was, he taught her to assist him in the prison hospital. Because of her conviction that prisoners were the unfortunates of society, more sinned against than sinners, she made a very sympathetic nurse. After her release she went to Vienna for additional training in nursing and obstetrical techniques. She even thought of studying medicine until it was pointed out to her that she could not combine the practice of medicine with membership in the Anarchist Party. Until she founded her magazine *Mother Earth*, which she published for twelve years until it was suppressed during World War I, she supported herself as nurse, midwife, and masseuse.

Emma Goldman earned the admiration of friends and foes for her heroic discipline, her unfailing devotion to her principles and her extraordinary mental endowments. Edward Corsi, Commissioner of Immigration, declared her to be "the most interesting radical ever to pass through the gates of Ellis Island."[1] A recent writer[2] describes her as "a woman of total sincerity, warm-hearted and cultivated, who . . . won the friendship and respect of many people who were not anarchists but who were impressed with her unfailing courage in support of freedom in all its forms." A fellow Anarchist spoke of her as possessing a

1. Edward Corsi, *Under the Shadow of Liberty* (New York, 1935).
2. James Joll, *The Anarchists* (Boston, 1964), p. 189.

force that was elemental "like wind or flood."[3] John Cournos, who was neither anarchist nor Socialist, described her "a dynamic personality, as sturdy as you make them." She drew into her circle not only radicals, but also a variety of old-fashioned liberals of old American lineage, some of whom were newspaper editors, lawyers, ministers, or just intellectuals. They raised large sums of money for bail for her and her friends, paid their fines, and offered their homes as meeting places. Among them were William Marion Reedy, editor of the *Saint Louis Mirror*, ex-Senator Charles Erskine Wood, Alden Freeman, son of a Standard Oil executive, the single-taxers Bolton Hall and Ernest Crosby, Gilbert E. Roe, Roger Baldwin, John Swinton, editor of *The New York Sun*, Hugh C. Pentecost, lawyer, Margaret Anderson, editor of the *Little Review*, Horace Traubel, biographer of Whitman, Frank Harris, editor of *Pearson's Magazine*, Bayard Boyesen, on the faculty of Columbia University, the wealthy Presbyterian Agnes Inglis of Detroit, and many others. They supported her because she preached much that liberal Americans could wholeheartedly endorse, such as the rights of labor, free speech, family limitation, and, after America's entry into World War I, resistance to the draft. A fascinating lecturer, she spoke to longshoremen and millionaires, working and professional women; in halls behind saloons, in drawing rooms, in mines hundreds of feet below the ground, from pulpits and soap boxes. Her peppery answers delighted university students, professional people, and Hyde Park audiences. She was high-principled, fearless, and incorruptible.

Though she had planned Frick's murder with Berkman, in her maturity she seems to have realized the irresponsibility of terroristic action. An idealist, she was intensely sensitive to human misery and wholeheartedly committed to alleviating economic and political shortcomings. Her assertion that she loved much about America and that she had become more American than Russian, has the ring of sincerity. She admitted her admiration for Jeffersonian democracy, but she felt that, like the America of Jefferson, the constitutional guarantees of freedom of speech and freedom of assembly had vanished long ago. What she particularly indicted were the "gag methods" of the police, the "unscrupulousness and inhumanity of the American courts," and the absence of tolerance for dissident opinions.

---

3. Lucy Robins Lang, *Tomorrow Is Beautiful* (New York, 1948).

By the time she was sentenced for her third time, her husband's citizenship had been revoked and she was liable to deportation. Her release from prison for obstructing the draft, coincided with the height of the "red scare"; In December of 1919 she and Alexander Berkman were among the two hundred forty-nine radicals deported on the S.S. Buford, nicknamed "The Soviet Ark." The disappointments they had encountered in America were pallid in comparison to what awaited them in revolutionary Russia. Instead of a glorious new world order, they found people starving, the Cheka in control, the jails filled, and executions taking place daily. Lenin told her and Berkman, when he had deigned to receive them, that they should have remained in America. They were excluded from Soviet affairs. Even as a nurse Emma Goldman could find no welcome in Russia. After almost two years' of desperate maneuverings, they considered themselves fortunate to be able to leave Russia. Thereafter, until her marriage to the Canadian James Colton, she was forced to wander, a stateless person on limited visas, from one European country to another. But nothing could dim her anarchist zeal. In 1938, two years before her death, she attended the Anarchist Congress in Spain.

In 1934 she was permitted to enter the United States for ninety days. Upon her death, however, she returned permanently to American soil. Like Bill Haywood, the "Wobbly" who had escaped to Russia by jumping bail, and others, who requested that their remains be interred in Waldheim Cemetery, where the Haymarket victims are buried, Emma Goldman also wished to be laid alongside them. One of her recent biographers claims that she never overcame the longing for America.[4] In death her wish was granted. Jo Davidson, sculptor and friend, designed a plaque for the headstone on her grave.

FROM *Living My Life**

We were struck by the great difference between the New Englanders and the Russian peasant. The latter seldom had enough for himself to eat, yet he would never fail to offer the stranger bread and kvass [cider]. The German peasants also as I remembered from my schooldays, would invite us

---

4. Richard Drinnon, *Rebel In Paradise* (Chicago, 1961).

*Emma Goldman, *Living My Life* (New York: Alfred A. Knopf, Inc., 1931). Reprinted by permission of the publishers.

to their best room, put milk and butter on the table and urge us to partake. But here in free America, where the farmers owned acres of land and much cattle, we were lucky to be admitted at all or be given a glass of water. Sasha [Alexander Berkman] used to say that the American farmer lacked sympathy and kindness because he himself had never known want. 'He is really a small capitalist,' he argued. . . .

It was a bright October day, the sun playing on the water as the barge sped on. [On the way to jail] Several newspaper men accompanied me, all pressing me for an interview. 'I travel in queenly state,' I remarked in light mood; 'just look at my satraps.' 'You can't squelch that kid,' a young reporter kept on saying, admiringly. When we reached the island [Blackwell's], I bade my escorts good-by, admonishing them not to write any more lies than they could help. I called out to them gaily that I would see them again within a year and then followed the Deputy Sheriff along the broad, tree-lined gravel walk to the prison entrance. There I turned towards the river, took a last deep breath of the free air, and stepped across the threshold of my new home. . . .

My three weeks in the Tombs had given me ample proof that the revolutionary contention that crime is the result of poverty is based on fact. Most of the defendants who were awaiting trial came from the lowest strata of society, men and women without friends, often without a home. . . . Among the seventy inmates in the penitentiary, there were no more than half a dozen who showed any intelligence whatever. The rest were outcasts without the least social consciousness. Their personal misfortunes filled their thoughts; they could not understand that they were victims, links in an endless chain of injustice and inequality. From early childhood they had known nothing but poverty, squalor, and want, and the same conditions were awaiting them on their release. . . .

Soon I took up my new work. The ward contained sixteen beds, most of them always filled. The various diseases were treated in the same room, from grave operations to tuberculosis, penumonia and chidlbirth. My hours were long and strenuous, the groans of the patients nerve-racking; but I loved my job. It gave me opportunity to come close to the sick women and bring a little cheer into their lives. . . . I had so much to give; it was a joy to share with my sisters who had neither friends nor attention. . . .

Of the friends I made on Blackwell's Island the priest was the most interesting. At first I felt antagonistic to him. I thought he was like the rest of the religious busybodies, but I soon found out that he wanted to talk only about books. . . . We would discuss his favourite composers—Bach, Beethoven and Brahms—and compare our views on poetry and social ideas. He presented me with an English-Latin dictionary as a gift, inscribed: 'With the highest respect, to Emma Goldman.' . . .

'Leon Czologosz and other men of his type,' I wrote in my article, . . . 'far from being depraved creatures of low instincts are in reality supersensitive human beings unable to bear up under too great social stress. They are driven to some violent expression, even at the sacrifice of their own lives, because they cannot supinely witness the suffering of their fellows. The blame for such acts must be laid at the door of those who are responsible for the injustice and inhumanity which dominate the world.' . . .

Anarchism asserts the possibility of an organization without discipline, fear or punishment and without the pressure of poverty: a new social organism, which will make an end to the struggle for the means of existence—the savage struggle which undermines the finest qualities in man and ever widens the social abyss. In short, Anarchism strives towards a social organization which will establish well-being for all. . . .

It struck me that behind the difference between American and French legal procedure was a fundamental difference in attitude to social revolt. Frenchmen had gained from their Revolution the understanding that institutions are neither sacred nor unalterable, and that social conditions are subject to change. Rebels are therefore considered in France the precursors of coming upheavals. . . . In America the ideals of the Revolution are dead-mummies that must not be touched. Hence the hatred and condemnation which meet the social and political rebel in the United States. . . .

Comrades, idealists, manufacturing a bomb in a congested tenement house! I was aghast at such irresponsibility. . . . With accusing clarity I now relived that nerve-wracking week in July 1892 [when Berkman had fashioned a home-made bomb]. In the zeal of fanaticism I had believed that the end justifies the means. It took years of experience and suffering to emancipate myself from the mad idea. Acts of violence committed as a protest against unbearable social wrongs—I still believed them inevitable. . . . But though my sympathies were with the man who protested against social crimes by a resort to extreme measures, I nevertheless felt now that I could never again participate in or approve of methods that jeopardized innocent lives. . . .

. . . All through the years we had been close to the pulse of Russia, close to her spirit and her superhuman struggle for liberation. But our lives were rooted in our adopted land. We had learned to love her physical grandeur and her beauty and to admire the men and women who were fighting for freedom, the Americans of the best calibre. I felt myself one of them, an American in the truest sense, spiritually rather than by the grace of a mere scrap of paper. For twenty-eight years I had lived, dreamed and worked for that America. . . .

. . . In response to my request for trinkets, for the inmates, . . . [I received] a huge consignment. . . . It was a problem to divide the gifts so as to give each what she might like best without arousing envy or suspicion of preference and favoritism. I called to my aid three of my neighbours, and with their expert advice and help, I played Santa Claus [at the Jefferson Penitentiary]. On Christmas Eve, while our fellow-prisoners were attending the movies, a matron accompanied us to unlock the doors, our aprons piled high with gifts. With gleeful secrecy we flitted along the tiers, visiting each cell in turn. . . . My Christmas in the Missouri penitentiary brought me greater joy than many previous ones outside. I was thankful to friends who had enabled me to bring a gleam of sunshine into the dark lives of my fellow-sufferers. . . .

I had always longed to revisit Russia, and after the February-October Revolution I had definitely decided to return to my native land to help in its reconstruction. But I wanted to go of my own free will, at my own expense, and I denied the right of the government to force me. I was aware of its brutal strength but I did not propose to submit without a fight. . . .

[In Russia] The intelligentsia, the men and women who had once been revolutionary torch-bearers, leaders of thoughts, writers and poets were as helpless as we and paralysed by the futility of individual effort. Most of their comrades and friends were already in prison or exile; some had been executed. . . . These Communist friends spent nights with us—talking, talking—but none of them dared raise his voice in open protest.

We did not realize, they said, the consequences it would involve. They would be excluded from the party, they and their families deprived of work and rations and literally condemned to death by starvation. Or they would simply vanish and no one would ever know what became of them. Yet it was not fear that numbed their will, they assured us. It was the utter uselessness of protest or appeal. Nothing, nothing could stop the chariot-wheel of the Communist State. . . .

. . . What a commentary on the Communist State outdoing Uncle Sam! He, poor boob, went only as far as deporting his foreign-born opponents. Lenin and Company, themselves political refugees from their native land only a short time ago, were now ordering the deportation of Russia's native sons, the best flower of her revolutionary past. . . .

Soviet Russia had become the modern socialist Lourdes, to which the blind and the lame, the deaf and the dumb were flocking for miraculous cures. I was filled with pity for these deluded ones, but I felt only contempt for those others who had come, had seen with open eyes and understood, and had been conquered. Of these was William Z. Foster, once the champion of revolutionary syndicalism in America. He was keen-eyed and he had come as a press correspondent. He went back to do Moscow's bidding. . . .

. . . There was still a large place in my heart for my erstwhile country, regardless of her shabby treatment. My love for all that is ideal, creative, and humane in her would not die, but I should rather never see America again if I could do so only by compromising my ideas.

Oscar Ameringer
Musician, Painter, Editor
1870-1943

What an idea to play around with amusing trifles . . . when the world was so obviously out of joint and no one but me to set it right! Life, for me, had become earnest, at least and rather more real, too.

This is how Oscar Ameringer felt after his conversion to Socialism via Henry George's *Progress and Poverty*. His was a most colorful career, spiced with adventure and many changes of fortune. In his birthplace, an Austrian village, he was the "town pariah," and the townspeople could see no other future for him except "gallows and hell or America." Shipped off in 1886, at the age of sixteen, his destination was Cincinnati. There he worked briefly at the trade his father had taught him—cabinet-making—but having received musical instruction in various brass instruments, he soon discovered a more agreeable way of supporting himself. Drifting in and out of various bands, which, he explains, were operated at that time by German saloon keepers, he traveled through the Ohio valley, where he frequently found himself stranded because the receipts were scanty, or because the treasurer had absconded with what money there was. But an engaging young man with warm brown eyes could always get food, a night's lodging, and often some loose change from a kindly farm couple. The friendly, hospitable towns of the Midwest represented to him "one America." Because other parts of the country made widely differing impressions on him, America appeared to him composed of "many Americans," and his peregrinations as a "roughneck Odyssey."

Among his other talents was a disposition to paint and *"die Lust zum fabulieren,"* as Goethe, his patron saint, referred to the inclination to write. Ameringer followed all three at various times in his life. A great advantage was his rollicking sense of humor, which enabled him to meet many setbacks with an uproarious guffaw rather than with a jaundiced eye. Later, the high jollity of his youth became tinged with bitter cynicism.

He stumbled into a new calling when he helped an epileptic boy to his home and discovered that his mother taught drawing and painting. She encouraged him to study drawing in an art school and soon he found himself painting wealthy farmers from life and farm photographs, while enjoying the hospitality of their comfortable homes, equipped with bathrooms, running water, and books. At the same time he discovered that humor magazines like *Judge* and *Puck* would print his contributions. His early writing experiences stood him in good stead, for after his conversion to Socialism he employed his journalistic talents in behalf of the labor press. An indication of his ability was a flattering offer to write for the Hearst papers, which he declined. . . .

How did he become a Socialist? By reading Henry George, Edward Bellamy, and the muckraking articles on business and high finance printed in *McClure's*. What he learned was enough to turn him from a successful insurance salesman into a "crusader" for a "new social order."

From then on he remained in the thick of social reform. As a strike organizer in New Orleans he discovered a "different America," and when he transferred his activities to Oklahoma, still "another America." In Oklahoma he found that sharecroppers on land owned by Indians were "worse fed, worse clothed, worse housed and more illiterate than the Chicago packing-house wops and Bohunks Upton Sinclair described in *The Jungle*." While running for various offices on the Socialist ticket in various places, he found time to raise money, to make speeches (with "clarinet obbligado"), to assist Victor Berger, and to edit various labor organs. He found still "another America" in the Illinois coal fields, where he edited the *Illinois Miner* for the United Mine Workers, and made it the "most readable family paper in America."

Beneath the high antics was a perceptive, dedicated individual who was aware of the good and bad in American life. Some of his ideas, such as an agricultural resettlement project for unemployed miners, anticipated the New Deal. Though he set it up, he failed in getting the Resettlement Administration to take it over, for which he indicted the "PhD.'s of the agency." Like all Socialists he was critical of America, because inequities and corrupt politics were allowed to exist and thus to impede the pursuit of happiness. Yet his faith in the "American way of practical thinking, the power of the ballot box and a genuine love of country," remained unshaken. When he was past seventy, the function of America was to him "not to be the richest, most powerful and most feared nation on earth, but the torchbearer of all that is good, true and beautiful on earth . . ."

FROM *If You Don't Weaken**

Looking back, these many years afterward, I can see clearly that nature had cut me out for an artist, musician, writer, or under exceptionally favorable circumstances, all three. For it was in these callings that I made my living for more than half a century and to them I returned always whenever the course of life had led me into other fields. . . .

---

*Oscar Ameringer, *If You Don't Weaken* (New York: Henry Holt & Co., 1940). Reprinted by permission.

. . . I have no history, if there be one, of the American Federation of Musicians at hand, but if I recollect rightly, this is how it came into existence. Some of us younger, and consequently more radical, musicians resented the treatment extended by our saloon-keeper band and orchestra masters. While there was no particular objection against beer, free lunches and loafing places, even a musicians wants to handle a few dimes now and then. As a result of this laudable ambition, some two dozen of us launched a short-lived co-operative saloon. . . . Our saloon musicians' headquarters was a few door [from] . . . the heart of the Cincinnati amusement center. The society we had organized bore the significant name of "Aschenbroetel Verein," or "Cinderella Society," out of which grew Local Number One of the American Federation of Musicians. . . .

I was making a fairly comfortable living painting landscapes and flower pieces in wooden bread bowls at one dollar a bowl. . . . I painted butterflies on ladies' white slippers and forget-me-nots on fronts of ladies' wrappers in the style popular at the time. I drew enlarged photographs in crayon and, toward the end, painted portraits from life in oil, aquarelle, pastels, or whatever the customer wanted. . . .

Much as I loved music, and the teaching of music, I was barely able to support my growing family. Something more substantial was required and I began to look around for it. A friend of my earlier days was now engaged in the life-insurance business in Columbus. He invited me to join him, and to Columbus I went. . . . I am persuaded that had I loved either life-insurance or money enough, I might well have made my fortune. . . . I could sell almost anything by selling myself. But before selling myself I had to believe in the immaculate conception of the thing I sold. And judging by my reading of the muckrakers, life insurance and high finance were a hell of a way from being immaculate. . . .

For myself, the die was cast. Up to then I had been a part-time world saver. Now I was a professional, on full time, and in every fiber of my being. This thing was too terrible to be tolerated. . . . The Oklahoma farmers' living standard was so far below that of the sweatshop workers of the New York east side before the Amalgamated Clothing Workers and International Ladies' Garment Workers Unions had mopped up that human cesspool, that comparison could not be thought of. . . .

I am not afraid of democracy. I have seen enough of life to realize that the only way to mislead the voting masses is to overwhelm them with lying appeals to their innate sympathy, decency and sense of justice. That was what so successfully swept America into the World War. [Like all Socialists Ameringer did not support the war effort.] Nor am I afraid of the rank and file. As my old friend, Carl Sandburg, once said, the common people have hung around for a long time. . . .

In my first years as editor of "The Illinois Miner" it became clear to me that, no matter what was done, not more than perhaps fifty-thousand out of the then ninety-thousand union members would find permanent employment in the mines of Illinois. . . . Why, I asked myself, let these men and their families decay in dying mining towns, waiting to hear mine whistles that were silenced forever? Outside of our English, Scotch, Welsh, and the small number of German miners, the overwhelming majority of the others, were not born miners, but rather sons of the soil. So why not restore them to the soil? . . . I talked my associates among the Illinois miners into the notion. . . . And so, as the only agricultural expert of the miners' union, I set forth in search of the right location on which to rear my subsistence-homestead Utopia. . . .

. . . Well, it's still projecting. Around a hundred families are living on it, raising cotton, corn, cows, pigs, chickens—and vegetables. When I last saw them, they all looked fairly well dressed and well fed. There is a good school, which even boasts a small library. The neat, whitepainted cottages are surrounded by flower and vegetable gardens. It really is a nice place, my garden home down in luxurious Louisiana. . . . It was, I admit it, an almost heart-breaking job. . . . It isn't all I had hoped it would be. But where twelve years ago there were eight square miles of jungle, populated by wild cats, hoot owls and skunks, there are now laughing fields and smiling children, Especially am I proud of some twenty colored families, for whom I had reserved forty acres each. They have not yet won their war against the jungle and poverty, but they will. . . .

Yet I do not despair. Long has been the road, strewn with

rocks and thorns, soaked with heart's blood, marked with tears, but an upward road always. Civilizations have risen and fallen. Great leaders of men have come and gone. Centuries of unbroken progress toward the better life have been followed by dark ages. But always, somewhere on this earth, was a people who preserved the inheritance of the race and carried it to greater heights. That you, my America, will be the carrier of the best of the ages and the herald of the better day is the prayer of my heart.

Edward Steiner
Minister, Social Scientist
1866-1956

> The American people have taken it for granted that a standard of living is a biological inheritance, and that in the Divine economy the American was born with a passion for colonial houses, and soap and water, while the immigrant came into the world fond of hovels, dirt and wheelbarrows.

Imagine an educated Austrian, follower of Tolstoy, forced into a sweatshop, then into the coal and iron mines, riding freight trains as a hobo, assaulted, robbed, beaten senseless, not once but several times, serving a jail sentence for a crime of which he was unaware, experiencing "the whole scale of hunger, sorrow and despair," and you have the story of Edward Steiner. It is a tale many immigrants could repeat, except that few were able to triumph over their difficulties as he did.

The fact that he was a university graduate helped him finally to extricate himself from the treadmill of hopelessness. A political indiscretion caused him to leave Austria in haste. In the 1880s—the time of his arrival—there was no demand for such training as he possessed. Consequently he was forced to turn to the sweatshop. Disgust with New York, hatred of the saloon, the baneful effects of which sickened him, and the hope that away from the city he might be able to live in the Tolstoyan way, made him belatedly follow Horace Greeley's advice to "go West." It took him first to the coal mines of Pennsylvania, where he earned himself a jail sentence as a result of going to work in a mine that was on strike; to Chicago, where he found "solid phalanxes of saloon" and where he again made the acquaintance of a "lock-up"; to the harvest fields of Minnesota, where the horrors of unemployment continued to pursue him.

The deprivations to which he was subjected as an alien caused a most profound change in the direction of his life. At first indifferent to religion, he became a profound believer in Jesus Christ and was eventually brought into the ministry. Also in consequence of the calamities he had suffered, he developed such an empathy for all unfortunates that he became the eloquent champion of the Negro, the laboring man, and, especially, the immigrant. Though he served as minister of several parishes for about ten years, he did not find his true vocation until he was called to Grinnell College to become professor of "Applied Christianity." In that post he acquired such a reputation as a social scientist that the most respected men in public service paid him homage. Horace Bridges,[1] himself foreign-born, and a leader of the Ethical Culture movement, called him, in the words of St. Augustine: that "Anima naturaliter," adding the word "Americana."

Edward Steiner learned to love America with a mystical feeling, despite the harsh treatment accorded to him during the early years of his life. But he never lost his loathing for the city of Chicago. He found the police of Chicago to be in league with the saloon, the brothels, the cheap lodging houses, protecting them in their exploitation of immigrants. Chicago was to him a "forbidding," a "pitiless" place.

In pleading for fairness to immigrants, at whom the shafts of the exclusionists were directed, Edward Steiner offered himself as an example of the tramp that had been jailed, who had trundled wheelbarrows, wielded a pick-axe when he was lucky enough to find work, and yet had eventually made a respected place for himself in American society. In his experiences there is an echo of Walt Whitman's words: "I was the man—I suffer'd —I was there."

FROM *From Alien to Citizen**

I should like to teach the strangers that there is a fair

---

1. Horace Bridges, *On Becoming An American* (Boston, 1918).

*Edward Steiner, *From Alien to Citizen* (New York: Fleming H. Revell Company, 1914). By permission of the publishers.

reward for hard struggle and an honest living wage for an honest day's work. That they must guard their health by abstinence from intoxicating drink, and I should like to prohibit its sale on board of ship and everywhere else. For to the immigrants, the ignorant immigrants, alcohol is a lying curse. They believe that it strengthens and that no hard labor can be done without it. . . . I should like to tell them also that their health will be guarded in mines and factories and that their bodies and souls have value to man and God. . . . I should like to point to the Goddess of Liberty and say that she welcomes all who come in her name, that she guarantees freedom to all who obey law, that our law is always reasonable and that, if it is a burden, it falls upon the shoulders of rich and poor alike. . . .

To recall prison experiences is not pleasant, and would not be profitable, if this were merely a narration of what happened to one individual, a quarter of a century ago. . . . The jail in which I found myself was an unredeemed, vermin-infested building, crowded by a motley multitude of strikers and strike breakers; bitter enemies all, their animosity begotten in the elemental struggle for bread, and hating one another with an unmodified primitive passion. . . . Poor food, vermin of many varieties and the various small tortures endured, were all as nothing to me compared with the fact that for more than six weeks I was permitted to be in that jail without a hearing; without even the slightest knowledge of why I had forfeited my liberty. . . .

Not only is ignorance of our laws and our language a fruitful cause of the delinquency of immigrants and their children, but the venality of police officials, the conditions of our courts and prisons, not only fail to inspire respect, but contribute much to the development of those criminal tendencies which nature has, to a degree, endowed all men.

Until very lately the immigrant in Chicago, unless he had waiting friends, found no gateway open to him except the saloon, the brothel, the cheap lodging house and finally the 'lock-up.'

The agencies which began the assimilative process were all anti-social, greedy for their prey, and, worst of all, the police was in league with them and protected them. There was nothing left to do but walk up and down in impotent rage and inveigh against a city which permitted its newest and most potential human material to be polluted, if not corrupted, at the very entrance into its life. . . .

To me Chicago is a marvel, made up as it is of over-lapping strata of aliens from beyond the sea and aliens cast from its surrounding prairies—all of them cast into her turmoil of labour, eating their bread by the sweat of their brow or by the shrewder method—eating it by the sweat of other men's brows. Chicago is a marvellous city to me; not because of the cattle she kills or the grains she speeds from her sheds or the piles of stones she has set into skeletons of steel; but because the human souls survives and men can get away from her without harm.

When I left Chicago for the Minnesota harvest fields I offered up a fervent prayer of thanksgiving for being able to go from it alive; although the coming and going are easier now and my sojourn always pleasant, I still have that same prayer on my lips whenever I leave Chicago. . . .

It would be futile to try to tell of the many jubilant notes which my seminary experiences brought into the hitherto minor chord of my life in America. One epoch-making event, however, I must record. During that period I became an American citizen. On a certain never-to-be-forgotten day I walked to the country seat, about seven miles away, to get my papers. What seemed to me should be a sacred rite proved to be an uninspiring performance. I entered a dingy office where a commonplace man, chewing tobacco, mumbled an oath which I repeated. Then he handed me a document for which I paid two dollars. When I held the long-coveted paper in my hand, the inspiring moment came, but it transpired in my own soul. ·. .

It is no wonder that strangers like myself love this country, and love it, perhaps, as the native never can. Frequently I have wished for the careless American citizen, who holds his franchise cheap, an experience like my own, that he might know the value of a freeman's birthright. It would be a glorious experience, I am sure, to feel that transition from subject to citizen, from scarcely being permitted to say 'I' to those great collective words: 'We, Fellow-citizens.' . . .

I was told repeatedly that I might stay with my church to a good old age if I left the saloon alone. I was perfectly willing to do that, had the saloon left me alone. Its mean, crafty, deadly influence was everywhere; not only in the drink it dispensed—that might have been the least of its brood of evils. It buttressed the brothel and spread poison, until its loathsome touch fell upon the mothers and the children. It corrupted the family, weakened legitimate business and even reached into the church, ready to throttle its spirit. . . .

My great aim now is to teach intelligent and religious men and women how to look at the unlike to learn to like them, how to break through prejudice so that the emotions are not conquered by hate, how to be able to stand in this conglomerate of races and nationalities which flow into our nation and to be able to say without cant: We the People. This path which I have marked out for myself is not an easy one; yet my doctrines do not readily arouse great opposition, although they are most radical and revolutionary. . . .

If to-morrow my part in the battle ends I shall thank God for the share I have had in it thus far, I shall thank God for the way He has led me into it; through hunger, homelessness and loneliness; the drudgery of work, the pangs of poverty and even the fires of affliction.

Alexander Berkman
Anarchist, Writer
1871-1936

> The People—the toilers of the world, the producers —comprise, to me, the universe. They alone count. The rest are parasites, who have no right to exist.

In July, 1892, Alexander Berkman made an attempt to kill Henry Clay Frick in retaliation for Frick's actions in the Homestead Steel Strike. According to Berkman's own statement, his attempted assassination was the "first terrorist act in America." He was given an unusually severe sentence—twenty-two years, commuted under a new law for good behavior to twelve years and ten months in the Western Penitentiary of Pennsylvania and one year in the workhouse. He entered prison at twenty-one and remained a captive until he was thirty-five years of age.

He had come from a well-to-do family in Russia, where he

had finished four years of the Classic Gymnasium in Kovno. He
had been a superior student. The death of his mother gave him
the opportunity to make a new start in America. He was sixteen
and the year was 1887, the heyday of anarchist agitation. He
had become infected by the teachings of nihilism through the
influence of an uncle who had come to an untimely end in
Russia. The boy had pictured America as "the land of noble
achievement, a glorious free country, where men walked erect
in the full stature of manhood—the very realization of my youthful dreams." Instead he found hunger, cold, and homelessness.
Embittered, he let Johann Most, disciple of Bakunin, become his
"first teacher in Anarchism." It was Alexander Berkman who
introduced Emma Goldman to Johann Most when she made her
first appearance in New York.

Though he and Emma Goldman shared the same convictions,
acted in unison, and upheld each other through thick and thin,
yet there was a palpable difference between them. She kept her
"heart young," as he remarked in a letter to her; she loved
people and beautiful things and considered much in America
good and beautiful. In Berkman all human impulses seemed to
to have been frozen. An intense fanatic, this "Savonarola of
Anarchism" never allowed himself to forget what the proper
attitude of a revolutionary should be: to live solely for "the
holy Cause—the People," and in so doing to expunge "mere
human sentiment." In conformance with Nietzsche's phrase: "How
to become what one is," he made himself become what he felt
himself to be.

A desolate picture of American society—consisting of misery
and exploitation of workers and unrelieved horror of prison life
—emerges from his writings. Because he spent fourteen years
in prison—between the age of twenty-one and thirty-five, he
knew no other America. He was certain to have denied that
there was any other America for his class.

Berkman's *Attentat* [act of political assassination], was an act
of immolation intended to dramatize Frick's betrayal of the steel
workers by importing Pinkerton agents to protect scabs. Though
Frick's wounds were slight, to Berkman's everlasting regret, he
received an unusually severe sentence. Had Berkman been
represented by counsel, his sentence might have been lighter,
also his case might later have been reopened. But considering
himself "morally innocent," he followed the practice among

anarchists in spurning legal aid and conducting his own defense. Had he been willing at the end of seven years to renounce anarchism, his sentence might have been commuted. But when he stood before the warden, he reiterated his anarchist convictions, fully aware that he was dooming himself to a continued existence in prison.

Like Thoreau, who said when he went to Walden that he intended to drive "life into a corner" and if it proved to be "mean . . . publish its meanness to the world," after his release Berkman set out to publish the meanness of his life before and during his years in prison. The picture of life in penal institutions—the degradations, the monstrous indifference of prison officials, the threat of homosexuality—suggest a version of the Inferno, except that his descriptions are not a product of the imagination. He declares: "I will echo their agony to the ears of the world. I have suffered with them, I have looked into the heart of pain and with its voice and anguish I will speak to humanity, to wake it from sloth and apathy, and lend hope to despair. His sincerity cannot be questioned.

In conformance with anarchist doctrine, he considered all prisoners, no matter how degraded, "les miserables," victims of society" and "social stupidity." Like all jailed anarchists he made the fullest use of the prison library. Because of his extensive reading, in which he was abetted by a kind and thoughtful prison chaplain, this man whose English was so poor at the time of his trial that he had to depend on a German interpreter, developed such remarkable fluency and style, that Emma Goldman was glad to leave the editing of her magazine, *Mother Earth*, to him.

The events of his later years emerge from Emma Goldman's story of her life, which she began while living in France, where her more affluent friends and admirers had bought a small home for her. After Berkman's memoirs had been rejected by all reputable publishing houses, she published it under the imprimatur of Mother Earth Publishing Company, having obtained the necessary funds from Lincoln Steffens and others. In 1917 he too was indicted for obstructing the draft and sentenced to two years' imprisonment in the Atlanta Penitentiary. He was one of the deportees on the S.S. Buford and he shared her bitter disappointment over the failure of the Russian Revolution. Together they left Russia, and though the sentiment that had brought them together had long since evaporated, they remained devoted to one another. Berkman made a precarious living as a writer and translator and whenever she was able to, she aided him financially. She relied on him to help her with her autobiography and to edit it.[1]

Ill and in need, Alexander Berkman committed suicide in Nice, an action he justified by "right of revolutionary ethics."

FROM *The Prison Memoirs of an Anarchist**

And now I am in America, the blessed land. The disillusion-ment, the disappointment, the vain struggles! . . . Now I see myself on a bench in Union Square Park . . . The night wind sweeps across the cheerless park, chilling us to the bone. I feel hungry and tired, fagged out by the day's fruitless search for work. . . . What is that pain I feel? . . . I feel a sharp sting as of a lash. Oh, it's in my soles! Bewildered I spring to my feet. A rough hand grabs me by the throat, and I face a policeman. . . .

East End, the fashionable residence quarters of Pittsburgh, lies basking in the afternoon sun. . . . A steady procession of equipages fills the avenue, the richly caparisoned horses and uniformed flunkies lending color and life to the scene. A cavalcade is passing me. The laughter of the ladies sounds joyous and care-free. Their happiness irritates me. I am think-ing of Homestead. In mind I see the sombre fence, the fortifi-cations and cannon; the piteous figure of the widow rises before me, the little children weeping, and I again I hear the anguished cry of a broken heart, a shattered brain. . . . And the fine ladies on horseback smile and laugh. What is the misery of the People to *them*? . . . Laugh! Laugh! . . .

How little I knew of America then! A free country, indeed, that hangs its noblest men. And the misery, the exploitation,—it's terrible. I must mention all this in court, in my defence. No, not defence—some fitter word. Explanation! Yes, my ex-planation. I need no defence: I don't consider myself guilty . . . I need no lawyers. They couldn't explain my case. I shall not talk to the reporters, either. They are a lying pack, those journalistic hounds of capitalism. . . .

---

1. Richard Drinnon, *Rebel in Paradise* (Chicago, 1961).

*Alexander Berkman, *Prison Memoirs of an Anarchist* (New York: Mother Earth Publishing Company, 1912).

. . . A revolutionist cannot be influenced by mere sentimentality. We bleed for the People, we suffer for them, but we know the real source of their misery. Our whole civilization, false to the core as it is, must be destroyed, to be born anew. Only with the abolition of exploitation will labor gain justice. Anarchism alone can save the world. . . .

The legal aspect aside, can the morality of the act be questioned? It is impossible to confound law with right; they are opposites. The law is immoral: it is the conspiracy of rulers and priests against the workers, to continue their subjection. To be law-abiding means to acquiesce, if not directly participate in that conspiracy. . . . The Law! It is the arch-crime of the centuries. The path of Man is soaked with the blood it has shed. Can this great criminal determine Right? Is a revolutionist to respect such a travesty? It would mean the perpetuation of human slavery. . . .

We, criminals? We, who are ever ready to give our lives for liberty, criminals? And they, our accusers? They break their own laws: they knew it was not legal to multiply the charges against me. They made six indictments out of one act, as if the minor 'offences' were not included in the major, made necessary by the deed itself? They thirsted for blood. Legally, they could not give me more than seven years. But I am an Anarchist. I had attempted the life of a great magnate; in him capitalism felt itself attacked. Of course, I knew they would take advantage in my refusal to be legally represented. . . . Well, I expected no less, and it makes no difference now. . . .

Four weeks of 'Pennsylvania diet' have reduced me almost to a skeleton. A slice of wheat bread with a cup of unsweetened black coffee is my sole meal, with twice a week dinner of vegetable soup, from which every trace of meat has been removed. Every Saturday I am conducted to the office, to be examined by the physician and weighed. The whole week I look forward to the brief respite from the terrible 'basket' cell. . . . The torture of the 'basket' is maddening; the constant dusk is driving me blind. Almost no light or air reaches me through the close wire netting covering the barred door. The foul odor is stifling; it grips my throat with deathly hold. The walls hem me in; daily they press closer upon me, till the cell seems to contract, and I feel crushed in the coffin of stone. . . .

Often the Chaplain pauses at my door, and speaks words of encouragement. I feel deeply moved by his sympathy, but my revolutionary traditions forbid the expression of my emotions; a cog in the machinery of oppression, he might mistake my gratitude for the obsequiousness of the fawning convict. But I hope he feels my appreciation in the simple 'thank you.'

I marvel at the inadequacy of my previous notions of 'the criminal.' I resent the presumption of 'science' that pretends to evolve the intricate convolutions of a living human brain out of the shape of a digit cut from a dead hand, and labels it 'criminal type.' Daily association dispels the myth of the 'species,' and reveals the individual. Growing intimacy discovers the humanity beneath fibers coarsened by lack of opportunity and brutalized by misery and fear. . . .

New guards—unless drafted from the police bureau—are almost without exception lenient and forbearing, often exceedingly humane. . . . Slowly the poison is instilled into the new guard. Within a short time the prisoners notice the first signs of change: he grows less tolerant and chummy, more irritated and distant. . . . In a moment of commiseration and pity, the officer is moved by the tearful pleadings of misery to carry a message to the sick wife or child of a prisoner. The latter confides the secret to some friend, or carelessly brags of his intimacy with the guard, and soon the keeper faces the Warden 'on charges,' and is deprived of a month's pay. . . . The instinct of self-preservation, harassed and menaced on every side, becomes more assertive, and the guard is soon drawn into the vortex of the 'system.' . . .

The narrower your horizon—the more absorbed you are in your immediate environment, and dependent upon it—the sooner you decay, morally and mentally. You can, in a measure, escape the sordidness of life only by living for something higher. . . .

It was the vision of a great ideal, the consciousness that I suffered for a great Cause, that sustained me. The very exaggeration of my self-estimate was a source of strength; I looked upon myself as a representative of a world movement; it was my duty to exemplify the spirit and the dignity of the ideas it embodied. I was not a prisoner, merely; I was an Anarchist in the hands of the enemy; as such it devolved upon me to maintain the manhood and self-respect my ideals signified.

Morris Hillquit
Lawyer, Political Theorist
1871-1933

> I am a Socialist because I cannot be anything else.
> I cannot accept the ugly world of capitalism, with
> its brutal struggles and needless suffering, its
> archaic and irrational economic structure, its cruel
> social contrasts, its moral callousness and spiritual
> degradation.

No one gravitated to social reform by a more direct route than the seventeen-year-old youth who had just arrived from Russia in the year 1888. He had received a classical education in the Gymnasium at Riga, where the cultural influences were German and the instruction was in Russian. Culturally at sea with the Jewish element of the East Side, the young man listened on summer nights to debates on political and social doctrines that were taking place between the young intellectuals of the East Side, whom the heat of the tenements had driven to the roofs. It was a time of social unrest and disappointment for newly arrived immigrants, and the young people, forlorn and unsure of themselves as he was, were searching for a creed to which they could dedicate themselves. Some espoused Positivism, some Anarchism, and others turned to Socialism. He allied himself immediately with the Social Democrats and when he reached the required minimum age of eighteen, he became a member of the Socialist Labor Party, as it was then called. From then on he never wavered in his adherence to Socialist ideals, despite the struggles and setbacks from which the movement was never free. Socialism became the *raison d'être* of his life.

In the early days of Socialist activity, Morris Hillquit organized unions, led strikes, and helped to edit the first Yiddish newspaper. This was before the days of Abraham Cahan's *Daily Forward*. After passing the examination for teaching English to foreigners, he taught evening school. Within six years he had completed the study of law at the New York University Law School, was admitted to the bar, and settled down to the practice of law.

By successive stages Morris Hillquit became the moving

force of the Socialist Party. Specifically, he served Socialism in two distinct ways: as a propagandist and as counsel for individuals whose political views had made them targets of suspicion and persecution. He defended Johann Most, the Anarchist, but could not get an acquittal for him, though the judge complimented him on his handling of the case. In the capacity of Socialist propagandist he took an active part in the reorganization of the party, in representing the party at meetings and debates, and as candidate for various political offices. He was twice nominated for the office of mayor of New York City and five times he sought a seat in Congress. Though he failed of election, it was often by very "narrow margins." Besides, he was frequently opposed by a coalition of Democrats and Republicans. He believed that the endorsement by the Socialist Party of woman suffrage in 1917, when he was a candidate for mayor, forced the other candidates to declare themselves in favor of the franchise for women. It became law in New York State before the nineteenth amendment was ratified.

Though many Socialists supported World War I, the official stand of the American Socialist Party was to disassociate itself from the war effort. Newly enacted legislation dealt harshly with dissenters. Morris Hillquit undertook the defense of many who found themselves persecuted during the Wilson administration. However, when Eugene Debs and Victor Berger were arraigned under the Espionage Act, Hillquit was unable to act in their behalf. Confined in a sanatorium, he could only watch the developments from his sick-bed. Eugene Debs, then sixty-two years of age, was given a ten year sentence and Victor Berger was convicted to serve twenty years.

In his dedication to Socialist goals, many of which were enacted into law during the twentieth century, lies his service to America.

FROM *Loose Leaves From a Busy Life**

The selfish positivist cult of individual perfection and personal salvation did not satisfy my social instincts.

The romanticism of the anarchists held no attraction for me. I always had a certain sense of realism, which rendered me

---

*Morris Hillquit, *Loose Leaves From a Busy Life* (New York: The Macmillan Company, 1934). Used by permission of the publishers.

immune from the intoxicating effect of the hollow revolutionary phrase. I could not envisage a great social, economic and moral world revolution accomplished by guerrilla warfare, dynamite bombs and theatrical conspiracies. I could not have taken the violent anarchist thunder seriously.

I was on the other hand deeply impressed with the practical idealism of Social Democracy. Socialism has never become a religious dogma to me. I accepted its philosophy as convincing on the whole, without insisting on every article of the Marxian creed for myself or my comrades. . . .

. . . What I endeavored to demonstate was . . . that trade unionism and Socialism sprang from the same economic conditions and necessities, that their ultimate goals were consciously or unconsciously identical, that one complemented the other and that both would gain by mutual understanding and practical cooperation. . . .

War was declared on April 6th, and the emergency convention of the [Socialist] Party opened in St. Louis the next day. It was a tense and nervous gathering of about two hundred delegates from all parts of the country. The sole business of the convention was to take a stand on the war just declared, and never did I witness a more solemn or dramatic proceeding. . . .

We put our whole soul into the proclamation, the agonized Socialist soul crying out in anguish against the savagery of war, against the needless sacrifice of American lives in the quarrels of clashing capitalist interests in Europe and against the atmosphere of passion, hatred, and terror which the war was sure to breed. . . .

I was opposed to the flotation of the Liberty bonds for several reasons. I believed that the cost of the war should be borne by the wealthy, and particularly by those who were amassing colossal fortunes in war industries, rather than by government loans calculated to burden the people for generations to come. I was repelled by the methods of moral terrorism employed in the sale of the bonds, and, holding the views on the war that I did, I felt that I could not in good conscience give it voluntary support. . . .

Yellow? I am thinking back to the hectic days of the [mayoralty] campaign [of 1917], the open or covert incitements to violence emanating from the press, the pulpit and war-frenzied 'leading citizens,' the threatening letters that came to me in almost every mail, the rows of sullen home-guard soldiers often surrounding my meetings, the Department of Justice shadowing me at every step and having stenographers to take down every word of my campaign speeches; I am thinking of the heavy atmosphere of hate and terrorism in which I constantly moved. It took infinitely greater physical and moral courage in those days to defend an unpopular minority position than to howl with the infuriated mob. . . .

My unprecedently large vote was by no means a personal triumph. It was a legitimate victory of the Socialist Party. While I was necessarily kept in the front line of the battle as the head of the party ticket and had to stand the brunt of the fight, the whole of the organized Socialist movement of New York was mobilized for active campaign work and all did yeoman service. . . . all of it was volunteer work, work of love, without recognition and without pay. . . .

Persecution under the Espionage Law became a veritable epidemic in the Socialist movement. Personally, I escaped unscathed to the deep chagrin of some of my patriotic contemporaries. One of New York's aggressive newspapers made it a habit to refer to me invariably as the 'unindicted Mr. Hillquit,' and other press suggestions in the nature of 'memento mori' were not lacking. . . .

I have never considered Socialism as purely or even mainly a political movement. Socialism is above all a philosophy of life and civilization. It aims at a saner, higher and nobler social order. . . . The progress of such a movement cannot be measured by any concrete tests. It can hardly be measured at all. Who can be so bold as to say that the Socialist propaganda has not left a deep imprint on American thought and mind? . . .

By violating my conscience I might have made peace with the existing order of things and found a comfortable place among the beneficiaries of the system. I might have joined one of the political parties of power and plunder and perhaps attained to a position of influence and 'honor.' . . . I should have felt dissatisfied and mean. I should have been deprived of all the joys of life that only an inspiring social ideal can impart, of the pleasure and comradeship of the best minds and noblest hearts in all lands, and, above all, of my own self respect. . . .

Charles P. Steinmetz
Scientist, Teacher
1865-1923

> We have been talking of the native-born American's 'assimilating' the immigrants. There can be no such thing; assimilation implies two parties becoming similar, but implies both changing.

This statement by an eminent scientist whose contribution to the furtherance of progress in America equals the highest made by any native or foreign-born scientist, one to whom all doors must have been open, implies a keen awareness of the relationship between foreign-born and native. Also it is clear he must have pondered the qualitative changes in identity which are the result of the assimilative process by which newcomers were able to merge with the American mass.

Charles Steinmetz was a Socialist, who in 1888 fled Germany because of fear of arrest. Consequently he may be classed with those whom political persecution drove out of their homelands. As a student at the University of Breslau, he came under police surveillance because his membership in the Social Democratic Party made him automatically an opponent of Bismarck's policies. He fled to Switzerland and forfeited the Ph.D. degree. He continued his studies in Switzerland, but in the year 1889, when a friend undertook to pay his passage to America and made himself financially responsible for him, he forsook Europe. He was twenty-three. Poor and physically disabled, he bore the gift of genius. At first he worked for a private employer, but soon joined the staff of the General Electric Company, where his electrical research made scientific history. Later he transferred his activities to Union College in Schenectady.

By his own admission he remained a Socialist and a dues-paying member of the Socialist Party. Though Morris Hillquit asserts ". . . he retained his ardent faith in Socialism and proclaimed it in unmistakable terms whenever and wherever he had the opportunity," one searches in vain for the kind of ringing statements characteristic of social rebels. He admits he had ". . . every reason to be personally satisfied." Apparently he was not unaware of the disparities existing between the various classes of American society, nor does he seem to have regarded it with indifference, for he continues guardedly: "I would far more enjoy my advantages if I knew that everybody else could enjoy the same."

Not only does he refrain from criticism of capitalist society, but he has some surprisingly good things to say about the beneficial aspects of large corporate enterprises.

FROM *America and the New Epoch**

When I landed in Castle Garden, from the steerage of a French liner, I had ten dollars and no job, and could speak no English. Now, personally I have no fault to find with existing society; it has given me everything I wanted; I have been successful professionally in engineering, and have every reason to be personally satisfied, and the only criticism which I can make is that I would far more enjoy my advantages if I knew that everybody else could enjoy the same. . . .

For several years I was employed by a small manufacturer; then for nearly a quarter century with a huge manufacturing corporation, and helped make it what it is to-day. Thus I have seen the working of small individualistic production—where every cent increase of wages appears so much out of the pockets of the owner—and of corporate production, and have realized, from my acquaintance with the inside workings of numerous large corporations, that the industrial corporation is not the greedy monster of popular misconception, bent only on exploitation, and have most decidedly come to the con- clusion that, even as crude and undeveloped the industrial corporation of to-day still is in its social activities, if I were an unknown and unimportant employee I would far rather take my chances with the impersonal, huge industrial cor- poration than with the most well meaning individual em- ployer. . . .

America is in a peculiar and very fortunate position. As a new country with vast capital in natural resources, and with a relatively low population density, but a rapidly growing population, it offers great opportunities of development. That part of the United States which is least favored by nature, but

---

*Charles P. Steinmetz, *America and the New Epoch,* (New York: Harper & Brothers, 1916). Reprinted by permission of Harper & Row.

which was settled first—the New England states—felt the pinch of the industrial problem already in the middle of the nineteenth century, but the problem was solved, at least temporarily, by forcibly excluding foreign competition from the United States, and so reserving the markets of the South and of the West to the industrial New England States. This was the issue on which the Civil War was fought; the abolishment of slavery was merely an incident of this economic issue. The Civil War thus was an economic war, just as every great war has been! It consolidated the United States industrially as one nation, while the Revolutionary War had made it politically one nation. . . .

. . . Thus the native does not assimilate the immigrant, but native and immigrant assimilate with each other, and the native as well as the immigrant changes, fortunately, for it would be a sad America if we still burned witches as the Puritan 'natives' did, if we still had the Blue Laws and the religious intolerance of the old New-Englanders. Or we may say, 'America assimilates all the immigrants coming to its shores into a new American nation.' But this nation is not like the Puritan or the Dutchman of New Amsterdam, or the German of '48, but has, more or less, the characteristics of all of these.

Mary Anderson
Labor Organizer and Official
1873-1960

> My ambition was to get better working conditions —and that included better wages—for women. I had found personally that it was very hard to live on the little we earned and I knew we could not do anything or get anywhere unless we were all together.

Among the throngs of Swedish immigrants who took the long voyage from Sweden to Michigan, magnet of many Scandinavians, was a modest, sixteen-year-old girl of sanguine temperament but meager education. Her hope was that she would not have to "work around the house," which she disliked. But when she realized that in a lumber town there was nothing else for a young woman to do, she went into housework and remained a "hired girl" for several years. Her complaint was that the work was "lonesome"; she had "nobody to talk to."

When she found a job as shoe stitcher in a Chicago factory, she liked it much better, because factory work made it possible to "make contacts with other people"; there was story-telling and laughter; it could be "great fun."

This woman reached an apex no sober immigrant would have dared to anticipate. From the job of shoe stitcher and member of the United Boot and Shoe Workers Union, she moved to the Women's Trade Union League. After organizing workers into unions, she would concentrate on keeping workers and employers from violating their agreements. Her watchword became "patient negotiation"; her purpose to avert unnecessary strikes, because they involve "so much suffering" and "if not justified . . . they do harm to the whole trade union movement." In 1918 it became necessary to enroll women workers in the war industries and Mary Anderson was offered the position of assistant to the chief, who was Mary van Kleeck, but in a little more than a year she became the head of the newly created Women's Bureau in the Department of Labor. She retained this job until her retirement in 1945.

In this position and in her various assignments—to the Peace Conference in Paris and as American representative to international labor organizations, she met and worked with some of the most prominent personages at home and abroad. In 1941, Smith College bestowed on this woman whose education had consisted of a few years schooling in a Lutheran parsonage, an honorary degree. When the King and Queen of England visited the White House, Eleanor Roosevelt decided to introduce Mary Anderson to them as a distinguished American woman.

How did she accomplish this rise from a lowly position to one of such importance? Her colleague, Mary van Kleeck, praised her "leadership, her wise judgment, steadiness of purpose, and deep spirit of kinship with all women in industry—born out of her own industrial experience." President Roosevelt mentioned "her rich common sense," and her "successful championship of always practical . . . programs." She herself shrewdly admits that she has had "a lot of luck," but that she has worked hard too ". . . to get some things done that needed to be done." One element that is implicit in this remarkable example of accomplishment is the factor of America, where success was created out of the conjunction of place, time, and personal ability.

FROM *Woman At Work**

I got a place in a lumberjack's boarding house washing dishes. It was very hard work. . . . I got two dollars a week and my board and lodging. We had to carry water and look out for fifteen or twenty lumberjacks. It was early morning work—and all-day-long work. There was a cook and two other women for housecleaning, making beds and laying the table, but I didn't know much of the language and I had nobody to talk to. It seemed to me that there was nothing in my life but dirty dishes to wash and a kitchen to clean up. . . .

I never got bored with that job [stitcher on shoes] because fitting the lining to the outside and stitching it had to be done carefully or else the next process, 'vamping,' could not be done. I always look back on my life in that factory, where six or seven hundred people worked, as very interesting because this was my first factory experience and I learned that factory life is not just the work at a machine. You make contacts with other people. . . . I didn't know what a union was, but I was ready to join because I wanted to be with others and do what they are doing, and that is what I thought the union meant. . . .

A good deal of time is wasted at every labor meeting. To deal with labor, you have to be patient while everyone learns to work together. I think patience is one of the greatest disciplines in working with human beings. Intellectuals often fail in their relations with labor because they have no realization of the fight labor has had to put up. . . .

In my day, I have received plenty of criticism, but I have not minded it. . . . I always did whatever job I had to do as well as I could under the circumstances and I never found that it was any help to anyone to get upset if things did not come out exactly as I had wanted them to. I think my work in trade union organization and arbitration taught me not to expect too much and to be satisfied with part of a cake if I could not get a whole one. . . .

---

* *Woman at Work: The Autobiography of Mary Anderson* by Mary Anderson and Mary Winslow. University of Minnesota Press, Minneapolis. © Copyright 1951 by the University of Minnesota.

This kind of prejudice and sentimentality about working women is one of the things we have had to combat all through the years. 'Woman's place is in the home' sounds like a fine slogan but it is completely false when you come to examine the real conditions. Everyone who knows anything about working women knows that they work to support themselves and to contribute to the support of their families. They do not do it for 'pin money' or for fun. . . .

Among all the discriminations against women, I think the agitation against the employment of married women is one of the most unjust and unsound. It is based on the false theory that all married women have someone to support them. That is a theory that we in the Women's Bureau have proved time and time again is not true. . . .

. . . I think our philosophy should be that education for trade unionists is a union responsibility. Any union that is worth its salt wants its members to understand the philosophy of the trade union movement, and I do not think this can be taught very well except under the auspices of the trade unions. A certain amount of academic education for all citizens is the responsibility of the state, but special education in the meaning and techniques of trade unionism can only come from the unions themselves. . . .

During the latter part of the war [WWII] I served on a confidential committee appointed by the State Department that was very interesting. We were trying to work up standards on labor conditions and social security that would be used later on at the peace conference. I was appointed chairman of the subcommittee on women. Finally, we issued an excellent report, the substance of which was eventually adopted at the conference of the International Labor Office in Philadelphia in 1944. In this statement were incorporated standards advocating equal pay for women and equal opportunities for them. This was not done without something of a struggle because by this time we had learned the lesson that the simple phrase 'Equal Pay for Equal Work' did not mean much when it came to actually applying it. . . .

Now, [after retirement] among other things, I am working for a federal law requiring equal pay for women. After we get that I know there will be something more to do to help improve conditions and opportunities for women. As long as I am able I shall keep on. . . .

Ludwig Lewisohn
Teacher, Critic, Novelist
1882-1955

> . . . The Man on the streets thinks that we have
> liberty. He has no true conception of its nature,
> and his spirit is corrupted by the brutal ro-
> manticism of success. For he is right in thinking
> that, within ever narrowing limits, he has one
> kind of liberty—the liberty of economic competi-
> tion.

In offering "the devastating truth" about America in his two
autobiographical statements, *Up-Stream* and *Mid-Channel*, Ludwig Lewisohn establishes himself as the most severe and most
vituperative critic among the foreign-born of the American way
of life. While the Anarchists, Socialists, and other theorists
understandably concentrate their attacks on America's economic
philosophy and the evils attributable to it, Lewisohn condemns
in thunderous phrases the whole fabric of our society—the
people as well as their ideals. America is the antagonist—
Lewisohn is the accuser.

Brought by his parents, cultured Germans, to South Carolina
in 1890 at the age of eight, he embraced the American ethos,
which he later opprobriously designated as "Anglo-American,"
without reservation. He responded to the moonlight-and-mag-
nolia beauty of the South so strongly that one is reminded of
Emily Dickinson's words—"Beauty crowds me till I die." He
was so attracted to the group spirit as it confronted him that
he "accepted Jesus as my personal Savior," taught Sunday School,
became a member of the Epworth League and felt himself to
be "an American, a Southerner and a Christian."

His disappointment was cumulative. He observed, at first
with sorrow, later with growing resentment, that his parents,
who felt closer to their American neighbors than to the un-
educated Jews of the town, were totally ignored. "Never a
footstep on the stairs," he lamented in his rhythmic, cadenced
English. By the time he graduated from the local college he
suspected that he was not being accepted as the Christian he
supposed himself to be. When the opportunity to teach English
at a near-by denominational school was withdrawn, and the

man who had extended the offer removed from the faculty, he suspected the reason—his Jewish origin. He began to wonder whether the "democratic spirit" and "equality of opportunity" were not empty phrases.

His doubts were confirmed at Columbia University where he enrolled for graduate study. A scholarship he needed desperately was refused; later he found himself ineligible to teach English. The admission by an official of the English department that his Jewish birth was a serious handicap drove him out before completing the requirements for the Ph.D. degree.

Eventually he secured a job in academe, not to teach English, but German, which had been his minor field of study. By then he was certain it was due to "Anglo-American prejudice." The designation "Anglo-American" meant the point of view that prevailed among those raised in the English social and literary tradition and is intended to convey the utmost scorn. It also includes a slavish subservience to what to him had come to mean "democratic pretensions" and other ideals he had decided were spurious, sterile, and hurtful. Yet he asserted: "I can never speak as an enemy of the Anglo-Saxon race."

Since he considered his experiences proof that "equality of opportunity" and the "democratic spirit" did not exist, his attack is centered on the "unveracity" of American ideals. Not only were they constantly being violated, he said, but the American people tacitly ignore the truth. For this and other reasons he declared the American people guilty of "moral illusionism," "duality of conscience," and "democratic pretensions." His indictment also included conformity—"following the herd"—materialism, and lack of intellectual appreciation. He flayed college teachers for "pinchbeck dignity," "lack of intellectual hardihood," and for their "angular straw minds"; students for being "trivial" and "conformists." (That American students are interested mainly in their diplomas has been commented on by many foreign-born intellectuals.) His special scorn is reserved for the grocers, undertakers, and insurance salesmen who are apt to compose the boards of trustees and who are "hopelessly committed to the status quo."

Aware of the depths of his indictment, he declared: "I have written of America for the simple reason that I am an American and I have spoken strongly for the equally simple reason that the measure of one's love and need is also the measure of one's disappointment and indignation."

Seven years later Lewisohn added a sequel to his first auto-biographical statement that is even more of a *confessio vitae* than the first. He had exiled himself to escape the scandal-mongers. His wife had refused to set him free and his name was being dragged into the mire. By then he had also discovered his *Eigenart* as Jew, which life in the Southern atmosphere where he had been brought up, had submerged. What made his hegira back to Europe possible, was Oswald Garrison Villard's interest in a series of articles on the colonization of Jews in Palestine to be printed in *The Nation*.

While the chief target of the first book was "the failure of democracy," the second jabs sporadically at the narrow and illiberal attitudes to divorce and the "Comstockian morality" he considered characteristic of American life. The book also provides the explanation for his decision to reintegrate himself in the Jewish fold. For this he holds "failure of Christianity" responsible. But the belligerence he displayed in his first book is muted and the verbal pyrotechnics are toned down.

Despite the many critical shafts directed at the dominance in America of Puritanism and "the moral self destruction of historical Christianity," there is evidence that he felt himself bound to the United States. He speaks of "home," of "our own people," and of "our country and myself."

Lewisohn returned "home." "The things that were in the saddle" drove him back. By that time many of the changes he had advocated, had occurred. The fact that many of the evils he had so passionately inveighed against, were becoming, as he had hoped they would, "obsolescent," strengthens the validity of his criticism. The vituperative tongue was a manifestation of his personality and his ability to handle the language, and should not invalidate the rightness of some of his arguments.

FROM *Up-Stream**

There are thousands of people among us who can find in my adventures a living symbol of theirs and in my conclusion a liberation of their own and in whom, as in me, this moment of history has burned away delusions to the last shred. But how many will admit this and not rather yield to the insidious

---

*From *Up-Stream*, by Ludwig Lewisohn. By permission of Liveright Publishers, New York. Copyright © Renewed 1952 by Ludwig Lewisohn.

fear of those to whom they owe deference or money or a social position in Gopher Prairie or Central City? . . .

. . . in the early nineties of the last century there lingered in that village [in South Carolina]—as there did doubtless in many other places—something of that honest simplcity, that true democratic kindliness which we like to associate with the years of the primitive Republic. . . . But as part of my imaginative inheritance as an American I won them by virtue of the two years of my childhood spent in St. Mark's in South Carolina. . . .

Our friend, Mrs. C., was a very fervent member of her church. She was too well bred to engage in crude proselytising. But, seeing that we observed no Jewish rites, she suggested that it would improve my English if I were to join her Sunday School class. My mother who had precious memories of snow-swept Christmas services in her native East Prussian village, made no objection. My father, an agnostic reared on Huxley and Haeckel, had no prejudices for or against any religious cult. . . .

Let any one who has an unclouded vision of our American life, and not least of the academic part of it, consider my undertaking [to embark on graduate studies at Columbia University.] . . . I had lived utterly for the things of the mind and the emotions. I was twenty years old and knew less of practical matters than a child of ten. I had no social adroitness but the most quivering sensitiveness and pride. I was passionately Anglo-American in my sympathies, I wanted above all things to be a poet in the English tongue, and my name and physiognomy were characteristically Jewish. I had ill-cut, provincial clothes and just enough money to get through one semester. . . .

. . . I am touching on this central weakness of the Anglo-American mind—its moral illusionism. That mind is generally quite sincere. It really arranges its own impulses and the impulses of other men in a rigid hierarchy of fixed norms. It has surrendered the right and the power of examining the contents of such concepts as 'right,' 'wrong,' 'pure,' 'democracy,' 'liberty,' 'progress,' or of bringing these conventionalized gestures of the mind to the test of experience. It has not, indeed, ever naively experienced anything. . . .

We boast our equality and freedom and call it Americanism

and speak of other countries with disdain. And so one is unwarned, encouraged and flung into the street. With exquisite courtesy, I admit. . . . It will be replied that there are a number of Jewish scholars in American colleges and universities. There are. The older men got in because nativistic anti-Semitism was not nearly as strong twenty-five years ago as it is to-day. But in regard to younger men I dare assert that in each case they were appointed through personal friendship. family or financial prestige or some other abnormal relenting of the iron prejudice which is the rule. . . .

. . . To the 'average, intelligent American' education, for which he is willing to deny himself and pay taxes, means—skill, information—at most accomplishment. . . . Our people do not believe in education at all—if education means a liberation of the mind or a heightened consciousness of the historic culture of mankind. Philosophy and morals are taken care of by the Fifth Street Baptist Church. College is to fit you to do things—to build bridges, cure diseases, teach French. It is not supposed to help you to be. . . .

Our man has the liberty of economic competition. . . . He can dream his favorite dream. Also he has a vote. He can choose between two candidates both offered him by essentially the same masters. . . . But once let him think and arise from the dull mass and cease worshipping the idols of the tribe and the market-place! If he speaks he will be gagged; if he acts he will be jailed.

FROM *Mid-Channel**

. . . My country and its Christian laws have no regard for love or virtue or the creative mind but give their support to legalized malignity and moral foulness, if only these mouth the moral saws of the market place. . . .

. . . There is no such thing as a man; only such a thing as a Frenchman, an Englishman, an American, a Spaniard, a German, a Greek, a Jew. The loftiest sage, whose works ultimately speak to all mankind, is deeply and inextricably rooted in his historical soil, even as the highest works of the human imagination are forever integrated with the consciousness of the folk from which they arose. . . .

---

*Ludwig Lewisohn, *Mid-Channel* (New York: Harper & Bros., 1929). Used by permission of Mrs. Louise Lewisohn.

I had come to the conclusion, then, that the greater part of my sore discontent with life had arisen for me not from my likeness to my American friends but from my special unlikeness to them. They followed, upon the whole, their traditions and instincts; I, instead of following mine of which I had long become aware, had been forced to try to mimic theirs and had been thought of as doing well in the degree in which my mimicry was successful. It was wholly forgotten by everyone that the better a man's mimicry of another is, the less human and the less like that other he becomes. The cleverest ape only loses the apishness that God gave him; he never becomes a man. . . .

In America, however, the distance between law and public convention on the one hand, and the minimum requirements of civilized existence on the other, is such that no decent man or woman can help being an actual or potential criminal. A state that forces its best citizens, the creators of its cultural values into constant law-dodging or law-breaking—it is an open secret to how many American thinkers, writers, scholars this applies—such a state is not, to put mildly, in a sound condition. . . .

One has never heard of a good artist who did not express himself through concrete and characteristic modes of being, and perceiving and reacting. Is not even music, the purest of the arts, tinged by ethnic color? A good deal of international Jewish art is unluckily not unlike Esperanto. And so it is also because I want my art to be sound that I find it necessary to be myself—a Jew. The creative act, whatever its material or its object, is fed by sources deep in the subconsciousness. A treatise could be written on art and the germ-plasm. If I contribute my mite toward preserving Israel, Israel also preserves me. . . .

It was clear that according to the powers that rule us [in America] I could do nothing right and that there was no health in me. Between those powers and myself there seemed no possibility of peace. Very early in life I had a most harmless little book confiscated by Comstock's officers; during the war I had been ostracised for insisting mildly enough on facts which no clever schoolboy thinks of denying to-day, when I tried to sanitate my moral life I was driven into exile. Now I had written a book, a thoroughly American book which the best thoroughly American critics were declaring an artistic

work of no ordinary importance, and there leaped out of
ambush the redoubtable solicitor brandishing Section 211 of
the Federal Criminal Code. . . .

When shall we deliver America, not of you, O learned counsel,
but of your power? For you sit in all the seats of the mighty,
in executive and legislative chambers, in all the departments
of the State, in the high chairs of judges. Year in and year
out you have dogged my footsteps . . . determined that
America and American life shall have no freedom nor beauty
nor creative power nor leave any memorial of having been.
We are much stronger than you, O weak and violent solicitors,
and you will only be remembered because we choose, now
and again, to mention you. But it is getting late in the world's
age for you. Mankind has work to do. Be humble and useful
and become herders of sheep. You will retain authority, but
it will do no harm.

John Cournos
Art Critic, Novelist, Poet
1881-

I was in a jungle, I did find myself *inferior* in a
sense to the beasts with stronger teeth and claws
than I had; teeth and claws which I sometimes
envied, since I lived in a society in which it was
hard to do without them.

In this statement there is an echo of the Darwinian theory
which received much credence during the period when industrial exploitation was in full swing. It places John Cournos
among the detractors of the American system, at least as it
prevailed between 1890 and 1930. Unlike Lewisohn, his attack
was not directed against American ideals, but at that aspect of
American life which exposed him, a young boy, to economic
competition and exploitation of the fiercest sort. Because mech-
anistic aspects of any society repelled him, he rejected Communism, asserting: "I do not want to worship the Machine
either under Capitalism or Communism."

He was ten in 1891 when his mother, minus her detested
second husband, who was to follow later, brought her brood

of children out of Russia. Their destination was Philadelphia, because he had read in his geography book that it was a city "famed for its philanthropic and educational institutions." The illusions he had formed about Philadelphia did not survive his first appearance on the street. Almost immediately circumstances forced him to go to work selling newspapers on street corners, regardless of weather, during the early morning hours before he was due at school. He tells a harrowing story of having a foot frozen and of being carried by a slightly older sister on her back, to a hospital. By the time he finished grammar school he had undergone so many gruesome experiences that the hatred he felt for a "machine civilization," seems understandable. The "City of Brotherly Love" became a place of horror, and life a succession of "corridors of struggle." His formal education was over at thirteen and the incidents in his life and the people through whom he learned the hard lessons of life, became his "universities."

An experience that burned itself into his memory with especial force was a job as bobbin-boy in a Philadelphia woolen mill. Though his sisters worked with him and their mother joined them occasionally to augment the family earnings, the combined wages were insufficient to secure the necessities for the family. It confirmed his view of America as "a trench of perpetual warfare with no hope of relief" and "the Jungle of Machines . . . seemed fiercer than in any jungle created by nature."

When he became an office boy in the editorial offices of the *Philadelphia Record,* fate proved kind for once, for it was a typical American opportunity. The editor in chief, a kindly man, asked him every evening if he had written an editorial yet. One evening the young man handed him an article on the Cuban war and the American jingoists. It was printed. When he became assistant editor, it was to him "another corridor of struggle conquered."

Thus he ascended the ladder. The consequence of having become friendly with a group of artists associated with the Pennsylvania Academy of Fine Arts, was a deepening interest in music, art, and books. The intensity of their feeling about art, awakened in him the ambition to become a writer. He learned so much about art from them that he began to write art criticism for the *Record* and the *Boston Transcript.* It was on his reputation as an art critic that he arranged to go to Europe after almost twenty years in Philadelphia. He had admitted: "I had run away, of course." In England, which he loved, he began his career as a novelist, producing several highly-thought-of novels. He is still active as an art critic today. He remained in England, except for occasional visits to America, until 1930.

In 1935 he offered as his opinion: "When America harnesses its spiritual energy as it has harnessed the Falls [Niagara Falls] it will become a great country, a marvelous country." But thirty years later, he still had reservations about America. His opinion is that "although America can be very generous, even kind, there is not enough awareness of spiritual and aesthetic values."[1] It would seem therefore that to John Cournos the time is not yet.

FROM *Autobiography**

Little did I comprehend then that the land of milk and honey had no geographical entity, that it was only in men's hearts, a dream serving as a lure, as a stimulation to activity, to struggle, to the creation of art and the achievement of heroic if not always noble deeds. . . .

. . . as I grew to manhood and thought and struggled and went through a diversity of experience, the conflict became a conscious one, developing definitely into a battle against the machine, against all the organized exploitation which has risen with the machine, and, above all, against that materialization of man which the machine has effected, creating the great issue of the age, the issue on which mankind today is split and for which it is yet to fight its greatest battles, on one side or the other. As a child I *felt* this discord between myself and the mechanized, materialized community, productive of poverty, of slums, of spiritual sloth; and only as my mind developed did I begin to rationalize my bitter resentment against a social order that permitted this. . . .

I do not deny that struggle has its own value. Aren't there better things to struggle for than bread and shelter? So much strength goes into this struggle, that there is not enough energy

---

1. Personal interview, 1963.

*John Cournos, *Autobiography* (New York: G. P. Putnam's Sons, 1935). Copyright 1935 by John Cournos.

left to fight for the things which beautify and ennoble. . . .

No, gentlemen. You who have put struggle in my way, you who say that struggle is good for me (what if it is!), I owe you no thanks. . . . my success (what there is of it) cannot condone your selfishness, your un-Christianness, your violation of the principles of the religion you profess. You Business Potentates, you Go-Getters, you Arbiters of Capitalist Society, you have built up an order which pens off the multitude, to whom now and then you fling a bone for them to fight about, and you call it the struggle of existence, and you say that this struggle is good, that it makes men active and ambitious and anxious to 'get on' and occasionally when you see a particularly strong 'competitor' in the pen you let him out to join you, which gives hope to the rest—you feed them on that, and up to a point keep them contented; you even contribute to charity: you give only to churches that they may keep the 'flocks' subservient to your 'ideals', to schools that they may teach and glorify your idea of competitive struggle, to hospitals that they may take me in and give me a soft bed only to fling me back afterwards into the fierce pen of Struggle. . . .

And into this world, into this to me incomprehensible background, I, a child of another world, was flung, expecting my fears of life, of insecurity, to be quieted, only to find them intensified. I had come, expecting to be accepted as a human being and to have the chance of developing as a human being. And what was I? A potential wage-slave, a potential buyer of things, a potential exploitee. America, in a way I could not explain at the time—for I was young and ignorant and had only my feelings to guide me—terrified me. . . . Without quite realizing it, I, a little boy, was fighting against the whole world, in which intuitively, if as yet dimly, I felt elements antagonistic not only to myself but to that host of millions caught in the meshes of its system and blindly contented with their lot; a world which, to put it bluntly, loudly proclaimed its profession of Christ and recrucified Him every day. . . .

If the Communists, from their own point of view, are justified in rejecting a spiritual fulcrum for moving the world, I contend that as an honest man, convinced of their error, I am equally justified in rejecting their world as in rejecting the Capitalist world which at least allows me (in this very instance) to express my views. . . .

. . . while still acting as office boy, I became a regular contributor to the paper. I wrote editorial paragraphs, contributed a column called 'The Reporter's Nosegay' which contained short paragraphs describing happenings about the city of an anecdotal nature. I translated . . . items from the German magazines . . . Moreover, I was paid space rates for my contributions, at the rate of five dollars a column, bringing my week's earnings up from four dollars to ten. . . .

Today I can confess that I have learned something from ever so many persons; that my whole education was, as it were, snatched from the fates even as rings are snatched on the twirling merry-go-round by eager, determined hands, with the greatest difficulty. Quite frankly, I took this from that person, that from this, and I bent what I took to my own ends and used it in my own way. . . . One pays for tuition at any university, and let no one think that I did not pay for mine, and an infinitely greater price: suffering. . . .

Only when America becomes filled with the ghosts of great men—may heaven speed the day! then only, and not until then, will America become a great country, the fountainhead of still more great men.

Abraham Mitrie Rihbany
Minister
1869-1944

> Here, as nowhere else on this planet, the "talented foreigner" finds the ample room and noble incentives necessary to reveal his talents and to enable him to attain the more abundant intellectual, political, social and moral life.

In 1891 a twenty-two year old Syrian youth, wearing a Turkish fez, set out for America on borrowed money. The road that led from Beirut to Alexandria, Marseilles, and Paris, was to stop temporarily in New York, then was to take him through parts of the American continent and end in Boston. In Marseilles he discarded his Turkish fez. Skipping centuries as he went from his primitive home in Asiatic Turkey to Europe and thence to America, the journey was one that took him through time as well as through space. In New York he found lowly employment among his own people. Because he had been educated in a Protestant missionary school and had taught its primary grades, he was considered learned. A Syrian merchant hired him as book-keeper, but he expected him to do the menial work as well.

After two years in New York he realized that life in the Syrian colony, was "simply Syria on a smaller scale." As soon as he had paid his debts, he was ready to go West to sample "the real life in America." His hope was to raise enough money for a college education by lecturing before churches and societies on the Holy Land and on oriental customs.

In the course of his peregrinations and struggles—with actual want and with the English language—Mr. Rihbany became such an effective speaker that he was able to acquire enough money to enter Ohio Wesleyan University. On a subsequent lecture circuit he was offered a pulpit, despite the fact that he had not even begun his theological training. After persistent urgings, he accepted.

Mr. Rihbany had been raised in the Greek Orthodox Church, but as a result of the influence of the mission school, he had converted to Protestantism in Syria. A deeply religious man, he saw his function as that of spiritual interpreter of "the gospel of Christ in the simplicity of the New Testament and not necessarily as it had been restated by any group of theologians."

Though he encountered opposition to his liberal interpretations in some of the parishes he served, he did not swerve from his determination that he follow "the open road of the religion of the spirit." He found the pulpit that fitted his convictions when he was called to the Church of the Disciples in Boston, which had been founded by the Transcendentalist minister, James Freeman Clarke, in the 1840s. That church had disposed of doctrinal conditions for membership. There Mr. Rihbany came to the end of his "Far Journey."

FROM *A Far Journey**

While I was at school, I heard much about America. I studied its geography, heard of its great liberator, Washington, and almost every Sunday listened to Mr. Pond and other

---

*Abraham Mitrie Rihbany, *A Far Journey* (Boston: Houghton Mifflin Company, 1913). By permission of the publishers.

preachers speak of the zeal of its people for missionary work among the heathen of the earth. . . . But more exciting tales about America came to me through returning Syrian immigrants. Most of them, being common laborers, knew, of course, very little of the real life of America. They spoke only of its wealth and how accessible it was, and how they themselves secured more money in America in a very few years than could be earned in Syria in two generations. More enlightened accounts of the great country beyond the seas came into Syria through a small minority of a better class of immigrants. From such descriptions I had a few glimpses of American civilization, of a land of free schools, free churches, and a multitude of other organizations which worked for human betterment. . . .

. . . At last America was within my reach. Would it be anything short of madness to let such a great privilege go by? I had to act on my own responsibility, but I remembered that when I dropped my tools as a stone-mason and went to school, I had to act on my own responsibility; when I left the Church of my fathers and became a Protestant, I had to follow my own course. Now I was called upon to make a third great decision, and to make it quickly. The wiser powers within and above me again asserted themselves, and I decided that I would go to America. . . .

. . . As our little party proceeded on across Battery Park toward Washington Street, I felt the need of new faculties to fit my new environment. . . . What was awaiting me in America, whose life, as I had been told, was so vast, so complex and so enlightened? Whatever the future had of 'wonder or surprise,' it seemed that merely being in the United States was enough of a blessing to call forth my profoundest gratitude. . . .

Notwithstanding my humble position as katib [bookkeeper who cleaned, swept and ran errands], I was not long in New York before I began to dream and see visions. How to acquire the priceless privilege of being an American citizen, was the first and foremost question in my mind. I was told that I did not need to be in such a hurry about this matter, but I thought differently, and . . . not quite six weeks after I had landed at Ellis Island, I appeared in the Court of Common pleas of the County of New York, accompanied by an inter-

preter, and asked to be 'admitted into American citizenship.'
. . . I felt such an inward sense of relief and exaltation that
my countryman, the interpreter, appeared to me to be an
alien. It seemed to me at the moment . . . that by that act
I had forever broken the shackles which had bound me and
my forefathers for ages to the chariots of tyrants, and had
become a citizen of a country whose chief function was to
make free, enlightened, useful men.

The sum total of my year-and-a half's experience in New
York convinced me that it was most difficult, if not impossible
for a foreigner to become really Americanized while living in
a colony of his own kinsmen. Just as the birth of a new species
can never take place without a radical break with the parent
stock, so the thorough transformation of a foreigner into an
American can never be accomplished without the complete
departure, inwardly and outwardly, of that individual from
his kindred. . . . I thought I could hear the same voice which
said to my namesake, Abraham, 'Get thee out of thy country,
and from thy kindred, and from thy father's house, into the
land that I will show thee. . . .

I was told while in Syria that in America money could be
picked up everywhere. That was not true. But I found that
infinitely better things than money—knowledge, freedom, self-
reliance, order, cleanliness, sovereign human right, self-govern-
ment, and all that these great accomplishments imply—can be
picked up everywhere in America by whosoever earnestly
seeks them. . . .

It was in that little town [in Ohio] . . . that I first heard
'America' sung. The line 'Land where my fathers died' stuck
in my throat. I envied every person in that audience who
could sing it truthfully. For years afterward, whenever I
tried to sing those words, I seemed to myself to be an intruder.
At last a new light broke upon my understanding. At last
I was led to realize that the fathers of my new and higher self
did live and die in America. I was born in Syria as a child,
but I was born in America as a man. All those who fought for
the freedom I enjoy, for the civic ideals I cherish, for the
simple but lofty virtues of the typical American home which
I love, were *my fathers!* . . .

Now, do you wish to know what riches I have gathered in
the New World? I will tell you. These are my riches, which

neither moth nor rust can corrupt. I have traveled from the primitive social life of a Syrian village to a great city which embodies the noblest traditions of the most enlightened country in the world. I have come from the bondage of Turkish rule to the priceless heritage of American citizenship. . . . I am rich in the sense that I am helping in my small way to solve America's great problems and to realize her wondrous possibilities. In this great country I have been taught to believe in and to labor for an enlightened and cooperative individualism, universal peace, free churches, and free schools. . . . I am privileged to occupy the office of a minister of religion —the holiest vocation in the possession of man.

Morris Raphael Cohen
Philosopher, Teacher, Author
1880-1947

> . . . when I think of what probably would have been my career had I remained in Russia and what little I could have accomplished there, it certainly seems very fortunate that I was able to come to these blessed United States, where I have been able to develop a career of some usefulness . . .

This modest assertion of a career of "some usefulness" understates the importance of Morris Raphael Cohen's influence on his students and contemporaries, to whom he was a symbol of "intellectual conscience." During the course of his academic career, he taught and lectured to fifteen thousand students throughout the United States, but his name is associated especially with the College of the City of New York, where he had been a student and where he developed into one of the most venerated teachers of that institution. His method was to "joggle the mind"; to "train thinkers," and to help them attain "intellectual independence."

His intellectual training was begun in Russia by an Orthodox Jewish grandfather, who taught him the Talmud, "the crown of Jewish education," before he was twelve. By the time he was brought to America in 1892, he had been introduced to Aristotle,

Maimonides, Josephus, and to secular books on social topics. In the public schools of Manhattan and Brooklyn he made such rapid progress that within three years after his arrival he took the entrance examination for City College, then a five year course, and scored the highest marks and won a gold medal.

During his college days he fell under the spell of the Scottish philosopher Thomas Davidson, who was attracting young intellectuals to the Educational Alliance, a settlement that helped to transform many young immigrants into New York's most illustrious citizens. So profound was Davidson's influence on his disciples that after his death Morris Cohen and others continued the project of providing education for East Side workers at the "Breadwinners' College" which Davidson had organized at the Educational Alliance. After graduating from City College Morris Cohen went on to Harvard to secure the Ph.D. degree in philosophy, then returned to City College to teach, first mathematics, then philosophy.

It would be hard to exaggerate the influence of this vital teacher on his students, or to overrate his contribution to the intellectual life of America. Justice Holmes is said to have remarked that he envied the youths who sat at his feet. As a philosopher he was committed to social reform and to a system of social jurisprudence. Though he believed that far-reaching improvements were not possible without a change in the economic set-up, he was averse to any sacrifice of democratic principles. He left an intellectual legacy of several hundred articles on philosophy, law, science, logic, and metaphysics, and several book-length works on philosophy and science, the legal system, and American liberalism. His career is a testimonial to the opportunities provided by the City of New York and its free institutions—the public schools, the settlement houses, the City College—to the intellectually gifted immigrant.

FROM *A Dreamer's Journey**

In September 1895, I entered the college which was to nurture and sustain me through the major part of my life. City College then, as in later years, offered a frugal though nourishing intellectual diet. Since the College was free, attend-

---

*Morris Raphael Cohen, *A Dreamer's Journey* (Boston: The Beacon Press, 1949). By permission of The Macmillan Company, N.Y.)

ance brought no social prestige. Since admission was not limited by race, class, creed or social status, it had to be limited by rigorous scholastic standards. Social life, sports, social polish, and the other superficial attractions of American college life were neglected. . . . In its earlier years the College student body was a fair cross section of the population of New York City. This meant that New Yorkers of many races and creeds could learn to understand each other in the formative years of college life. . . .

The life of the East Side in the days of my adolescence was characterized by a feverish intensity of intellectual life and a peculiar restlessness. . . . So it was that many of the first generation and many more of the second, despite the difficulties of a new environment and a strange language, brought to the tasks which the New World presented a force that was more than the force of any single individual. . . . Opinions may differ as to the worth of many of the enterprises to which this force was directed. The second generation had its boxers, gamblers and shyster lawyers, as well as great judges, teachers and scientists. Doctors, movie magnates, writers, merchants, philanthropists, communists or defenders of corporate wealth all showed an intensity that must have seemed a bit outlandish to the more comfortable and easy-going segments of the American population. . . .

What ensued was a struggle between the old and the new ideals, resulting in a conflict between the older and younger generations fraught with heart-rending consequences. Homes ceased to be places of peace and in the ensuing discord much of the proverbial strength of the Jewish family was lost. . . . There was scarcely a Jewish home on the East Side that was free from this friction between parents and children. This explosive tension made it possible for the same family to produce saints and sinners, philosophers and gunmen. . . .

Apart from its intellectual opportunities Harvard helped me to learn how to get along with people of radically different backgrounds. . . . I came to appreciate ever more clearly how important a part of education it is to get to know well people with whom at the beginning we have no sympathy, people who do not immediately strike responsive chords in our hearts. Only so, I came to realize, does one achieve spiritual growth. . . .

... As a son of immigrant parents I shared with my students [as a teacher at City College] their background, their interests and their limitations. My students were, on the whole, relatively emancipated in social matters and politics as well as in religion. ... And breaking away from it left them ready and eager to adopt all sorts of substitutes. ... I therefore saw no adequate opportunity for teaching philosophy along traditional lines. ...

Whatever my failings as a teacher, I tried to tell my students what I thought they ought to hear, rather than what I thought they would like to hear. The process of demolishing youthful illusions would have hurt sensitive students even if I had been more circumspect than I knew how to be in salving tender feelings. Actually I found the method of treatment by shock the most effective of leading students to appreciate the nature and dimensions of ignorance. ... This made the expression of student esteem and affection that came to me in the late years of my career at City College especially moving. ...

Of course if you claim to be in possession of a special revelation, then you have a mortgage on the truth of the universe, the other fellow can have nothing true to tell you, and the thing to do is to hold on to your revealed truth with all the ardor that is in you. But then the other fellow is just as certain that he alone has all the truth and there is no use in any argumentation. But if you take your stand on human history and human reason, and recognize, for example, that the claim to the possession of a special revelation of the Jew is, as such, not a bit better than that of the Christian or the Mohammedan, or any of the ten thousand other claims, then, it seemed to me, you must grant that each possesses both truth and error. ...

... In that literal sense of the word we are all assimilationists. On the other hand, it seems an entirely vain and undignified attitude to attempt to imitate the manners or mores of those about us, if that means ignoring our own past experience and traditions which have molded us. Not only does self-respect militate against such an attitude but we can be better Americans, if, instead of being blind imitators, we approach American civilization critically and try to contribute something distinctive to the general fund of its spiritual goods. ...

The promise of America is the promise of freedom for the development of human energy, liberated by free education and the abolition of hereditary class distinctions. . . . The overwhelming majority of Jewish immigrants and their descendants in this country have committed their lives to the basic principle of American democracy—that here in these United States men and women of many different backgrounds may co-operate, bringing each his own contribution to a greater civilization than has yet existed. The dynamic principle of American Jewish life is to be found neither in the wiping out of special gifts nor in a withdrawal to the desert but rather in the fruitful bringing together of Jewish and non-Jewish cultural values in the common enterprises of liberal democracy.

Mary Antin
1881-1949

> The public school has done its best for us foreigners and for the country, when it has made us into good Americans. I am glad it is mine to tell how the miracle was wrought in one case.

The story of Mary Antin's early years in the environs of Boston—crucial years of poverty, Americanization, and spiritual growth, is a version of the Cinderella theme, minus the stepmother and the jealous stepsisters. Nor is there any mention of a prince; he came along later. It is a tale of the pang, the fear, the "joy and wonder" of growing up in America, which has not lost its potency today. The heartfelt, worshipful conviction that she had indeed reached the "Promised Land" lingers in its pages. Hers is an Anne Frank story with a happy ending.

Mary Antin was born in a Russian ghetto, where, as she explains, all Jewish children learned fear early—fear of the Cross and what it portended, and fear of the Czar. In 1893 at the age of twelve, she came to the "coveted shore," in the vicinity where Puritans had landed. One idyllic summer at what is now historic Revere Beach, where her father had set up a refreshment stand, was followed by a succession of slum homes in the west and north ends of Boston. There, the author says, "the poor immigrants foregather, to live, for the most part, as unkempt, halfwashed, toiling, unaspiring foreigners; pitiful in the eyes of social missionaries, the despair of the boards of health, the hope of ward politicians, the touchstone of American democracy." There came her initiation into American life through the public school and its teachers—the Miss Nixons, Miss Dillinghams, Miss Dwights, whom many foreign-born have recognized as "the heroines of America." They taught, pruned, encouraged her; school principals singled her out for praise, which proved a balm not only to her and her parents, but to the immigrant community as well, who saw in her success hope for their children, regardless of whether they showed any inclinations to follow in her footsteps. Clay in the hands of her teachers, she was "made over." The only real fear she knew was of a terrifying landlady, whose rent was rarely paid on time and who could not understand why an immigrant girl should be kept in school instead of going to work and helping to pay the rent.

Mary Antin went on to Boston Latin School and from there to Barnard College. Her decision to take the "backward" look at that time of her life was induced by the realization that "one who has completed early in life a distinct task may stop to give an account of it. One who has encountered unusual adventures under vanishing conditions may pause to describe them before passing into the stable world." By then Mary Antin had lived her "simple life so intensely, so thoughtfully, as to have discovered in [her] own experiences an interpretation of the universal life."

Having become "other than the person" she had been, she felt impelled to tell the story of an earlier Mary Antin.

FROM *The Promised Land**

What more could America give a child? Ah, much more! As I read how the patriots planned the Revolution, and the women gave their sons to die in battle, and the heroes led to victory, and the rejoicing people set up the Republic, it dawned on me gradually what was meant by *my country.* The people all desiring noble things, and striving for them together, defying their oppressors, giving their lives for each other—all this it was that made *my country.* It was not a thing

---

*Mary Antin, *The Promised Land* (Boston: Houghton Mifflin Company, 1912). Used by permission of the publishers.

that I *understood*. But I knew one could say "my country" and *feel* it, as one felt 'God' or 'myself.' My teacher, my schoolmates, Miss Dillingham, George Washington himself could not mean more than when I said "my country," after I had once felt it. For the Country was for all Citizens, and *I was a Citizen. . . .*

It did require strength to lift the burden of life, in the gray morning, on Dover Street; especially on Saturday morning. Perhaps my mother's pack was the heaviest to lift. To the man of the house, poverty is a bulky dragon with gripping talons and poisonous breath; but he bellows in the open, and it is possible to give him knightly battle, with the full swing of the angry arm that cuts to the enemy's vitals. To the housewife, want is an insidious myriapod creature that crawls in the dark, mates with its own offspring, breeds all the year round, persists like leprosy. The woman has an endless, inglorious struggle with the pest; her triumphs are too petty for applause, her failures too mean for notice. Care, to the man, is a hound to be kept in leash and mastered. To the woman, care is a secret parasite that infects the blood. . . .

I wanted to apologize [to their landlady], but Mrs. Hutch didn't give me a chance. If she had been harsh before, she was terrific now. . . . Wasn't it enough that I and my family lived on her, that I must . . . rile her with my talk about college—*college!* these beggars!—and laugh in her face? . . . And do you think I'll keep you till you to to college? *You,* learning geometry! Did you ever figure out how much rent your father owes me? . . . You ought to go to work, if you know enough to do one sensible thing. *College!* Go home and tell your father never to send you again . . .'

My cough had been pretty bad—kept me awake nights. My voice gave out frequently. The teachers had spoken to me several times, suggesting that I ought to see a doctor. Of course the teachers did not know that I could not afford a doctor, but I could go to the free dispensary, and I did. They told me to come again, and again, and I lost precious hours sitting the waiting-room, watching for my turn. I was examined, thumped, studied, and sent out with prescriptions and innumerable directions. All that was said about food, fresh air, sunny rooms, etc., was, of course, impossible; but I would try the medicine. A bottle of medicine was a definite thing with a fixed price. . . . Once you began with milk and eggs and such things there was no end of it. . . . No; the medicine bottle was the only safe thing. . . .

I must not fail to testify that in America a child of the slums owns the land and all that is good in it. All the beautiful things I saw belonged to me, if I wanted to use them; all the beautiful things I desired aproached me. I did not need to seek my kingdom. I had only to be worthy, and it came to me, even on Dover Street. . . . Steadily as I worked to win America, America advanced to lie at my feet. I was an heir, on Dover Street, awaiting maturity. I was a princess waiting to be led to the throne. . . .

Having traced the way an immigrant child may take from the ship through the public schools, passed on from hand to hand by the ready teachers; through free libraries and lecture halls, inspired by every occasion of civic consciousness; dragging through the slums the weight of private disadvantage, but heartened for the effort by public opportunity; welcomed at a hundred open doors of instruction, initiated with pomp and splendor and flags unfurled; seeking, in American minds, the American way, and finding it in the thoughts of the noble, —striving against the odds of foreign birth and poverty, and winning, through the use of abundant opportunity, a place as enviable as that of any native child,—having traced the footsteps of the young immigrant almost to the college gate, the rest of the course may be left to the imagination.

Elizabeth G. Stern (Leah Morton)
Social Worker, Writer
1890-1954

> I wanted to be free to live as I believed, in every way. I wanted first the right to find out what I believed, what my faith was.

America gave her that opportunity. This daughter of an Orthodox rabbi, who had left his birth-place—Russia—in order, as he said, to give to his children " a new life and religious freedom," found in America a tremendously expanded horizon. Brought to the vicinity of Pittsburgh during her infancy, in the early 1890s, she seized the opportunity of securing a college education, of asserting her independence against the Orthodoxy

231

of her father, and of planning her life in a manner that could not have been thought of in the Russian Pale. During her search for an identity of her own, she was to marry a non-Jew, follow several careers, reassess her heritage and make her contribution: as a social worker, and in helping to break down the barriers against married women, which, she says, were rigidly maintained at the turn of the century.

The first fact that confronted her after she had concluded her training as a social worker was that anyone who admitted to a Jewish background was not acceptable to the boards of the new settlements that had sprung up through the benevolence of private donors. When she finally secured the opportunity to use her training, it was to lead to marriage with the man on whose staff she worked, and, consequently, to a break with her father who looked upon a daughter married out of the Jewish faith, as dead.

She had two handicaps to overcome—that of her Jewish birth and that of being a woman. In the days before World War I, married women who were mothers, were not expected to seek work, unless they were widows, or their husbands were incapacitated. The opinion was widely held that women belonged at home and that no woman could do "other work better than housework." The woman who had husband and children and still sought the opportunity to exercise her training, was rebuffed and criticised. As the mother of a child, Elizabeth Stern considered herself fortunate to be permitted to teach evening classes at a settlement. Even her liberal-minded husband would have been happier if she had contented herself with a volunteer job. After the birth of a second child, she sought an outlet in writing, because she knew that if she attempted to go back to her work, she would embarrass her husband and incur criticism. During the period when she concentrated on writing, she contributed to magazines and became the author of several books on social problems. When a long and serious illness incapacitated her husband and it became necessary for her to go back to steady employment, it was as personnel manager of a department store. Through the intercession of a prominent woman, she was chosen after years of rebuff to be headworker in a settlement. She relinquished that post when an unusual opportunity was offered her husband in New York.

In the course of her life, she came to realize that she could not silence the claims of her Jewish heritage. She tried to solve the main problem of a mixed marriage by not raising her children in any specific religion. Her husband agreed that "their children's creed must be their own, just as their work, their love later, is to be their own, not their father's or mine." The children, too, encountered prejudice. But she held fast to her conviction that they must be kept aware of the heritage that had come to them through their mother.

To all immigrants defection from family life was a matter of tragic import. Therefore the problems of this individual, bearing on abandonment of religious and family traditions, illustrates one of the most serious threats immigrant families faced as they watched the disintegration of their values in their American children.

FROM *I Am a Woman—And a Jew**

Our father prayed now. [Day of Atonement—Jewish holiday] It was surely a strange sight. The river along which we stood was the Ohio. Great boats were steaming up its waters; giant loads of steel and iron to build the railroads and the shops and factories of the twentieth century were passing us. Opposite our shore, far in the distance on the other side, burned furnaces of steel. . . . And my father spoke in a tongue written more than five thousand years ago, prayed as his forefathers on an ancient river, the Jordan, had prayed, with the same simplicity and unaltered faith. He prayed that his sins should be washed away by the waters before us. . . . From that day . . . I did not accept anything he told me about our faith until I had analyzed it myself. . . .

My father put down his paper, and spoke with scorn: 'This is the sort of Jew they say is American, who changes his face, changes his name; and he changes, too, the honor standards of Jewish womanhood for his daughter.' My own father had not changed his name, nor his face by shaving off the beard required by Mosaic law. Only I had almost disgraced the honor of Jewish womanhood, by dancing with a Gentile! . . .

I, like my husband, entered social work in its beginnings, when those who have made it first found its scope. We have seen its mistakes and its achievements. We know its limitations and its grandeurs. . . . But the social worker generally, now

*Elizabeth G. Stern, *I am a Woman—And a Jew* (New York: Dodd, Mead & Co., 1926). By permission of the publishers.

233

as in the beginning, has a situation no other worker faces. He does work requiring the most highly skilled training, long training; he does it as a professional worker with honor from the community—but his job is never his own, as is the doctor's, the lawyer's, the minister's. He is the employee of his board, to be engaged or dismissed at their pleasure, to have the work he created with human beings and lives (about which his own life is twined in the doing) cut off, without choice on his part, by the pleasure of his board. . . .

In New York, where the whole city seemed to be a New Jerusalem, entirely different from our small city, in which the Jews were few in number, the people who were not Jews felt toward Jews in two distinct ways. One group I could not talk to; the other troubled and embarrassed me. . . . The first group felt that all Jews were shrewd, sharp and bound to be successful. They did not credit them with any ethical ideals, except a bizarre sort of honor that held with their own people, like thieves with one another. . . . They, (the non-Jews) themselves made themselves the hangers-on of Jews; they came to Jewish homes, ate Jewish meals and even attended Jewish religious ceremonies, such as weddings or funerals. But all the time, they never for a moment permitted their Jews to forget that they saw them as Jews, the Jews of Dickens, ridiculous, kind, and very keen at making money. . . .

. . . eighteen years ago, for a woman to be pregnant and to expect to hold a job would have been horrifying, so unnatural a thing, that even to think of it was impossible to me. An 'expectant mother' waited for her infant, and thereafter she devoted herself to it. Whatever nonsense she might have have picked up about wanting a career (and, perhaps, she was not so much to blame for wishing these inconsequential, unimportant activities in the absence of her natural work) was, it was assumed, simply blown away like chaff before the wind of reality, when her real and her one job came—to be a mother. . . .

It was time to think out my problem of my being a Jewess among the other religious groups I met at my work and in our social life. . . . In the store, most of the young women were Catholics; the older women were Protestant. The men in the sales force and among the floorwalkers also, were Protestant; the delivery men and those doing the rougher work were more often Catholic. This was, of course, because the harder, rougher work was done by immigrant workers. . . . The departments where highest-class goods were sold—to 'swell customers' —were in the hands of American women and of selected American girls. . . .

. . . No people on earth has been driven, so harried as has been the Jew. No race has suffered so deeply, so long. One sanctuary the Jew has always had, however. That has been his home, his family. . . . The Jewish family has become not only a social institution, but a refuge in which God and love come together. . . . That is why the Jew cannot marry out of his folk, even when there are no religious ties to hold him back. . . .

My great-uncle had been a physician, but he had been the one Jewish student in the whole province . . . My daughter, almost a whole century later, in the United States of America, came with the name of a Gentile father, and because her mother was a Jewess, she, too, was to be allowed in, or squeezed out—by a quota that decided how many 'Jews' could receive an education. . . .

My own self I gave to my husband in marriage, and it meant happiness to me. But within me was something that I could give to no one—that belonged to my people. . . . It was myself, Jewess. It was what I had passed on to my children. That I wanted them to know and to find a glory in knowing.

Felix Frankfurter
Lawyer, Teacher, Justice of the Supreme Court
1883-1965

> I do take law very seriously, deeply seriously, because fragile as reason is and limited as law is as the expression of the institutionalized medium of reason, that's all we have standing between us and the tyranny of mere will and the cruelty of unbridled, undisciplined feeling.

In the career of Felix Frankfurter, the two most significant aspects of the immigrant experience are made vividly clear:

that immigrants found all avenues of advancement no less widely open to them than to natives; the contribution some immigrants were consequently enabled to make to American life.

Fortunately there exists a personal statement by Justice Frankfurter that casts some illumination on his background and on his early life as an immigrant boy. This information is contained in a published record of question-and-answer sessions conducted by Harlan B. Phillipps of Columbia University's Oral History Research Offices. Though Justice Frankfurter was reticent about his personal life, a few strands pertaining to his life and career can be disentangled from his observations about people and their interplay with history, which form the bulk of his reminiscences.

He was brought to America in 1894 from Vienna when he was a little less than twelve. His family was ". . . not bookish so much as intellectual"; his father's brother was the librarian at the University of Vienna and in his nephew's opinion, "a vastly, oppressively learned man." In one of his rare subjective moods he remarks about his mother: "She was wise enough not to say [to a friend]: 'Oh yes, my little boy, he's the smartest boy that ever was!'" Another reference to his mother occurs when he repeats his reply to President Roosevelt when notified by telephone that he had been nominated to the Supreme Court: "I can say that I wish my mother were alive."

He went to public school, then to the College of the City of New York, that training ground of many of New York's ambitious immigrants. Justice Frankfurter does not seem to have harbored the worshipful feeling for his alma mater, that his friend, Morris Raphael Cohen, harbored and never lost. Felix Frankfurter reserved his adoration for the Harvard Law School, that, to him "most democratic institution," where he had learned to care "passionately about the clean administration of justice" and which would turn him into "a romantic believer in reason."

Shortly after his graduation from Harvard Law School in 1906, he found himself assistant to Attorney General Henry L. Stimson. It was an ideal job for a lawyer who did not want to have to "deal with clients." Stimson became one of the young man's idols; the other idols were Harvard professors. When Stimson was named Secretary of War under Taft, Frankfurter became his special assistant and "junior partner." Asked to remain under President Wilson's new Secretary of War, he stayed until, in 1914, he was called to join the law faculty at Harvard. He was then thirty-one.

When war broke out in 1917, Secretary of War Newton D. Baker asked him to come down to Washington for a week-end, but he remained until 1919. His functions were several: to act as chairman of the President's Mediation Commission and to be permanent chairman of the War Labor Policies Board. He also undertook several overseas missions for the government.

In 1932 he refused an appointment to the Supreme Judicial Court of Massachusetts, the position Oliver Wendell Holmes Jr. had occupied before being named to the Supreme Court. He also declined the office of Solicitor General under President Franklin D. Roosevelt. In those days he was looked upon in some circles as somewhat of a radical, principally because of an article he had written on the Sacco-Vanzetti trial. This, President Roosevelt pointed out to him, would be held against him if he named him to the Supreme Court. Another disadvantage, of which the President reminded him "unsmilingly," was "your race." Yet, when he was finally nominated in 1939, he was confirmed without a dissenting voice. By contrast Louis D. Brandeis' nomination was achieved by a vote of forty-seven to twenty-two after five months of wrangling.[1]

As a Justice of the Supreme Court, Felix Frankfurter reached the highest public position ever attained by any of America's foreign-born. What he said about William Jennings Bryan, one of his earlier heroes, may be applied to him: "He was an excitement."

FROM *Felix Frankfurter Reminisces**

I was pitched into a class. I was in a daze. I don't know where they put me originally, but I finally ended up in the first class. Even that was intellectually much below my knowledge content, but English, of course, was a great barrier. We had a teacher, a middle-aged Irish woman, named Miss Hogan.

---

1. Alpheus Thomas Mason, *Brandeis: A Free Man's Life* (New York, 1946).

*Felix Frankfurter, *Felix Frankfurter Reminisces,* Recorded in Talks with Dr. Harlan B. Phillips. Reprinted by permission of Reynal & Company, Inc. Copyright © 1960 by Harlan B. Phillips.

I suppose she was one of my greatest benefactors in life because she was a lady of the old school. . . . She evidently saw this ardent kid who had by that time picked up some English—I'm not a linguist and haven't got a good ear for languages—but she told the boys that if somebody was caught speaking German with me, she would punish him. . . . It was wonderful for me that speaking English was enforced upon my environment in school, all thanks to Miss Hogan. . . .

. . . I read a lot, a terrible lot. At college I discovered what was the Lenox Library, which is now the Frick. . . . The reading room there was quite unfrequented. It was such a cool. quiet place—serene rather than cool. . . . I would just look at everything on the open shelves, commentaries on Shakespeare, and so on. I was a browser, and there you could browse. . . .

I have a quasi-religious feeling about the Harvard Law School. I regard it as the most democratic institution I know anything about. By 'democratic,' I mean regard for the intrinsic and for nothing else. There weren't any courses on ethics, but the place was permeated by ethical presuppositions and assumptions and standards. On the whole, to this day I am rather leery of explicit ethical instruction. It is something that you ought to breathe in. . . .

Certainly I was brought up in what might be called an ethical tradition. You were decent. You were respectful. You believed in certain verities. You were supposed to be truthful. Now, where I got these from: I might say my mother's milk, except I know damn well that milk carries no ethical instruction. . . .

One day he [a classmate from Maine] said to me, 'I think I ought to tell you something. Do you realize—you probably don't—that you're the first Jew I ever met in my life who wasn't a village peddler in my little village up in Maine? It was through him that I had notions about Jews—unclean,' and so on. This grand fellow gave me as good a glimpse as I would get from those big-worded, sociological, jargonized books on some aspects of anti-Semitism. . . . He was telling me what it meant to meet a Jew—he said so in so many words—who was clean, who was a nice lad and who was respected by the students at the Harvard Law School. He said that was a terrific experience for him. . . .

Sure it was exciting—my years in the United States Attorney's Office. In the first place, having the government as a client you never have to defend a case that you don't believe in, because in cases that had no merit, you'd say, 'No, Uncle Sam doesn't do this.' You don't indict people who oughtn't to be indicted when the United States Attorney was as scrupulous as Mr. Stimson was! . . . This was an incredibly effective and wholly scrupulous man. When he went out to raid a place with a search warrant—not only wouldn't he do it without a search warrant, but he'd send youngsters like me or Tom Thacher with whom I shared a room, later Judge Thacher, to see to it that the raiding officer kept within the limits of the search warrant. . . .

I was more and more confirmed in my own slow feelings of disharmony between myself and Jewish rituals and the synagogue. . . . Certainly it was not later than my junior year in college, I think, while I was in the midst of a Yom Kippur service that I looked around as pious Jews were beating their breasts with intensity of feeling and anguishing sincerity and I remember with the greatest vividness thinking that it was unfair of me, a kind of desecration for me to be in the room with these people to whom these things had the meaning they had for them when for me they had no other meaning than adhering to a creed that meant something to my parents but had ceased to have meaning for me. . . . I left the service in the middle of it, never to return to this day. By leaving the synagogue I did not, of course, cease to be a Jew or cease to be concerned with whatever affects the fate of Jews. . . .

Now I want to conclude about going on the Supreme Court. Why did I at once when the President said, 'Unless you give me an unsurmountable reason' acquiesce, I haven't any idea. I just haven't. I'm not implying one way or the other, but I don't know what I would have done if I had been asked to go on the Supreme Court in January 1939, had the world remained at peace as it was before Hitler changed its face for a time . . . but what spoke through me, I'm confident, was that in the context of world affairs in 1939, with all the brutal, barbaric behavior of Germany and generally the infection that was caused thereby elsewhere in the spread of anti-Semitism, and not least in this country, for the President of the United States to appoint a Jew to the Supreme Court had such significance for me to make it impossible to have said 'no.'

Samuel Chotzinoff
Musician, Belletrist
1889-1964

> The America of Horatio Alger contained, curiously enough, no Jews. . . . There were rich and poor, but the rich could suddenly become poor, and the poor gradually became rich. . . . As I read my very first Alger book, I fancied that the author was writing about me.

The contribution of the Russian-born Samuel Chotzinoff was to be primarily in music, as pianist, accompanist, critic, radio and television director, and, to judge by the tone of his writings, also to be an apostle of joy and beauty to those with whom he came into contact.

The Chotzinoff family reached America in two stages. Deceived by a dishonest travel agent they found themselves, to their immense surprise, dumped in London. There, the doughty mother succeeded in tracing the only distant relative the family possessed, by interviewing, day after day, a stream of men at the corners of London's Jewish section. With his help they were able to embark within a little more than a year for the second part of their hegira—America. The year was 1896 and Samuel was seven. The boy drifted, as if propelled by an unseen force, towards the study of the piano. As his talents became more pronounced, he found professional musicians and teachers eager to help him. His boyhood reached a climax at sixteen when he made his debut as a pianist at the Educational Alliance, that breeding ground of character and talent for East Side residents.

Another climactic event occurred when he became Efrem Zimbalist's accompanist on a highly successful tour of the United States. He was then twenty-two and had finished his studies at Columbia University. He was also the accompanist of Alma Gluck, the singer, and of Jascha Heifetz, whose sister he married. In his maturity he became a music critic and music director for the National Broadcasting Company radio and television network. His death cancelled the hope that he would write a third book of reminiscences of his later years.

FROM *A Lost Paradise**

This, then, was America! At the moment it was decidly
disappointing. And where was my father's cousin from Passaic?
Perhaps he had not heard about our record-breaking journey.
But he had heard, for a man suddenly emerged from the gloom
and with open umbrella in his hand was advancing on us.
My father ran to meet him, and the rest of us waited breath-
lessly. Strangely enough, they did not embrace when they
met. They talked long and earnestly. At length, my father,
turned and walked slowly toward us, the man right behind
him. My father's face was white. 'This is *not* America!' he at
last brought out. 'We are in London!' . . .

. . . A little over a year after we left Russia, we sailed from
Liverpool on the S.S. "St. Paul." . . . When the "St. Paul"
reached New York, we were met by my father's second cousin,
the junk dealer. This kinsman's name was Gold. It had been
Goldstein, but on his arrival in America he had thus shortened
it at the friendly suggestion of an immigration officer . . .
Now, on the pier, our cousin urged my father to perform a
similar operation on our own 'useless' family name, as he
termed it . . . He now demanded to be told what possible good
the last two syllables of our name could be us in a country
so dynamic and so impatient of nonessentials as America. 'For
here,' Mr. Gold said triumphantly— . . . 'Time is money.' . . .

It was now almost a year since I had begun to study the
piano [and] . . . my mother and sisters were clamoring to
hear me play so as to judge for themselves the extent of the
progress I claimed to have made. I felt sure of making an
impression on *them*, and it only remained for me to get
permission to invite my family to Miss Taffel's front room
during one of my practice hours. . . . when my mother and
sisters sat down on the Wiener chairs in the front room . . .
I could see in their faces that my mother and sisters were
quite unprepared for the facility I exhibited and the feeling
I put into the music.

On the sidewalk, my mother kissed me extravagantly and

---

*Samuel Chotzinoff, *A Lost Paradise* (New York: Alfred A. Knopf, Inc.,
1955). By permission of the publishers.

cried, in full view of boys playing prisoner's base. My sisters
were more circumspect, though I saw their eyes fill with
tears. . . .

I now became aware of America, where before I had been
aware only of a few square miles in New York's East Side.
. . . Then Chubb [a Christian boy who had become his
friend] disturbed the serenity of my first summer in Water-
bury. One morning when we were wrestling on his lawn,
while Jessie [his sister] sat reading and chewing gum on the
steps of their porch, I gained the advantage over him for the
first time in our battles. . . . Jessie, seeing how close I appeared
to be to victory, spurred me on with words of encouragement . . . I had already firmly pinned his shoulder down with
my knee when Chubb screamed: 'No you don't, *sheeny!*' The
appellation had its intended effect. My grip relaxed and the
next moment Chubb had rolled over me and had me under
him, both my shoulders securely touching the ground. As I
rose and dusted myself off, his sister cried: 'Shame on you,
Chubb!' and Chubb reported: 'Well, he *is* a sheeny!' And to
me: 'You are, you know! *You* killed Christ, didn't you?' I
denied the charge vehemently. Chubb went on: 'Well, if you
didn't, your *father* did. He's got a beard.' I stood helplessly
shaking my head, and Jessie came over and put her arms
around me. 'Stop that, you brute!' she screamed at her brother.
But he wouldn't be stopped. 'Your grandfather—your great-
great-great-great grandfather did it. *He* killed Christ. Yes he
did. And on Passover you drink Christian blood. Everybody
knows that! . . . I made for my hide-out on the hill. There
I threw myself on the ground and wept bitter tears. . . .

. . . Molly [a sister] gave birth to a son. At my suggestion
the infant was named Walt Whitman, whose poetry both Molly
and I constantly read. . . . I nicknamed my new nephew
'Whitty,' and only his parents, Hannah, [another sister] and
I knew the secret of its origin. I hoped that the child would
grow up to be a poet like his namesake, or, at least a good-
hearted, well read, sensitive man. . . .

After an eternity Mr. Franco raised his stick. After another
his arm descended and from behind me came the soft opening
syncopated D minor chords of the concerto. I played at the
right moment, a little timidly. My fear about not coming in
at the right moment had been groundless! The broken octaves

in the left hand were better. I began to grow confident. My playing *sounded.* . . . Long before the cadenza, I felt at ease. . . . I was conscious in the midst of the intricacies of the cadenza, that I was feeling *pleasure.* . . . When I took my final bow, my sister Sarah advanced to the stage and held up a bouquet of four roses wrapped in a Jewish newspaper.

FROM *Day's At The Morn**

The year is 1907. I am eighteen years of age. We have moved from Rivington Street to Henry Street for no valid reason, except that people on the East Side were expected to move frequently. But I am closer to the Educational Alliance and Katz's music store, for me the cultural centers of the East Side, both of them on East Broadway, a block or so away from our new quarters. . . .

Two obstacles stood in the way of my studying at Columbia. One was the entrance exam, the other the tuition fee. The first was easier to solve than the second. . . . After nine months of concentrated study of the required subjects, I felt prepared to take the entrance examination. But how and where to raise the great sum of $150, the first year's tuition? . . .

At a loss where to turn, I confided in Mrs. Lesser [the wife of an East Side dentist]. To my astonishment Mrs. Lesser had an immediate solution. This was to have Dr. Lesser advance me the money against the piano lessons I would give their children. . . . The doctor gave me $150 in ten-dollar bills, and asked for no receipt. In due course I took the examinations, which I passed with fair marks . . . and paid out $150 to the college bursar. . . .

. . . Mr. Belasco . . . was going to produce [a play] in the fall . . . The play was about a famous concert pianist. Mr. Leo Dietrichstein, the actor who was to play the part of the concert pianist, was, I was told, no pianist himself. . . . But in the play he was required to play, or, at any rate to appear to play, in full view of the audience. The difference would be solved by having Mr. Dietrichstein pretend to play on a dummy piano, while a real pianist played backstage. . . . And, indeed, he did ask me, the next moment, if I would be

---

*Day's At The Morn by Samuel Chotzinoff. Copyright ©1964 by Pauline Chotzinoff. Reprinted by permission of Harper & Row, Publishers.

interested in the job . . . I was speechless from gratitude and joy . . .

Never had I been so occupied as now. Between my last class at Columbia and the evening performance at the Belasco, I had barely time to attend to my pupils at home. My homework I did at the theatre between the Tenth Rhapsody, which opened the play, and "Warum," which came in the middle of the second act. Between "Warum" and the very end of the last act, when I played some scales and arpeggios, I had another three-quarters for study. . . .

In early spring, I finally realized my childhood ambition to live in a brownstone house on East Broadway. . . . Once, on leaning out of the window, I was able to distinguish above the general din a disputation on a Biblical matter. And scanning the block, I made out at a distance of perhaps three hundred feet two bearded figures gesticulating wildly. . . . Soon one of them, apparently outraged by the absurdity or the enormity of the other's argument, suddenly ran across the street in protest, and finding his companion hot after him, as suddenly recrossed. In this zigzag fashion the two came into view and proceeded in the direction of the river. I followed them with my eyes till they dwindled quite away. . . .

We [he was accompanying Zimbalist] finished together, and my ordeal was at an end. I felt I had done very well under the circumstances, and I was pleased, though not surprised, when Mr. Zimbalist said, 'Vahnderful; are you sure you never saw the concerto before?' Then and there he engaged me for the tour. . . . I could never attain his stature as an artist. But I could be his musical disciple. I could try to emulate his unusual qualities as a man, his benevolent sophistication and his exquisite manners. . . .

That night when I undressed and got into bed, my mother came to me in the dark and hugged and kissed me and wept for joy. She told me that when she saw me come out on the stage of Carnegie Hall, she knew complete fulfillment for the first time in her life—everything she had ever hoped for had come to pass. Now she had nothing more to live for except to see me married and the father of a son like me. . . .

[At the end of the concert tour] I went outside and stood on the steps of the hotel. . . . I looked down at myself, and a feeling of self-sufficiency and confidence stole over me. It

244

was a pleasurable and a defiant feeling. . . . I now found pleasure in being left alone by Efrem. I needed no one! My ideas, my thoughts, my memories and my imagination were enough for me.

Leonard Covello
Teacher
1887-

> "Narduccio!" she said "Narduccio *mio!* The gold you will find in America will not be in the streets, as they say. It will be in the dreams you will realize—in the golden dreams of the future."

These were the parting words of his grandmother. The "gold" he found was an inspired career as a teacher and his "golden dreams" were centered on the young people—preponderantly the children of immigrants whom he helped to find themselves. Born in southern Italy, birthplace of the most contemned class of immigrants, he was brought to New York in 1896 at the age of nine. In East Harlem, focal point for Italian immigrants, he experienced the whole gamut of frustrations to which immigrants were prone—poverty, insecurity, the need to contribute a child's labor, his mother's lingering illness and untimely death. Like his countryman, Edward Corsi, whom he preceded to America by a little more than a decade, he found inspiration in the social agency that was later to be renamed Haarlem House. He dropped out of high school to go to work, but returned to finish, then won a Pulitzer scholarship to Columbia College, to find himself upon graduation elected to Phi Beta Kappa.

While working for the master's degree, he accepted what he thought would be a temporary job teaching French at De Witt Clinton High School. There he succeeded in introducing the study of Italian into the high school curriculum and in bringing about several innovations that contributed to the permanent enrichment of the lives of pupils from diverse foreign backgrounds. He reached the apogee of his career with his appointment as principal of Benjamin Franklin High School, a melting pot for immigrant children of the twentieth century—where Negroes who had emigrated from the deep South, and Puerto Ricans

245

commingled with sons of Italians and other European immigrant stocks.

Since his own immigrant experience had taught him that in immigrant areas not only the children but the whole family had to be educated, his approach was to work wherever possible with the families of the boys and to introduce intercultural outlets that would encourage participation of parents and the community.

As a teacher for almost half a century and as principal for twenty-two years in an area of the city with the highest crime potential, this gifted teacher trained innumerable future citizens and turned many from delinquency into the paths of usefulness. Therein lies his main contribution to American life. Upon his retirement he became an educational consultant for the Migration Division of Puerto Rico's Department of Labor.

FROM *The Heart is the Teacher**

In this long lifetime of teaching, I have learned much about the ways of immigrant people and their American-born children. . . . I know what the American school can do to maintain family unity. I also know how the school can function as the integrating force in our democracy and in the molding of young citizens. . . . For only he who has suffered, directly or indirectly, the degrading insults of *wop* or *nigger* or *spick* or *mick* or *kike*—or whatever else the unwanted or newcomer to this land is called—can readily understand. . . .

The cobbled streets. The endless, monotonous rows of tenement buildings that shut out the sky. . . . Dank hallways. Long flights of wooden stairs and the toilet in the hall. And the water, which to my mother was one of the greatest wonders of America—water with just the twist of a handle, and only a few paces from the kitchen. It took her a long time to get used to this luxury. Water and a few other conveniences were the compensations the New World had to offer. . . .

. . . Our people had the worst possible jobs—jobs that paid little and were very uncertain. A stonemason worked ten hours a day for a dollar and a quarter—if there was work. When there was snow or rain or ice there was no work at all.

During slack periods men just hung around the house or played "boccie" down in the vacant lot or played cards in the kitchen or in the café. They did not talk about their troubles, but their games did not have the usual gusto. The children especially could sense their feeling of helplessness in this land which offered little more than strangeness and hardship. . . .

Very early the essential difference between working hard in Italy and working hard in America became apparent to us who were young. In Italy it was work and work hard with no hope of any future. . . . But here in America we began to understand—faintly at first, without full comprehension—that there was a chance that another world existed beyond the tenements in which we lived and that it was just possible to reach out into that world and one day become part of it. The possibility of going to high school, maybe even college, opened the vista of another life to us. . . .

. . . . Even I, as close as I was to the older people, could only imagine what it meant for them to leave 'the golden years' behind to seek the elusive pot of gold at the end of the rainbow. No wonder the shrinking within themselves. No wonder the 'living burial' in the graveyard filled with kindred spirits known as the slum area. Who but the few really bold and the reckless and the strong could survive? For the others, what was left of their bubble but the water which came at a turn of the tap, the toilet in the hall, the electric light, the subway that rattled them to work for a nickel—and their children? Their children! That was it. The rewards for all this sacrifice would come through the children. . . .

. . . With experience I had learned things about my role as a teacher. I learned how much there was to know about the people I was trying to teach. . . . When talking to one of my boys, the first question I asked was where he lived. I sought to project myself outside and beyond the walls of the school and visualize the block where he lived, the home from which he came, and the conversation that took place in the evening around his dinner table. Only in this way could I understand him better. And only by understanding him could I help him. . . .

The real educational problem among the Italians and Jews of yesterday and the Puerto Ricans of today lies in the emotional conflicts that are particularly tormenting to the boy whose parents are deeply oriented by centuries of foreign tradition and custom. The feeling of scorn and shame that builds in these children because of the pressure of adverse opinion from outside often produces antisocial attitudes dangerous to the boy and to the community—in short, the delinquent. . . .

[His reaction to a gang fight] On the spot, we invited several hundred parents of the boys into the school auditorium where we could talk to them. I assured them that there was nothing to worry about and that their boys were perfectly safe in the classrooms with the Negro pupils. 'Come on,' I said, 'you've all been in America long enough to know what it is. People who struggle for bread can't hate each other.' Sal Pergola spoke to the Italian parents, using the Neapolitan dialect. 'Go home. Make the spaghetti sauce. Take care of the washing before your husbands come home. . . . Let us handle things.' Another teacher spoke in Spanish, and pretty soon the parents began to rise and file out of the assembly, feeling a little foolish. . . .

One thing the New York City schools need is more teachers who speak the immigrant's language. Yet, there are schools where they not only do not use the bilingual teacher but make it a policy to use classroom teachers who do not know Spanish, feeling that the foreign language would be used as a crutch by teacher and pupil. . . . The bilingual teacher is a necessity in our schools. . . .

I believe and will always believe in the potential in every boy to lead a good and useful life—if we adults will only care enough, take the time and the trouble and the expense to develop this potential. . . . Half a century as a teacher leads me to the conclusion that the battle for a better world will be won or lost in our schools.

Michael Shadid
Physician
1882-

This country has given me wealth and freedom and opportunity far beyond the wildest dreams of anyone in Syria, and I wanted to repay it in some measure by working, not just for myself alone, but for the people as a whole.

On the eve of Michael Shadid's departure for America, an uncle, who was a priest, said to him: "In America you can be a force for either good or evil, as you choose." Having grown up in a primitive village in Syria, where there were no doctors, and in Beirut, where American doctors were the saviors of the sick, the youth had dreamt of becoming a physician and of healing the sick in just such little places as the one in which he had been born. In America he realized his ambition; he became a doctor. As a practitioner of medicine, he found "the force for the good," as well as the opportunity to serve the people, and thus, America.

When he left his homeland in 1898 he was sixteen and had received the equivalent of a high school education in the preparatory department of the American University at Beirut. There he had found more than instruction; he had been "introduced to the American way of life." He could speak English. Like his older countryman, Abraham Rihbany, who had left Syria a few years earlier, Machael Shadid discarded his Turkish fez at Marseilles. But unlike Rihbany, who did not like selling silks from door to door, Michael Shadid did not find the peddling of jewelry disagreeable. Traveling as far west as the Rockies, he earned enough money selling trinkets from door to door to enable him not only to pay back the loan that had made his emigration possible, but to bring his mother and brother to America; then to "peddle his way" first to a little college in Texas, and within four years after arrival, to enter the medical school at Washington University at St. Louis.

As soon as Dr. Shadid entered "country practice" in Missouri and Oklahoma, he realized that even a small medical bill often necessitated mortgaging one's farm. The fact that he kept returning to Chicago and New York for further specialized training, made him known as "the specialist doctor" and augmented his practice steadily. He was an already successful physician when the realization struck him that he had not carried out his intention to "do something as a contribution to human uplift." The effect was that he was instantly transformed into an impassioned medical reformer who set out to establish a cooperative hospital at Elk City, Oklahoma, during the decade of the thirties. It became "America's First Cooperative Hospital." The purpose was to bring superior medical care at reasonable costs to the people of the community. Despite loss of income and the bitterest opposition from the American Medical Association, which included a whispering campaign, threats to deprive him of his license, and the possibility of expulsion from the state medical society, Dr. Shadid refused to allow himself to be intimidated.

Eventually bouquets replaced brickbats. His hospital plan became the model for other cooperative health plans. He was offered the nomination for Congress several times, which he refused. His satisfaction came from the fact that he did not have to hear that pitiful query from some poor anxious person— "How much, doctor?"

FROM *Doctor for the People**

When I came to Beirut [at eleven], I found not only the largest and most prosperous city along the eastern coast of the Mediterranean, but also a part of America. Here in this Near East city of two hundred thousand people was an outpost of American civilization, a typical Middle-Western college with a campus of forty acres and twelve fine buildings: the American University of Beirut. And here too was Dr. George Post, famed throughout Syria for his skill and his almost miraculous surgery, the man who became my ideal, inspiring me with a burning determination to become a doctor. . . .

It was natural that my thoughts should turn to America, the Land of Opportunity, the land I had come to know and love through my association with its outpost in Beirut. And so, when a distant relative returned from New York for a visit in Beirut, this idea again came to mind, and many a family conclave was held to discuss the possibilities of emigration. My mother finally consulted our American kinsman, telling him of my ambitions, my studies, my desire to make something of myself in this world. She felt that in America I could reach my goal more easily than I could in Syria. . . .

But the twenty-one miserable days of the crossing were forgotten in the first sight of the Statue of Liberty, my first glimpse of America. It seemed to be a prophecy and a promise

---

*Michael Shadid, *Doctor for the People* (New York: Vanguard Press, Inc., 1939). Used by permission.

of everything we had dreamed about—freedom from oppression, opportunity to earn one's living decently, even to grow wealthy, to study and learn—perhaps even to become a doctor. . . .

In the next two years I covered almost all of the United States east of the Rocky Mountains, with the exception of the North East. In that time I became thoroughly acquainted with America and the American way of life. . . . I talked with cotton farmers in the South, wheat farmers on the plains, truck farmers in the East; I traveled in trains with small businessmen, ate with day-laborers, discussed politics with storekeepers, and the weather with everyone. My love for my new homeland grew deeper as I saw people of all nationalities working and living together, trying to build a great nation with freedom and opportunity for all. . . .

. . . One day in 1902 I found myself in a little town in Texas, looking at a crowd of young people on a college campus . . . Here again was the America I had first known in far-off Beirut—the American University seemed transplanted back to its original soil. . . . I asked the way to the dean's office, and with my satchel of jewelry in one hand and my hat in the other, I went in to see him. I told him of my life, my previous studies in Beirut, my constant reading during the last few years, my burning ambition to become a doctor. . . . He welcomed me warmly, and for the three remaining months of the semester I was the happiest of students. . . .

. . . When I treated poor patients for nothing . . . I naturally gave them the same care as I gave patients who could pay. I realized that in reality my chief incentive to do good work, to learn more, to make myself a better doctor, lay not in earning money, but in the satisfaction of achieving results, making sick people well. True, I had to earn money to support myself and my family, but I knew that I could do my best work and get the greatest of pleasure from it if I could work for the sake of the work alone and forget all thought of money. If only the town . . . could arrange for me to receive a salary sufficient to maintain my family, in return for which I should look after the health of the townspeople, what good could not be done! . . .

. . . Here was one more flaw in the system of medical practice—that decent hard-working people could not receive

251

good medical care without the fear of financial ruin. . . . My regular bill would have been enough to force him [a farmer] to sell his farm and his livestock. Even my 'small bill' would have been sufficient to put a heavy mortgage on his place, with exorbitant interest rates. . . .

. . . one spring day in 1928 I drew up a balance sheet, not primarily a financial one, but of my life as a whole. As far as money was concerned, I had done well. But I was not really satisfied. I had started out my life as a doctor with high ideals and with the ambition of doing my share in improving social conditions. What had become of my dreams of my returning to my native land as a great healer and surgeon?

. . . The result of my stock-taking was that I packed my things and with my oldest daughter, Ruth, set off for Syria. Ruth would be my barometer, for from her reaction I would know how her sisters and brothers would take to the transplanting. . . . Ruth was visibly shocked and frightened. She didn't even want to land, and asked if we couldn't return to the United States at once. . . . We went back to Elk City, and that town has remained our home and the center of my activities to the present day. . . .

. . . It happens that I am a great believer in the wisdom and the power of the people; in other words, a great believer in true democracy. And consequently I think the people should have all the facts, enter into the discussion, and have some say in determining the kind of medical care they should receive. . . .

'I plead for the Community Hospital, which is the first co-operative hospital in the nation. I plead for the fifteen thousand men, women and children, who put a hundred and fifty thousand dollars into the hospital, from their pittances, and the hundred thousand men, women and children in the Farmers' Union in this state who are going to have access to this, and similar, hospitals on a basis they can afford. I plead for the underprivileged, the disinherited, and the poor . . .'

When I think back to the days in 1931 when the Community Hospital was just a hole in the ground and I was considered by many to be a swindler, it is hard to recall that our future could ever have looked so black. Now the hospital, thrice-enlarged, stands firm; it is solvent, well staffed and secure in the esteem of the people. And I am once more a respectable citizen—not a demon with radical ideas trying to overthrow our system.

Marcus E. Ravage
Journalist
1884-

> Yes, we immigrants have a real claim on America. Every one of us who did not grow faint-hearted at the start of the battle and has stuck it out has earned a share in America by the ancient right of conquest. . . . We are not what we were when you saw us landing from the Ellis Island ferry. Our own kinsfolk do not know us when they come over. We sometimes hardly know ourselves.

A most perceptive analysis of the difficulties of adjustment to American life, is offered by Marcus E. Ravage. In the role of an "Everyman" among immigrants, he holds up a double picture of of the two stages of assimilation. He first illuminates life in New York, or, place of arrival, the "America of the aliens," with all its painful disillusionments and flounderings; the second picture reveals the feelings of inferiority that assail the incompletely Americanized alien who seeks to invade the "America of the Americans," in his own case, the University of Missouri. What he emphasizes is that the second phase of the "making over" process involved a new series of exposures to self-doubt, insecurity, and loss of pride. Furthermore, a new set of sacrifices, perhaps ever more painful than the first, was inevitably demanded.

Of Roumanian birth, he left his natal place in 1900, when the exodus from that Balkan state became a tidal wave. A combination of factors—economic depression and persecution of the Jews induced an "immigrant fever" so virulent, that in order to hasten their departure, people formed themselves into "walking groups," literally attempting to walk to the nearest point of embarkation. Driven by a desperate need to believe what he had been told about America, the youth of sixteen hypnotized himself into accepting as fact a most absurdly exaggerated version of life in the new world. Reality brought crushing disappointment.

253

The New Americans

The young man had hoped to become a physician. The fact that no hindrance other than money (which one could earn), was placed in the path of aspirants toward higher education, provided a powerful incentive to overcome this obstacle. After six years of onerous work, he was able to matriculate at the University of Missouri. But instead of studying medicine as he had planned, the attraction of English studies won out. What he proves is that in the "America of the Americans," all aliens who were only partially assimilated, could expect only new and painful humiliations. To find acceptance they had to cast off their "old skins" entirely. This involved sacrifice, for the inevitable outcome was complete alienation from their own people, who interpreted the desire to become like the Americans, as a repudiation of themselves and their values.

Mr. Ravage's exposition of the psychological problems of immigrants was considered so valid, that his book was used as a text for the study of Americanization problems. The conclusion seems therefore justified that this attempt to make the alien more understandable to Americans, is a significant contribution.

FROM *An American in the Making**

Oh, if I could only show you America as we of the oppressed peoples see it! If I could bring home to you even the smallest fraction of this sacrifice and this upheaval, the dreaming and the strife, the agony and the heartache, the endless disappointments, the   yearning and the despair—all of which must be ours before we can make a home for our battered spirits in this land of yours. Perhaps, if we be young, we dream of riches and adventure, and if we be grown men we may merely seek a haven for our outraged human souls and a safe retreat for our hungry wives and children. . . .

It seems to be assumed by the self-complacent native that we immigrants are at once and overwhelmingly captivated by America and all things American. . . . Why should we not be happy? Have we not left our own country because we were in one way or another discontented there? . . . If the alien were dissatisfied with America, would he not be taking back the first steamer instead of inviting his friends and family to follow him? . . .

---

*Marcus E. Ravage, *An American in the Making* (New York: Harper & Bros., 1917). Reprinted by permission of Harper & Row.

What were the reasons [for disappointment]? . . . Well, there were a variety of them: To begin with, the alien who comes here from Europe is not the raw material that Americans suppose him to be. He is not a blank sheet to be written on as you see fit. He has not sprung out of nowhere. Quite the contrary. He brings with him a deep-rooted tradition, a system of culture and tastes and habits—a point of view which is as ancient as his national experience and which has been engendered in him by his race and his environment. And it is this thing—this entire Old World soul of his—that comes in conflict with America as soon as he has landed. . . .

. . . I know that the idea prevalent among Americans is that the alien imports his slums with him to the detriment of his adopted country, that the squalor and the misery and the filth of the foreign quarters in the large cities of the United States are characteristic of the native life of the peoples who live in those quarters. But this is an error and a slander. . . . So far is the immigrant from being accustomed to such living conditions that the first thing that repels him . . . is the realization of the dreadful level of life to which his fellows have sunk. . . .

Yes, I hated America very earnestly on my first acquaintance with her. And yet I must confess here and now that for a whole year every letter that came from my parents in Vaslui, was an offer to return home, and that I steadily refused to accept it. Those letters . . . added their very considerable share to the tragic burden of my readjustment, for my parents suggested that, if I liked America well enough to remain there, they would endeavor to raise the money and join me. And to this I was constrained to reply: 'Vaslui is not for me, and America is not for you, dear parents mine.' . . .

. . . My good friends are unwilling to see that the alien has as much to teach as to learn, that the readjustment is inevitably a matter of give and take, and that he only begins to feel at home in this new country when he has succeeded in blending his own culture and ideas and mode of life with those of the people that came here before him. Your self-complacent native takes stock of the Americanized alien and cries, delightedly: 'See how America has changed him.' But I suppose he would be greatly astonished if the immigrant were to answer, with equal truth: 'Look how I have changed America!' . . .

255

For I need hardly tell you that becoming an American is spiritual adventure of the most volcanic variety. . . . It cannot be too often repeated that the shedding of one's nationality and the assumption of another is something more than a matter of perfunctory formalities and solemn oaths to a flag and a constitution. . . . Vowing allegiance to the state is one thing. But renouncing your priceless inherited identity and blending your individual soul with the soul of an alien people is quite another affair. . . .

During that remainder of that first week in Missouri I found out what it is to be a stranger in a foreign land; . . . In the first two months I had, and lost, a half-dozen room-mates. Do what I might, I could not make them stay with me. . . . I spent many sleepless nights trying to figure out the thing. It wounded my self-esteem to find my society so offensive to everybody. . . .

Perhaps the greatest stumbling-block in the way of my re-adjustment was the emphasis my Missourian placed on what he called my good manners. . . . *Did* he have manners? My father would not have thought so. . . . what are good manners in one country are extremely bad manners in another. . . .

My experience with Harvey [a college class-mate] and with Americans in general have bred in me the conviction that no one should be granted citizen's papers unless he can 'see' a joke. A man has not even begun the process of readjustment as long as he still stares blankly at the sallies of native humor . . .

So to New York I went [at the end of the first year at college], and lived through the last and bitterest episode in the romance of readjustment. During that whole strenuous year, while I was fighting my battle for America, I had never for a moment stopped to figure the price it was costing me. I had not dreamt that my mere going to Missouri had opened up a gulf between me and the world I had come from, and that every step I was taking toward my ultimate goal was a stride away from everything that had once been mine, that had once been myself. . . .

No, there was no sense deceiving myself, the East Side had somehow ceased to be my world. I had thought a few days ago that I was going home. I had yelled to Harvey from the train as it was pulling out of the station at Columbia, 'I am going home, old man!' But I had merely come to another strange land. In that fall I would return to that other exile. I was, indeed, a man without a country. . . .

And in the fall I went back . . . When I reached the campus I was surprised to see how many people knew me. Scores of them came up and slapped me on the back and shook hands in their hearty, boisterous fashion, and hoped that I had had a jolly summer . . . It took me off my feet, this sudden geniality of my fellows toward me . . . I felt my heart going out to my new friends. I had become one of them.

Constantine Panunzio
Minister, Social Worker, Teacher, Writer
1884-

> Like myself, every immigrant brings something with him from his native land which is worthy of perpetuation, and which, if properly encouraged and developed, may become a contribution to our national life.

At the turn of the century the tolerance of Americans for unrestricted admission of aliens reached a low ebb. The reason was the steadily mounting influx of Southern and Eastern Europeans. Contemned as "dagoes," "sheenies," and "Bohunks," these immigrants found themselves victims of sneers, insults, and discrimination. Their helplessness encouraged outright dishonesty and treachery. The contemptuous attitude which some Americans showed to hapless foreigners forms the basis of a serious complaint by this native of southern Italy. The avowed purpose of offering his experiences for publication, was to "open the eyes" of well-meaning Americans to injustice and to point out what "helps or hinders *the many* in or from becoming useful American citizens."

He was a nineteen-year-old sailor on an Italian cargo ship who deserted in Boston in the year 1902. His intention was not to remain, but to find another freighter, where he hoped to be less harshly treated than on the ship on which he had arrived, or, if it proved impossible to find a berth on an Italian merchant ship, to work long enough to earn his fare home. He came from a genteel family, but since he was friendless and tongue-tied, he fell into the hands of a *padrone*, who shipped him off to a lumbercamp in Maine. There he found himself in a virtual state of peonage. The attempt to earn the money needed for his return to Italy, was foiled by dishonest Americans, who deceived him, defrauded him of his wages, and used him as a cat's paw for purposes which he, in his ignorance, could not recognize as unlawful. When he took someone's advice to "hop a freight train," which he did not know was a misdemeanor, he landed in jail. An understanding judge set him free and thus implanted in him an abiding confidence in the integrity of judges and a violent distrust of policemen, whose callousness and brutality he had experienced on several occasions. Not until he found work in the home of a decent farming couple in Maine, did he get his first taste of "the real America I came to love." They showed him a new path to follow, which led through the Protestant religion to the Wesleyan seminary, subsequently to Wesleyan University at Middletown, Connecticut, and eventually to the Boston University School of Theology. He admits that it was not until he was well advanced in his school work that he began to acquire an "American consciousness."

But even after his ordination as a minister, he did not escape the epithets "dago," and (since he was dark-skinned) "sheeny." American churchgoers objected to having a minister with such an "outlandish name." In some churches he was considered "too much of an Italian," in others, "too little of an Italian."

Eventually he left the pulpit to turn to social service. In his work as superintendent of a settlement house in the North End of Boston, he found snobbery, disregard, and contempt for immigrant traditions. American employers were willing to finance Americanization classes, while at the same time woefully underpaying their laborers.

During World War I he served with the Y.M.C.A. in the Italian theater of war. He could have remained in Italy, where all doors were open to him, but he chose to return. His commitment to America is expressed in these words:

> I am not blind to Thy failings, but Thy virtue and Thy glory far outshine them. Whatever betide, I am Thine and I claim Thee as my own.

Mr. Panunzio became known as an educator and writer.

FROM *The Soul of an Immigrant**

. . . I took my sea chest, my sailor bag and all I had and set foot on American soil. . . . Of immigration laws I had not even a knowledge of their existence; of the English language I knew not a word; of friends I had none in Boston or elsewhere in America to whom I might turn for counsel or help. I had exactly fifty cents remaining out of a dollar which the captain had finally seen fit to give me. . . . not having money with which to purchase shelter, I stayed on the recreation pier. . . . One night, very weary and lonely, I lay upon a bench and soon dozed off into a light sleep. The next thing I knew I cried out in bitter pain and fright. A policeman had stolen up to me very quietly and with his club had dealt me a heavy blow upon the soles of my feet. He drove me away and I think I cried; I cried my first American cry. . . .

It may be in place here to say a word relative to the reason why . . . so many Italians in coming to America find their way to what I had called "peek and shuvle." It is a matter of common knowledge, at least among students of immigration, that a very large percentage of Italian immigrants were 'contadini' or farm laborers in Italy. . . . more nearly serfs working on landed estates and seldom owning their own land . . . There is another factor to be considered, and that is that the 'padrone' perhaps makes a greater per capita percentage in connection with securing . . . workers for construction purposes than in any other line; and therefore he becomes a walking delegate about the streets of Italian colonies spreading the word that only 'peek and shuvle' is available. . . .

. . . I went to Mr. Annis and asked him to pay me. . . . It was then that the truth came out. He laughed me out of court and with a sneer upon his lips which I remember to this very day, he handed me a five-dollar bill and said that was all he could pay me (he owed me eighty-five dollars in wages) . . . It was as if the very earth had crumbled away under my feet; I was bitterly angry; I hated the man and I hated America with all the strength of my young soul. . . .

. . . Here in the face of cruel injustice and seeking a means

---

*Constantine Panunzio, *The Soul of an Immigrant* (New York: The Macmillan Company, 1921). Used by permission.

of securing justice, I had been hurled into prison. What would they do with me now? . . . Would they burn me? Hang me? Shoot me . . . How could I, with my scanty knowledge of English, explain my innocence? . . . Now and then the sharp realization of what had happened came over me, and I would cry out in sheer bewilderment. I called for 'mother' as only a child can cry when utterly lost and in despair. . . .

The moment I stepped into the courtroom and looked into the kindly face of the judge a feeling of hope came over me. I felt certain I was looking into the face of a friend who would comprehend. . . . Instinctively I knew that I was standing before a man who would deal justly and kindly with me. . . .

. . . There where I was to get my first glimpse of what I thought was a representative American community [in Maine] I had heard the vilest and most profane language. Unprofessional prostitution was not uncommon. Liquor was sold in open defiance of the law. Threats of murder were frequently heard; lawlessness in game hunting was the boast of all; cattle stealing was not unknown, and there in that little hamlet of not over five hundred souls were to be found some of the worst microbes of our national life. . . .

All that my life in school and college meant to me, I cannot define. . . . Here in America I had earned my way through school and college. I had worked as janitor, tailor, woodsman, night watchman, mail clerk and respectable people thought no less of me for so doing. . . . The American in me was unconsciously growing. I borrowed no money until I was compelled to do so and then I returned it as soon as possible. I took pride in my toil and in being independent. . . .

. . . It seems easy to want to Americanize the foreigner at a distance or to delegate the task to some one else, but when they get too near us, then the line is sharply drawn, not on the basis of true merit, but simply because one is a 'foreigner.' The result is seen in 'little Italies,' 'little Polands,' little Ghettoes,' and the like . . .

. . . I said: 'Mr.—I am sorry that you take this attitude toward the matter. Please remember that when you have trouble in your factory, when you hear of labor difficulties of various kinds; when you hear of I.W.W.'s and anarchism, of bombs and the like, that it is the spirit back of your 'damn the dagoes' that is responsible in no small degree for these difficulties. . . .

. . . Not only were all the constructive forces of American society absent from the community, [where the settlement house was located] but also some of it very worst features seemed to have been systematically poured into the neighborhood to prey upon the life of the people in their all too apparent helplessness. There within that half mile square were no less than one hundred-eleven saloons . . . there in this neighborhood were also fifty-three of the worst imaginable institutions; poolrooms and bowling alleys, dance halls and gambling dens, brothels and the like. The fact was that this community, . . . in the absence of the constructive will of any one group of people, was leading a life almost completely separated from the life of America. . . .

I take my hat off to the typical American and I am profoundly grateful to have known him, speaks he a 'slanted' tongue or a mellifluous or ever so pure a brogue. So long as he is the embodiment of the spirit of America, he is my man. He . . . who is idealistic and yet practical; who emphasizes worth above appearance and who greets the unseen with a buoyant cheer—he is my man—he is my American. . . .

Maurice Hindus
Journalist, Novelist
1890-

> I was glad I had fled from New York and had come to Mount Brookville. It was the America I had yearned for and needed to know. . . . Here one nook of the vast world of mankind in which neither race nor religion nor class mattered. Made up dirt farmers, it extended a glad "howdy" to all others who sought to whip their living out of the soil. Protestant as it was, I had never known it to manifest, in word or act, any antipathy, toward Jew or alien.

Having been brought up on a farm in pre-revolutionary Russia Maurice Hindus was predisposed towards the view of life espoused by Rousseau, Jefferson, and Crevecoeur. A belief

261

in the moral superiority of people living close to the earth, mixed with a love of woods, fields, and streams, had entered deeply into his being. His father had been an improvident "koolak," who did not have "to wait for the Revolution to liquidate him." In 1905 his widowed but intrepid mother brought her children to New York. At first the fifteen-year old boy was impressed with the abundance of foods considered luxuries in Russia and with the fact that everyone wore shoes, socks, and used handkerchiefs. The soda fountains, the glossily wrapped chocolate bars and machine-made cigarettes—wonders of the machine age—delighted him. But the thrill soon wore off. The appetite for white bread left him and instead he felt hungry for the black bread of his former days. Working in dingy lofts amid noise and clutter, made him yearn for his old surroundings. When he lost his job during the "slack season," the difference between a money and an agricultural economy, where "the garden, the cows, the hens were a guarantee against destitution," became glaringly apparent. The asphalt pavements, the filth and smell of the streets, the murk of the East River, the "Keep Off the Grass" signs, and other restraints of urban life, turned New York into "arid zones" for him. He had entered Stuyvesant High School within a year of arrival and looked forward to continuing his studies, but the strain of working and attending school at the same time, soon affected his health. Going from clinic to clinic awakened "an irrepressible longing," for his "lost green world." An employment agency supplying help to upstate farmers found him a job as "hired man in an American village."

There he found the "real America." In studying the contrasts between the way of life in his "old village" and "the American village," he discovered the raw material for what would become his career. He was to be a writer and an interpreter of diverse cultures in different areas of the world, including Asia. He would continue to compare his two "green worlds," one in Russia, the other in America, and the way each was to change —the Russian one through the influence of the revolution, the American through the effects of the depression.

His first task was to get "the hang of things" in regard to his work and to learn to understand the people among whom he had placed himself. Struck by their tolerance, good will, fair play, and scrupulous honesty, he came to realize a variety of characteristics of American rural life: even dogs (unlike Russian dogs), were "accustomed to the language of friendship" and were therefore not to be feared; American cows were pampered, they were not supposed to be yelled at, let alone kicked, they were given names and their stalls were white-washed, well-lighted and clean. He was amazed at the variety of tools and the intelligence that underlay their planning and execution; by the fact that barns, houses, mailboxes were left unlocked; that a straying calf was immediately returned; that no one stole fruits or vegetables. The self-sufficiency of the people, their stern self-control (particularly at funerals) and the fact that he could perceive no animosity toward people of different religions struck him as "the most extraordinary reality in the civilization of Mount Brookville" (name disguised).

While he worked as a farm hand, he prepared himself for the Regents examination, and at the end of three years was permitted to enter Colgate University (which the Baptist minister had suggested). After the revolution he began to return to Russia periodically and to write his books, in which he gave authoritative appraisals of the progress of the agricultural experiments introduced by the Soviet regime. Mr. Hindus is also the author of several novels.

FROM *Green Worlds**

. . . I had finished public school in town [in Russia] a good school, but the road futher was now blocked because of race and poverty. Over there [in America] the road would open again, and perhaps . . . [his mother's] dream of seeing me become a 'learned' man would come true. The other children might likewise go to school. Schools would be free, and neither poverty nor race would keep the doors closed. That much she had been assured,—and that was one of the chief reasons why she decided to leave the old home. . . .

All that I had heard of sugar was true. . . . there was lots of it, and it was cheap, and its use in the accepted form meant no special extravagance. . . . True also were the stories of white bread. . . . Magnificently true were the stories of handkerchiefs and shoes. Here even I had to have a handkerchief,

---

*Maurice Hindus, *Green Worlds* (New York: Doubleday & Company, Inc., 1938). Reprinted by permission of the author.

and not only on the Sabbath and on holidays but on weekdays.
. . . Most true was the story of cigarette paper, too true.
Nobody used wrapping paper, copybook paper, newspaper,
for the rolling of cigarettes and, what was more hardly anybody made his own, anyway. . . .

In the old village our garden, our few strips of land, our
cow, our hens were a guarantee against absolute destitution.
Besides, there was also a neighbor who would lend us, or
any other family in need, a sack of rye or potatoes until the
next harvest was gathered. . . . Here, in the moneyed economy
of the modern city, his job was all a man had to lean on for
his bread. . . . The glamor of the American dollar, of which
I had heard so much in the old village vanished, had indeed
turned into an evil omen. . . . If only because of the guarantee
against destitution which it afforded, I should some day go
back to the land. There man could never be as tragically
helpless as in the city, with the job in a shop as the sole way
of earning a living. . . .

Then, one day as I was on my way home from the clinic,
an inner voice whispered, 'Why don't you go to an American
village?' Why not, indeed? The more I thought of it, the more
hopeful and exciting it became. Eventually I was hoping to
leave New York anyway. I was only waiting until I had completed my course in high school. I had set my mind and
heart on an agricultural career—through college and to a
farm of my own . . . I should find a highschool in an American
village and go to college there, and meanwhile I should be
striking roots in the American soil. . . .

In the old village I had been living in the age of wood.
In Mount Brookville I was living in the age of steel, and the
transition from one to the other was the most exciting and
most enlightening experience I have ever known. It was higher
learning at its most robust and noblest. . . .

I had worked for Jim nearly a year and a half, and in time
his house and his farm had become almost a home to me.
Never had I known him to accord privileges to himself at
the table or in the house that he didn't share with me and
the other hired man. Emphatic in speech and simple in mode
of living, he had been to me not only an employer, but a
friend and a teacher. . . .

Jim owed me money, but I was indebted to him for the

sturdy education he had given me. It was he who had taught me most of what I had learned about "the hang of things" on an American farm and his discourses on bees, people, politics, life were always a source of enlightenment and diversion. He had uncovered to me the rough grandeur and the mighty lightheartedness of America, also its superb fearlessness of man, God and government. Years, indeed a lifetime, of sojourn in New York and a whole library of books could never have so amply disclosed to me the outward and inward realities of America, its true heart and mind, as he had by his words and deeds. . . .

. . . I had no thought that I was on my way not only to college but to a destiny and a profession of which at the time I had not dreamed. Nor had I the least inkling of how priceless Jim's 'higher learning' would be in later years, when I was to write my books on Russia. Indeed, without this learning I very much doubt that those books would ever have been written.

Carl Christian Jensen
Social Scientist, Criminologist
1888-

> I started my life work a romantic uplifter, bent on one heroic task: to shoulder the underworld and raise it out of the drainage level.

Among those who found the current of their lives redirected into channels that were not open to them in their homelands, was Carl Christian Jensen. Of Danish birth, he emigrated in 1906 at the age of eighteen, alone. Since he had neither relatives nor friends in America, he was immediately thrown on his own resources. His education was of the scantiest, since he came from the "lowest layer," where, he says, "a trade ranked and was a climb because of the long apprenticeship."

In very short order he became acquainted with breadlines and nickel Bowery hotels. He was prone to religious fervor, which sent him to a waterfront mission where he wrestled with tramps, alcoholics, and lonesome servant girls. When he had risen to the job of electrician's apprentice, he became acquainted with a teen-age girl who had worked as a servant. After their marriage it was she who encouraged him in his ambition to acquire a college education. The road led first to a seminary where missionaries were trained, then to college and to a graduate fellowship.

After he had received the equivalent of a secondary education, he transferred to the University of Minnesota, where he maintained himself and his family by acting as janitor, morgue attendant, lay preacher, and handyman. His wife attended classes and worked at domestic jobs. At college he was attracted to such divergent careers as the medical missionary field, literature, biology, and mathematics. He chose the profession of the social scientist so that he could help in "giving a shoulder." In his own words, he chose to become a "Romantic Uplifter."

Mr. Jensen makes it clear that his decision to dedicate himself to social betterment was dictated not only by a sense of obligation to humanity, which his religious orientation fostered, but also by gratitude for having been "uplifted" to heights to which "in the old country only nobility and clergy rose."

FROM *An American Saga**

I never quite got over my second childhood. I doubt that any immigrant ever does—with his hasty often harsh attuning to the new world. My first birth was distant and dim and unreal. . . . Not so my second childhood. I was born full-grown, so to speak, and, therefore was aware of my new birth. . . .

On my arrival I was in possession of a twenty-dollar gold piece, five silver dollars, a pocket Bible, and a good watch. My sailor bag was full of working clothes. . . . The next day sailor tramps borrowed my gold piece. And when the rest of my money was spent I took refuge in the open, cuddling up in a pile of straw that kept the cement from freezing on the foundation of a new sky-scraper. There my sailor bag was stolen the first night. . . .

Along thirty miles of water front I wandered in search of work—around Manhattan Island, on the Brooklyn, Jersey City, Hoboken and Staten Island wharves—, waiting through rain

*Carl Christian Jensen, *An American Saga* (Boston: Little, Brown & Company, 1927). Used by permission of the author.

and sleet and snow with gangs of longshoremen to reach the boss before he finished picking the men he wanted. It took strength when a steamer arrived, to break the brawny barriers and stem the tides of human muscles. Strong men crushed each other to the ground in their passion for work. . . .

One day I came upon a man bent over a sewing machine in a dingy sweatshop, a pale, thinly bearded Jew with the melancholy glow of his race burning in his eyes. He had suffered his share in this life, having been driven from Moscow into the Siberian ice, during his student days, from whence he had made his escape to America. . . . He was tutoring a youngster in mathematics, he told me. Mathematics! 'If I took lessons, could I also enter Cooper Union?' I asked eagerly. 'One dollar I'll pay you every week.' He looked me over for head to foot—especially my head. 'Yes,' he said. 'I'll teach you.'

Twice in my life sublime ecstasy has caught me, like the moon the sea: at my entrance into the New World through the Broadway canyon, and at my first glimpse of Alma Mater. . . .

Shortage of money shut me out of the medical field, and I turned to sociology, applied and pure. Seventeen theories showed me the methods of healing social ills. I diagnosed society, and filled out prescriptions. Criminology, juvenile delinquency, child welfare, called for workers—a new profession which was hitched to all the arts and sciences, and which later took me to Manhattan for graduate studies, into prisons and criminal courts, hospitals for the insane and schools for the feeble-minded, in an optimistic attempt to lift the underworld. . . .

The Sunshine Society found me a preacher's outfit, and when I grew worldly, a Tuxedo. But I had already found myself a plainer place for clothes, the County morgue. . . . I fumigated the morgue clothing in a drygoods box, and washed it in gallons of gasoline, and aired it thoroughly . . . I was fastidious in my choice, and looked for well-dressed strangers, young and unclaimed. . . . Tramps and suicides I passed up. . . .

I had no magic lamp at my command to help me find the antechambers of the underworld, nor a host of supernatural servants, as had the heroes of myth and fairy tale. But I thrust old theories aside and set out on new quests. And whether I were locked up with a ward of insane or with a prison hall of murderers, or I taught handicraft to a class of feeble-minded children, or I was trailing a fiend the night long through the haunts of Manhattan, badge on my chest, gun and blackjack on my hip, I found the same clue common to all living things, man as well as beast: a wild urge for food and for love, to keep his flesh and his kind alive. . . .

I chummed with magistrates and higher judges; with district attorneys and their assistants; with shysters and criminal lawyers; with court interpreters, turn-keys, and probation officers. I discussed elemental problems with teachers of public schools, social workers, health nurses, doctors of city clinics; with priests, parsons and rabbis. And I studied Freud, Kempf, Watson, White and many other noted scientists. . . .

I went South with a staff of scientists to study the convict in the swamps along the Gulf. . . . Thirty-five hundred convicts—Negroes, Mexicans, whites opened up their hearts to let me glance at their scrolls within. They sketched their lives in trenchant strokes, confiding their family, school, industrial and criminal history to me.

Edward Corsi
Social Worker, Commissioner of Immigration
1897-

> . . . Uncle Sam has not always dealt intelligently or humanely with immigrants— . . . at times they have been treated more like stupid animals than intelligent future citizens.

One who followed Edward Steiner's footsteps in carrying out the Biblical command "He shall be thy spokesman unto the people," was Edward Corsi. Born approximately thirty years after Steiner, in the Abruzzi region of Italy, he was brought to America in 1907, the year of our heaviest immigration, when several shiploads daily waited to discharge their human cargo. His father, a disciple of Mazzini and editor of a liberal paper, had dropped dead at the moment when he was attempting to address an audience to express his thanks for having been elected to the

Italian Parliament. His memory became the boy's lodestar. All who were under the yoke of privation, and particularly those who, like himself, had come to America as aliens, found in Edward Corsi a sympathetic supporter.

The ten-year old boy had heard fantastic stories about the ease and plenty awaiting immigrants in New York and had therefore longed "passionately to come here." Instead the family found itself plunged into the bitterest disillusionment. The step-father, who had resigned his commission as an officer in the Italian army, could find employment only at the most onerous jobs. The mother, sickened by tenement conditions, sank deeper and deeper into illness and despair until she was forced to return to Italy, there to die within the year. They were so poverty-stricken that Edward and his brother were sent to pick lumps of coal on the railroad tracks, where, in consequence, Edward's brother lost an arm. Edward augmented the family income by rising at four to do the chores of a lamplighter. The only oasis in the desert of want was the settlement house of the neighborhood, later to become Haarlem House. There the boy found inspiration and guidance. Of Haarlem House he says: "It became an instrument of my own ideals and purposes and shaped my ambitions."

During the bitter years of his youth, the young man kept up his studies. After finishing the law course at Fordham University and doing his stint in the army, he became known to American readers of *Outlook* Magazine as the reporter who described conditions in Mexico in the early 1920's and who gave them a picture of Italy under Mussolini in the *New York World*. In 1930 he supervised the federal census in Manhattan, thus gaining additional insights into the lives of the foreign-born.

At his desk at the settlement house, where he had returned as a full-time worker, he received in 1931 the summons from the White House to become Commissioner of Immigration. As he expected, deportation became "the big business" in Ellis Island during his term in office. The year 1932 was the first in more than one hundred years when more people left America than those who sought entrance. It was his responsibility to sign deportation orders and to see that deportees were properly expelled from the United States. Corsi found this duty so "bitter" that he might have said with Dante: ". . . and I alone/Prepared myself the conflict to sustain,/Both of sad pity and that perilous

269

road,/Which my unerring memory shall retrace/." People to be deported were to him "these unfortunate souls, who brought a lump to my throat."

In 1934 he accepted the post of Director of Relief for New York City, because he felt he would be returning to his "first love, active social service." His vocation as social scientist seems an outgrowth of his background. Remembering his immigrant experiences, he could not be indifferent to anyone in adverse circumstances.

FROM *In the Shadow of Liberty**

I am sure our life on the East Side was typical of the lives of thousands upon thousands of immigrant families. It was a continuous struggle. There were many time when we had nothing to eat in the house. There was one period when my stepfather was out of work for eighteen months. . . .

Every person, black or white, in this country, is an immigrant or descendant of immigrants. The black immigration was largely forced, the white largely spontaneous. . . . Some had come at a time when the labor of extra hands was desperately desired, even prayed for. Other had come at moments when they could not hope to be anything but a burden on the population already here. . . . [During the last decades of the nineteenth century] the sources of immigration shifted from western to eastern and southern Europe. We received not only new races but new and distinct civilizations. . . . Only at this point did our country become the true 'melting-pot' of the world. . . .

Now that I am no longer at the Island and can speak more freely, I must confess that the duties of deportation were never very pleasant to me and often very bitter. Our deportation laws are inexorable and in many cases inhuman, particularly as they apply to men and women of honest behavior whose only crime is that they dared enter the promised land without conforming to law. I have seen hundreds of such persons forced back to the countries they came from, penniless and at times without coats on their backs. I have seen families separated, never to be reunited—mothers torn from their chil-

*Edward Corsi, *In the Shadow of Liberty* (New York: The Macmillan Company, 1934). Used by permission of the publishers.

dren, husbands from their wives, and no one in the United States, not even the President himself, able to prevent it. . . .

I will not discuss the value of American opportunity. But that it is to many the pot of gold at the end of the rainbow I have had deeply impressed upon me during my service at the Island. Sometimes I myself have been forced to shatter the hopes and render useless all the enormous efforts that have been expended in bringing the alien illegally into the country. . . .

Here is the law [anti-Red immigration law of 1918]. If an alien anarchist arrives at the gate, he is to be excluded. If a member of an alien organization who proceeds to foment organized crime under the guise of political propaganda is discovered among us, he ought to be expelled. However, nothing in the whole content of the law from which we have quoted indicates that the accused is to be denied the protection of our laws while he is a resident among us. No department at Washington, not even the Department of Justice, is permitted to hang a man without a trial. . . . It is apparently possible for an agent of a department to enter a man's house and arrest him, take him to jail, to Ellis Island, thence to be sent to the country of his birth, because of his political opinions. This man may leave behind him a wife and a group of American-born children who are citizens. Forever separated from him, they may become public charges. . . .

It is an inspiring sight to watch a mighty parade, to hear martial music . . . But how different and what a contrast is an army in retreat! The broken ranks, the maimed and wounded, the dying, the desperately struggling, proceeding anywhere but toward the original objective. Such is the contrast between the caravan of immigration to America, and the exodus of those hapless ones, who, old and broken, defeated, discouraged, the better parts of their lives spent in vain, often turn in refuge toward their homelands after disappointment in America! . . .

Perhaps my greatest success in striking a responsive chord in the heart of the alien and in the foreign-language press of New York came with the opening of the Commissioner's door to the aliens themselves. . . . They frequently asked for appointments, and I saw them as soon as possible. Perhaps I spoke their languages, and if so they were immediately at ease, unburdening to me their grievances and difficulties. Many made valuable suggestions, and often those talks were responsible for the prevention of injustices. . . .

My more insistent and persistent effort was toward the realization of the alien as a human being, to be considered from humane standards and treated not as a potential contestant for American labor, but as a potential citizen of these United States, sharing its life and adopting its customs. We, therefore, with whom he came in contact as representatives of his new government could best shape his future attitude toward this country and its laws. We had our chance with him first, and were responsible for giving him a sympathetic understanding which no subsequent contact with less scrupulous individuals could alter.

Pascal d'Angelo
Laborer, Poet
1894-

> I thought to myself, why, I am nothing more than a dog. A dog. But a dog is silent and slinks away when whipped, while I am filled with the urge to cry out, to cry out disconnected words, expression of pains, anything to cry out.

One must read the record of this "son of Italy" to realize what pain some immigrants endured in this land of ours before the faintest ray of hope pierced the darkness of their lives. To many, less brave, less heroically persistent than this untutored descendant of "paisanos," that moment never came. Some gave up and went home, back to the miseries from which they had hoped to escape; others stayed, getting more bowed, more splay-backed, to carry their physical burdens and their heartaches to the end of their appointed days.

This native of the Abruzzi, a region inhabited by "a people of seers and poets," a region Hemingway praised for having "the most beautiful spring in Italy" and for breeding one of his most moral characters, the priest Rinaldi, in his novel *Farewell to Arms*, was the son of sharecroppers who had known the most abject poverty. Some of these "paisanos" worked the land on a "one-fifth basis"—four-fifths to the landlord, one-fifth for themselves and their families. The yield was generally insufficient even for the barest necessities. Near-starvation drove his father to decide to leave home and family. Pascal, a boy of sixteen, decided to join his father in search of bread and wages. The story he tells of working on road gangs, in railroad yards, of the exploitation and cheating, frequently by their own country-men, their helplessness and despair, would fill any well-meaning American with shame and disbelief. His father decided to return home, because he found he was no better off in America, but the young man chose to remain.

He learned English by memorizing words from a small Web-ster's dictionary he bought for twenty-five cents. Living in an old box car, he began to write poetry. It was a bitter road to travel. He continued digging ditches, roads, and doing other pick and shovel jobs, considering himself fortunate when he could work and thus earn the necessities of life. His worst period came when he decided to break out for New York, in order to hasten his recognition as poet. Neither cold, hunger, dirt, bleak-ness broke his determination to become recognized; nor did the constant stream of rejections. Despairingly he entered a contest conducted by *The Nation.* Carl van Doren's recognition of his talent brought the turn in his fortune.

FROM *Pascal d'Angelo, Son of Italy**

Our people have to emigrate. It is a matter of too much boundless life and too little space. We feel tied up there. Every bit of cultivable soil is owned by those fortunate few who lord over us. . . . And what is it that saves the man and keeps him from being ground under the hard power of neces-sity? —The New World! . . .

In this country immigrants of the same town stick together like a swarm of bees from the same hive and work wherever the foreman or 'boss' finds a job for the gang. . . . And we set to digging and handling our picks and shovels, and I have been handling them ever since. . . .

. . . You cannot feel from the cold roads and steel tracks all the pains, the heartaches and the anger I felt at the bru-

*Pascal d'Angelo, *Pascal d'Angelo, Son of Italy* (New York: The Mac-millan Company, 1924). Used by permission of the publishers.

tality of enforced labor. Yet we had to live. We laborers had to live. We sell our lives, our youth, our health—and what do we get for it? A meager living. . . .

[A friend speaking:] 'This is a peculiar country. I can never understand these people in America and their cold ways. They will go to the funeral of their best friend and keep a straight face. I believe they feel ashamed if in a moment of forgetfulness they've turned to look at a flower or a beautiful sunset! . . .

The commissary system prevails throughout this country. In its most extreme workings it results in perpetual peonage of the unlucky laborers who get caught. Usually the lure is high wages and free transportation. My own uncle . . . was attracted to a place in Florida where he was held eight months before he was able to effect an escape. The food they gave him was vile and the living conditions were unspeakable. The laborers —white men—were guarded by ferocious Negroes with guns which they used at the least excuse. . . .

Something had grown in me during my stay in America. Something was keeping me in this wonderful perilous land where I had suffered so much and where I had so much more to suffer. Should I quit this great America without a chance to really know it? Again I shook my head. There was a lingering suspicion that somewhere in this vast country an opening existed, that somewhere I would strike the light. I could not remain in the darkness perpetually. . . .

But work continual, hard, fatiguing work made my attempts at writing few and shortlived. I always was and am a pick and shovel man. That's all I am able to do, and that's what I am forced to do, even now. . . .

[A friend speaking] 'Pascal, what hope is there for any laborer in this world? Look at me: besides being an illiterate, I am as you see me . . . a deformed hunchback [from carrying burdens]. . . . And you, who they say, can write English —what good does it do to know the language of America while working here? You are not getting a cent more than a parrot like me who goes wherever they take him. You live in the same box car. You eat the same food. And if you stay here long enough, you will become the same as I. Look at me and you are looking into the mirror of your future! . . .

I reflected: what was one little starvation more or less in a man's life, especially in that of a self-anointed poet? Within a few years we would be gone, so why not sing our songs in the meanwhile? . . .

. . . I had learned to have faith in the future. . . . No matter how bad things were, a turn would inevitably come—as long as I did not give up. I was sure of it. But how much I had to suffer until the change came! What a thorny, heartbreaking road it was! . . .

The literary world began to take me up as a great curiosity and I was literally feasted, welcomed and stared at. Letters of congratulations and appreciation came from the various sections of America, from Boston to 'Frisco. . . . But more sincere and dearer to my heart were the tributes of my fellow workers who recognized that at last one of them had risen from the ditches and quicksands of toil to speak his heart to the upper world. . . .

Claude McKay
Poet, Novelist
1890-1948

> I desired to achieve something new, something in the spirit and accent of America. Against its mighty throbbing force, its grand energy and power and bigness, its bitterness burning in my black body, I would raise my voice to make a canticle of my reaction.

In Claude McKay we have a non-European newcomer to America. It can come as no surprise that his estimate is based on his special situation as a Negro. Born and raised in the British West Indies, he hoped to find on the North American continent a greater challenge for his talents. Jamaica seemed to him "too small for high achievement"; he wanted a wider audience. He found here challenge enough, as well as widened opportunities, but the cultural climate of the United States, which denies to Negroes acceptance as participating members of American society, deepened his hurt and insecurity. He found out that even among intellectuals a party may become "frostbitten" when a Negro is present. His resentment sent him wandering over many parts of Europe and North Africa—"a black Diogenes exploring the whole world with . . . [an] African lamp." After a decade of sampling various cultures, he was drawn back to America.

He had had a "peasant childhood" in the hills of Jamaica. His father, a man of stature among the blacks, was a friend of missionaries. The boy's education had come from a "free-thinker" school-teacher brother, for whom a missionary had secured the chance for a college education. Following his brother around to various villages, he read omnivorously and became a free-thinker himself at an early age. The attempt at writing verse was an early manifestation of his talents, in which he was encouraged by an English gentleman who had some of his verses published under the title *Jamaica Song and Story.* In 1911 the desire to complete his education in the United States brought him to Kansas State College. But he did not finish. Instead he turned "vagabond with a purpose." The purpose was to "graduate as a poet," while supporting himself as porter, longshoreman, waiter, valet, and so forth.

After his discovery by Frank Harris, who was then editor of *Pearson's Magazine,* he took off for London. There he spent "the most miserable of years" and was glad to escape to the Negro pale in America."

Upon his return he found a sponsor in Max Eastman, who appointed him associate editor of *The Liberator.* Though he mingled freely with intellectual whites, he frequently found himself in the role of "He Who Gets Slapped," especially when his friends, Max Eastman and Eugen Boissevain (later the husband of Edna St. Vincent Millay), were forced to eat in a restaurant kitchen with him, because a Negro could not be served in a public restaurant. In Russia he was lionized and everywhere else, he asserts, he was treated with altogether more consideration than in America or in England.

Claude McKay's restlessness is clearly attributable to the desire to escape from "the suffocating ghetto of color consciousness"—which drove Richard Wright and other prominent Negroes out of America. His comments have a familiar ring. They sound like an echo of much that has been said by Civil Rights leaders, except that McKay's statement was made in 1937 when "the great modern Negro leader" he hoped for was not even remotely on the horizon. The following poem "If We Must Die" became a powerful rallying cry among intellectual Negroes.

If We Must Die

If we must die, let it not be like hogs
Hunted and penned in an inglorious spot,
While round us bark the mad and hungry dogs,
Making their mock at our accursed lot.
If we must die, Oh let us nobly die,
So that our precious blood may not be shed
In vain; then even the monsters we defy
Shall be constrained to honor us though dead!
Oh kinsmen! we must meet the common foe!
Though far outnumbered let us show us brave,
And for their thousand blows deal one death-blow!
What though before us lies the open grave?
Like men we'll face the murderous cowardly pack,
Pressed to the wall, dying, but fighting back!

FROM *A Long Way From Home**

The phrase 'white friend' used by a Negro among Negroes is so significant in color and emotion, in creating a subtle feeling of social snobbery and superiority, that I have sometimes wondered what is the exact effect of 'colored friend' when employed by a white among whites. . . . I know the reactions and the nuances must be very different within the two groups. . . . Perhaps I have been impractical in putting the emotional above the social value of friendship, but neither the color of my friends, nor the color of their money, nor the color of their class has ever been of much significance to me. It was more the color of their minds, the warmth and depth of their sensibility and affection that influenced me. . . .

Only super-souls among the whites can maintain intimate association with colored people against the insults and insinuations of the general white public and even the colored public. Yet no white person, however sympathetic, can feel fully the corroding bitterness of color discrimination. Only the black victim can. . . .

It was one of the most miserable meals I ever ate. I felt

*Claude McKay, *A Long Way From Home* (New York: Lee Furman, Inc., 1937).

not only my own humiliation, but more keenly the humiliation that my presence had forced upon my friends. The discomfort of the hot, bustling kitchen, the uncongenial surroundings—their splendid gesture, but God! . . . it was too much. I did not want friends to make such sacrifices for me. If I had to suffer in hell, I did not want to make others suffer there too. . . . I am not white steel and stone. . . .

Poor, painful black face, intruding into the holy places of the whites. How like a specter you haunt the pale devils! Always at their elbow, always darkly peering through the window, giving them no rest, no peace. How they burn up their energies trying to keep you out! How apologetic and uneasy they are—yes, even the best of them, poor devils—when you force an entrance, Blackface, facetiously, incorrigibly, smiling or disturbingly composed. Shock them out of their complacency, Blackface; make them uncomfortable; make them unhappy! Give them no peace, no rest. How can they bear your presence, Blackface, great, unappeasable ghost of Western civilization! . . .

It is hell to belong to a suppressed minority and outcast group. For to most members of the powerful majority, you are not a person; you are a problem. . . . As a member of a weak minority, you are not supposed to criticize your friends of the strong majority. You will be damned mean and ungrateful. Therefore you and your group must be content with lower critical standards. . . .

Right here in New York there are children of mixed parentage, who have actually hated their white mothers after they had grown up to understanding. When they came up against the full force of the great white city on the outside and went home to face a helpless white mother (a symbol of that white prejudice) it was more than their Negroid souls could stand. . . .

. Well, whatever the white folks do and say, the Negro race will finally have to face the need to save itself. The whites have done the blacks some great wrongs, but also they have done some good. They have brought to them the benefits of modern civilization. They can still do a lot more, but one thing they cannot do: they cannot give Negroes the gift of a soul —a group soul. . . .

Such is my opinion for all that it may be worth. I suppose

I have a poet's right to imagine a great modern Negro leader. At least I would like to celebrate him in a monument of verse. For I have nothing to give but my singing. All my life I have been a troubadour wanderer, nourishing myself mainly on the poetry of existence. And all I offer here is the distilled poetry of my experience.

Louis Adamic
Journalist, Writer
1899-1951

> That was life: bird ate fish, somebody else ate bird, and so on. . . . The go-getting capitalist and the poor workin'-stiff belonged to two different species as widely separated as the hell-diver and the fish.

One of the foreign-born who interpreted American life in Darwinian terms, was Louis Adamic. A twentieth-century immigrant from what is now Yugoslavia, his experiences during the twenties confirmed his conviction that America was a "jungle," not only for foreigners but for natives as well. He held that even "the great Hoover" was "a rather typical product of the jungle" and had been destroyed by it.

Unlike many immigrants who claim to have been led by tales of returned countrymen to expect the impossible, Adamic admits he had been warned. A Slovenian who had returned ill and disillusioned after years of working in the mines drew a harsh picture of America for him as a land that "swallowed foreigners" and looked upon them as "dung . . . the fertilizer feeding the roots of America's present and future greatness." But he would not believe it. In 1913, a fourteen-year-old schoolboy, he took part in a patriotic demonstration against the Austrian government and was expelled from the Gymnasium. Unwilling to study for the priesthood, he won the consent of his parents to try his luck overseas, but he had to promise his mother he would not work underground. At first he was lucky in finding a job on a Slovenian paper and a home with the editor's family, but before long he was confronted with a succession of hardships which caused him to enlist in the army before he was out of his teens.

After his return from the battlefields of France, joblessness pursued him and he was forced to go to sea. Though he was a veteran, the decade of the twenties was for him no "prosperity decade." Hunting for work on the west coast, he was exposed to the influence of the "Wobblies" and thus found further confirmation for his thesis that America was "more of a jungle than a civilization—a land of deep economic, social, spiritual, and intellectual chaos and distress, in which by far the most precious possession a sensitive and intelligent person can have is an active sense of humor." *Laughing in the Jungle* was a form of whistling in the dark. After a period of difficulty he passed an examination for a clerical post at the municipal port of San Pedro in California, and there found some security and the opportunity to develop as a writer.

As late as 1938 Adamic continued to refer to America as a "jungle." Nevertheless he admitted he had become "fascinated by the country, starting to love it, identifying myself with it, calling myself an American."[1] Between 1932 and his death in 1951 he wrote more than two dozen volumes, some of which have foreign themes and others a purely American background. During World War II he offered the plan that "we [Americans of foreign descent] make the passage back to Europe in person, and while administering relief and reconstruction convey as much as we could of our American experience in democracy."[2] After an invitation by President Franklin D. Roosevelt to dinner at the White House (which forms the subject of another book)[3] his suggestion "to educate Europeans in democracy" bore fruit in the appointment of foreign-born administrators in occupied countries.

At the age of fifty-two Adamic ended his life by suicide.

FROM *Laughing in the Jungle**

[Adamic quotes a returned immigrant] America the jungle swallows many people who go there to work. She squeezes

---

1. Louis Adamic, *Grandsons* (New York, 1935).

2. Louis Adamic, *Two-Way Passage* (New York, 1941).

3. *Ibid.*

*Abridged from *Laughing in the Jungle* by Louis Adamic; Copyright 1932 by Louis Adamic; renewed 1960 by Stella Adamic. Reprinted by permission of Harper & Row, Publishers.

the strength out of them, unless they are wise or lucky enough to escape before it is too late. . . . we helped to build these buildings [the skyscrapers of New York]—we Slovenians and Croatians and Slovaks and other people who went to America to work. We helped to build many other cities there . . . and railroads and bridges, all made of steel which our people make in the mills. Our men from the Balkans are the best steel-workers in America. The framework of America is made of steel.

. . . America is the Land of Promise to them. She lures them over by the thousands and hundreds of thousands—people from many countries, not only from Carniola. She needs their hands even more than they need her dollars, and makes use of them. Once upon a time immigrants were called 'dung' in America; that was a good name for them. They were the fertilizer feeding the roots of America's present and future greatness. They are still 'dung.' The roots of America's greatness still feed on them. . . . Life in America is a scramble. More people are swept under than rise to riches. . . .

[The author speaking] The great majority of immigrants who plunged into the turmoil of America, from the most intelligent to the least, were naturally bewildered, or numbed by the impact of the country upon their senses and their minds. Their first concern upon arrival was to find people of their own nationality, in whose midst they might orient themselves. One could seldom, if ever, get a job in one's old line. In America there was no stability, which was almost the keynote of life in the European countries before the World War. . . . The more pronounced the difference in language, ways and conditions in America and in the immigrant's own country, the more urgent it was for him to seek out his countrymen. . . .

Of a sudden I perceived that America was a veritable battle-ground of tremendous and savage forces. People were shot down, killed in open warfare. And then I began to understand —not quite, of course, but it was a beginning—such incidents as the so-called Ludlow massacre in Colorado in 1913, and the dyamitings in Los Angeles and elsewhere in the preceding few years that I had seen referred to in various papers and magazines. . . .

When, finally, I was down to my last five dollars, I went to the sergeant and told him to take me to the recruiting-office. I was not yet a citizen, but had taken out my first papers, which was all that was required for a foreign-born applicant for enlistment. . . .

[In New York—at the end of WWI] . . . as the wagon shook over the cobbles, little pieces of coal dropped onto the streets. They were immediately picked up by two small girls clad, so far as I could see, in threadbare, torn dresses that barely reached to their knees—and I was cold in my heavy army overcoat. They were immigrant children, no doubt. . . .

. . . The fall of 1922 was the tailend of the first post-World-War economic depression in the United States. The Legion's employment-office was jammed with shabby, frustrated, bewildered, half-starved and profane ex-service men, many of whom, like myself, had recently come to Los Angeles, thinking the city really was 'the white spot on America's industrial map,' as advertised by the Chamber of Commerce in Eastern papers and magazines. But jobs were scarce. The side streets east of Main, where the commercial employment agencies were located, teemed with unemployed men, some of them willing to work at anything for any money. . . .

For several years I agreed with Mencken that the sensible thing to do for a sensitive and intelligent person who could not help being interested in the American scene was to look upon it—upon the whole 'gross glittering, excessively dynamic, infinitely grotesque drama of American life'—with detachment, as a 'circus show.' . . .

I had not come to America . . . to become rich; nor . . . to escape from myself . . . ; nor, like most immigrants to slave at whatever task I could find. Rather, I had come to experience America, to explore the great jungle, to adventure in understanding—and here I was. . . . I was twenty-nine years old and I had been in the United States half of my life, but so far, I thought, America had scarcely touched me. . . . She was neither dragging me down, nor pulling me up. I 'played safe,' as a sensible adventurer should do in a jungle. I laughed and stayed sane and healthy. . . .

An astonishing place, America. One cannot love, nor hate it. It is terrible, magnificent and funny, vacillating between the sublime and the ridiculous. A place of contrasts and contradictions. . . . It is, I repeat for the nth time, a jungle. It is impossible to really figure it out in any fundamental sense.

. . . It is futile to try to change or influence it deeply; it is immune to reform, and within it—within the jungle—operate tremendous economic and other forces that seem to have got out of human control. . . .

. . . There is a mocking elusiveness about American life that appeals to my sense of the dramatic. Sometimes I think that there is in America, in her drive and rush, in her cock-eyed sense of values and her resultant discontent, a high promise—may be a false one, but nevertheless it catches and fires one's fancy, and one begins to think and feel in terms of the vast, varied, painful, effervescent tragi*comic* (emphasis on the comic) life of the country.

Stoyan Christowe
Journalist, Writer
1899-

Again he turned to me. As he spoke he held his right hand stretched out, with the first two fingers in the sun bunched as though he were going to cross himself.

'You belong to America. America belongs to you. You don't know how fortunate you are.'

'I do.'

This colloquy took place between Stoyan Christowe after his return to the Balkans in 1928 as special correspondent for the *Chicago Daily News* and the foremost Bulgarian intellectual, poet, critic, translator, and teacher, and it sums up Christowe's feeling for America. Fifteen years stretched between Christowe's emigration in 1913 and his return to his native land. His almost mystic love for the very earth of this continent, induced by his intimate contact with the soil while he worked on the Great Northern Railroad, had transformed him so that he had come to feel like a foreigner with his own people. He spoke his native language so haltingly, that when he was received by King Boris of Bulgaria, he asked permission to speak in English, which the king understood better than Christowe could speak Bulgarian. He disappointed his people by being "an American first," whereas they expected him "to be a Macedonian first, a

writer and an American afterward." He was glad to escpae
"toward home, toward America" before he became "re-Bal-
kanized" and lost fluency in the English language.

He was fourteen and a student at a Gymnasium in Macedonia,
then a Turkish province, when he was struck by "Americamania"
—the disease that swept the Balkans at the turn of the century.
Accompanied by a male relative, he left for America in 1913.
Upon arrival they proceeded to St. Louis, where a large group
of townsmen had found work at the Terminal Roundhouse, at
that time "the pride of America," as a railroad depot.

Disillusionment at the contrast between what he had heard
and what he found, came as a matter of course. He did not
want a job at the carshop; it frightened him. After four months
of job hunting he found work in a factory which made the
skin of his palms as tough as parchment. His uncle died and
in death became one of those whom Archibald MacLeish meant
when wrote in "Burying Ground by the Ties":

It was not to lie in the bottom we came out
And the trains going over us here in the dry hollows . . .

His passionate love affair with America began when at fifteen
he joined a railroad gang of one hundred men, who were to
lay tracks in Montana for the Great Northern. As a member
of "the antheap" laboring in the vastness and bleakness of the
empty plains, he became enamored in a physical sense of the
land that was yielding itself up to their purposes. His job was
to lay "shims" between the rails to prevent them from touching
and to create the empty spaces that would allow them to ex-
pand during hot weather. During the winter he lived in an
abandoned box-car near a town with a Carnegie library and
taught himself English with the help of a Webster dictionary
and a Kittredge grammar he had retrieved from a trainwreck.
After four years as a trackhand he took himself to Chicago with
a thousand dollars in savings and the determination to go to
college. Learning the language was to be "the passkey to my
America."

Graduation from Valparaiso University found him pursuing
a new goal—that of gaining admittance to the newspaper and
magazine world. Though the process of acceptance was slow,
he succeeded in getting a foothold as a book reviewer and as

a writer of special articles and short stories. It was then he received the assignment to return to the Balkans as foreign correspondent. From there was to come his first book-length volume. Later he was to write books which are a blend of foreign and American themes. He is still active as a book reviewer.

FROM *This Is My Country**

. . . America had reached across the spaces and invaded my being. I went about moping, irritable, constantly dreaming of the New World. I even refused to do any work at home, or in the fields. My father became furious and did everything possible, short of using the stick, to break the spell. At long length, however, the truth sank into his head that the only way to cure the malady was with a dose of the serum that had caused it. . . . [A departing immigrant] agreed to take me along and look after me as far as St. Louis, where I had an uncle. . . .

We were not debarked at the pier but were transferred on to a ferry and taken direct to the 'Island,' where the ferry disgorged us and we formed queues. . . . Nordics, Latins, Slavs, Jews, greedy-eyed and dreamy-eyed, raw human fodder for the capacious intestines of America, we shuffled along toward the forbidding brick building. It was a purgatory we had to pass through before we could enter America. . . .

Most of [our] villagers worked in roundhouses. . . . Here the engines were fire-knocked, wiped, repaired, refueled and otherwise put into shape for their new trips. . . . In my new overalls and jacket, my new shoes, the cotton mittens on my hands, the black canvas cap with the shiny visor pulled over my forehead, I must have looked like a miniature model of a working man. . . . Was the whole thing a deception? All these legends about America? Was this how money was earned in the New World? . . . There stretched before me an endless chain of hellish days. I saw myself reaching with the tongs into the flames, thousands, millions of times, to pull out enough pennies to take me back into the old country. . . .

My American world was still very circumscribed, extending

---

*From *This Is My Country* by Stoyan Christowe. Copyright 1938, © 1966 by Stoyan Christowe. Published by J. B. Lippincott Company.

no farther than the shoe factory, with an occasional visit to the nickelodeons. . . . However, what I lacked in actual, concrete contact with the American world, I made up in my study of the English language. This I undertook systematically, from books. Andon . . . told me something which proved of immense value to me. He said that I should never learn a word unless I also learned how to spell it. . . .

At last we started for Montana. . . . The journey of a thousand miles from St. Paul to our destination in Montana in those rattling bunk-cars was an ordeal that I still remember after so many years. . . . The camp did not constitute a train by itself, but was always attached to a freight train. For some reason which I never divined it was anathema to the crews. Some conductors were kinder than others and asked the engineers to go easy on us. But those freight-train engineers were unused to carrying human beings and subjected us to repeated shocks. Some of us bore the torture in silence; other jabbered and cursed angrily. . . .

We strung thousand of rails through Montana, strung them uphill, and across bridges, and fitted them around bends. . . . From all of . . . [the men] I learned something of America, for everyone brought with him his own America, which I added to mine, like little stones to a varicolored mosaic. And the pattern of America grew and expanded in my mind, so that I was greatly pleased with myself and with the work I was doing. Every time the Fast Mail swept like a whirlwind through the plain, carrying the United States mail and bags of gold from St. Paul to Tacoma, I felt elated that the wheels rolled upon steel I had helped lay to the ground. . . .

I was forever preoccupied with the English language. Word by word, idiom by idiom the language revealed itself to me, each word unveiling its meaning like a woman lifting up her veil to expose her features. And each word with its specific meaning illumined some dark corners of the civilization into which I was stitching myself inextricably. . . .

With my growing knowledge of the language America itself grew before my vision, etched itself out more clearly, and captivated my soul more enduringly. There began to seep through my being, like a strong potion, a vitalizing American magic. My young body became possessed of a passionate yearning to be absorbed by America. I longed, like a youth in love, to lay my head upon the breast of America. . . .

I came to Chicago not so eager to look for a job as to orientate myself regarding my new America. So far I had been in an immigrant America. The real, the actual America had called out to me with a natural procreative passion. . . . I decided to enter some school in the fall and wrote to Valparaiso University for a catalogue. . . . My English might still be hesitant, and my own self might still be in ferment, but my goal was clear and simple. . . .

[After graduation from college] . . . My English having gone through various stages of turbulence and fermentation, had now settled and clarified itself, as much as it ever would. America, . . . had seeped into every tissue and fiber of my being; had, in fact, completely infused itself into my consciousness that a strange feeling came over me whenever I stopped and recalled the fact that I was not born here. My village, my father, all my background . . . seemed very unreal. . . . I really had been reborn. . . .

The offer to become secretary of the Bulgarian consulate was a slap on my American cheek. It was a negation of all that I had . . . struggled and suffered and had made myself ridiculous and had gone through this painful slow process, blindly fumbling and gestating in that 'infinite teeming womb' of which Whitman sang, in order to find myself as a foreign official in the country which I loved more than my own. . . .

. . . when I decided to visit the Balkans I believed that my Americanism had 'jelled' and that there was no danger of its going precipitate on me. In that I was not deceived. . . . So poignant was the nostalgia for America at times that I could hug a Ford just because it was made there. Some homely and typical bit of America, such as an electric sign blinking EAT as you drove in a car at night through some small town, would spring in my mind and keep blinking there . . .

Angelo Pellegrini
Teacher
1904-

. . . I perceived a truth, clear and compelling as if it had been a revelation: *I am not an Italian; I am an American. I issued from my Mother's*

> *womb in Italy; but I was born in America . . .*
> Whatever purposes I might have had in life,
> could be achieved nowhere else.

This startling insight came to Angelo Pellegrini while he was
visiting his native land, Italy. He had lived in the state of
Washington for thirty-six years, ever since he had been brought
there in 1913, a boy of nine. He had received his first impression
of America as a land of great prodigality when he had consumed his first American breakfast. This impression of great
waste was augmented after their arrival in the little western
lumber town, when he beheld a huge conveyor with a fire
below in which day and night burned lumber unfit for the
market. Some of the lumber, which the boys retrieved from
the maws of the machine, went to furnish the wood necessary
for repairs to their house and for firewood.

While still in his teens he had made the decision not to
throw his heritage as an Italian overboard, but "to pursue
simultaneously the culture of . . . [his] parents and that of
. . . [his] new country." Consequently he was able to fuse the
humanistic influence of his background with the democratic
conditions of America. In time he became a *Western* college man
and a *Western* Ph.D., as he designated himself, because the
"Western university which . . . [he] attended, contributed
enormously to . . . [his] basic attitudes."

In 1949 he went back to Italy as a teacher of literature
on a Guggenheim grant to gather material "on the Italian
immigrant's assimilation and contribution to America." It was
also an inner quest: to see "the spiritual content" of his native
land and to determine to what extent he was an American and
not merely a transplanted Italian who was still sensitive to
the refrain that "certain aspects of life in Italy were superior
to life in America."

The siren song was that one could live "more humanely" in
Italy. Also it had been dinned into his ears that Americans were
ruled by "gross materialism," "lack of spirituality," that they
were preoccupied with "commerce, dollars and speed"; that
what matters in America is quantity, not quality. The confirmation he found was that the opportunity to "live humanely" in
Italy was out of reach for people of his class and that he could
not have lived "humanely" had his parents remained in Italy.
He realized there was more than a likelihood that, like his

father, he would not have gone beyond the third grade. The irrefutable logic of what he saw and experienced, convinced him that Italians were more "money-mad than Americans" (Edward Bok said the same thing about the Dutch) and that "speed was practiced more assiduously by Italians than by Americans." Instead of spiritual values, he found a highly flourishing "cult of the Dynamo." He came to the conclusion that though some American esthetes had sought spiritual values across the sea, "America has the broad view of what constitutes values," because a "basic spiritual value . . . [is] the right of all men to self-realization." The opportunity for "self-realization," he realized, was no more prevalent in the Italy of 1949 than it had been in 1903, when his father had left "in search of bread." Beside bread, he had made it possible for his son to find "a fullness of life" beyond his own comprehension.

Mr. Pellegrini returned in a worshipful mood, induced by the conviction that in his native land he had found "the meaning of America." His reaction bears out the theory propounded by Michael Pupin,[1] himself of foreign birth, that the foreign-born who go back to visit their countries of origin, return with a greater appreciation of America. In fact, Pupin advocated that periodic visits by the foreign-born to their native lands be made "obligatory."

FROM *Immigrant's Return**

At long last we had arrived in America! . . . The Pellegrinis were not rejected . . . we moved to the third layer of reality —lush, bountiful America! The age of fear and anxiety and nightmares was past, we were definitely, in the promised land, in the green pastures. There may be better fare than the American breakfast to justify the ways of God to man, If so, it has not been my good fortune to ingest it. . . . As much as we could eat of anything. All for one price. *Just ask for it!* So that was America! Just ask for it! Or, *just reach for it!*

Sistro had sold father a six-room house for five hundred dollars. In that house were four fixtures which made us feel

---

1. Michael Pupin, *From Immigrant to Inventor* (New York, 1923).

*Angelo Pellegrini, *Immigrant's Return* (New York: The Macmillan Company, 1953). Used by permission of the publishers.

like aristocrats; hot and cold running water, electric light, a wood range in the kitchen and a wood heater in the living room. May I be permitted a modicum of imprudence and mention another fixture? We had what was very likely the finest outdoor privy in America. . . . [Later] over a period of years, we converted American waste [lumber] to our own uses. We enlarged the house, built a barn, chicken coops, rabbit hutches, and a pigsty. And always there was enough wood stacked in the shed, and in reserve on the outside, to last the family for two or three years. . . .

We had brought to America strong backs and a willingness to work. Gradually, as we realized that work was rewarded with abundance, willingness had been transmuted into . . . an enthusiasm for labor that no one of us had lost to this day. The habits that a grim landscape in Italy had forced upon us became the means of our liberations from the fear of want. . . . Not even during depressions, hard times, brief periods of unemployment, were we ever in doubt that our domestic economy was on firm footing. . . .

. . . The immigrants from southern Europe were not in a friendly and sympathetic atmosphere before World War I; and this was true in a high degree of provincial America of the Far West. We had come to America in search of bread, and so felt the inferiority of beggars. Everything which was different about us—our behavior, our diet, our groping, uncertain speech—we interpreted in terms of that inferiority. Many of the natives were kind and generous, but others spared no effort to let us know that we were intruders and undesirables. . . .

When I entered high school I was still trailing clouds, not of glory, but of the young manure gatherer in Italy. To be sure I had made my peace with the immigrant heritage. I had survived the danger of attempting to disguise my alien birth by such silly means as Anglicizing my name, expunging garlic from my diet, and proclaiming allegiance to mashed potatoes and gravy. In and out of the classroom I peppered my speech with Italian phrases and paraded my knowledge of another language, another people, another land. But I had not succeeded, or at least I felt that I had not succeeded, in gaining acceptance by my contemporaries on my own terms: as an authentic American who prefered Gorgonzola to apple pie. . . .

My matriculation in the University in the fall of 1922, viewed quite impersonally, was an important event because it was the symbol of a triumph of the New World over the Old, a triumph of which I was not so much the agent as the beneficiary. . . . It is a fact that if my parents had had their way I should never have gone to college. . . . They had come to the New World too late to learn to behave as Americans. . . . But I was also ready to defy his [father's] authority for the first time in my life had he stubbornly refused to grant my request. I was absolutely determined. America was in my blood. . . .

When I went to Italy I had no doubt that I should learn much about the meaning of 'living humanely.' In fact, I could almost say that I went there for precisely that purpose. . . . I found speed; I found commercialism. I also found cosmetic America, jazz America, movie America, Coca-Cola America. And a passionate interest in the America made up of such tawdry elements as these and an urgent and avid desire on the part of many to come to the America they so pitifully misunderstand! . . .

I had realized long before that that emigration to America had meant for me the difference between growth and stagnation; that it had changed the whole course of my life; that it had given me freedom to pursue the profession of my choice; and that it had made me quite happy. But I had never felt the weight of this truth with such convulsive immediacy as I did during the days we spent with the people who had been my childhood friends. . . . America had rescued me from Casabianca. She had given me bread and an education. Then, at her expense she had sent me back for a brief period of study so that I might interpret from a larger view the contributions Italian immigrants were making to American culture. . . .

But the vision cleared on the train from Rome to Genoa . . . I could not think of remaining years apart from the mountains, the plains, the rivers, the skyscrapers, the mad vitality, the jet-bursts of energy, the commercial piety, the loony cults, the drunkenness, the sobriety, the clean-cut, the square jaw, the pedestrian earnestness, the quick insight, the belly laugh, the bubbling-roaring irrepressible melting-pot—America! . . .

So it was from the vantage point of his native village . . . that the migrant [himself] had been able to perceive most

clearly the meaning of America . . . In the great public-
school system from the elementary grades through the university he had found teachers who had helped him plot his
course and in whom democracy and kindliness were a living
faith. And when he reached his middle years his success
could be best described as little else than an accumulated
indebtedness. To proclaim it publicly, he felt, was a fitting
conclusion to his story.

David Cornel De Jong
Poet, Novelist, Writer
1905-

> Mother asked: "And now, when are we going back
>   to Holland?"
> Father said calmly: "We are not going back."
> "I don't want to stay here where we've had noth-
>   ing but grief, humiliation, poverty and suf-
>   fering," she cried.
> "That's why we are staying here," he answered,
>   "Now that we've had all that, it's time to
>   see what America can really offer us."

So spoke the father of David Cornel De Jong after two years
of agonizing struggles. What America was to offer them was
increased economic security and acceptance by the Hollanders
of Grand Rapids, Michigan. The father would earn better wages
and would thus be enabled to provide a more comfortable
home for his family. David was to find his vocation and to
establish himself as a writer.

At the time of his arrival in 1917, David, the elder of two
sons, was twelve. In his judgment his parents, upright, rather
prissy Hollanders, had emigrated for "really . . . no pressing
reasons." They encountered their first shock at Ellis Island,
where they were roughly handled by immigration officials. But
worse was to come in Grand Rapids, Michigan, so beloved of
the Dutch since the first emigrant group had settled there in
1850.

What they found there besides economic hardship and the
misfortunes of death and protracted illness, was such meanness
and cruelty at the hands of their countrymen, that, years later,

David de Jong could not bring himself "quite to the point of forgivingness." Repellently unfeeling and un-Christian these Dutch, themselves immigrants a decade or two ago, or at best a generation removed from their immigrant forbears, would find it possible to deny a request for a pitcher of water, which flowed from their faucets, whereas the newcomers were forced to draw theirs from a rusty pump outside. The author draws an awful picture of the Dutch in America. No help or sympathy was given to the mother as she lay ill for months, while a new-born baby slowly wasted away and the rest lived in utter neglect. The Dutch-American children, unrestrained by their parents, pelted the newly arrived boys with stones or rotten fruit and taunted them with obscene words. The adults took cognizance of the family only when they wanted to sell them old clothes or old furniture.

By contrast, the Americans, for whom the boys removed snow and rubbish, did not persecute them or treat them as "monstrosities." Sometimes the Americans pampered them and showed them distinct kindness. It was because of the contrast between his own people and the Americans that the boy began to love Americans and America. This sentiment grew into "a stronger love, respect and faith than . . . [he] ever had for Holland."

Though at fifteen it seemed to him as if business school were destined to be the highest rung he could climb, he acquired not only a college education (Calvin College, Michigan), but was able to continue studying at several graduate schools. In his immigrant experience and in his knowledge of life in Holland, he found some of the themes for his writings. David Cornel De Jong belongs to those who found in their foreign birth the spur to make miracles of accomplishment possible in the American environment.

FROM *With a Dutch Accent**

And then, suddenly, in spite of the fact that we had an-ticipated it for days, there was America, the Statue of Liberty and New York's wonderful towers. How could it be, I wondered, that after having been so impatient to get there, I suddenly

*David Cornel De Jong, *With a Dutch Accent* (New York: Harper & Bros., 1944). By permission of the author.

293

seemed almost frightened by America now that we had
arrived. Was it because our uncertain future was only becoming concrete and unescapable, and that uncertainy had
to become part and parcel of me like any previous actuality?
. . . We had left home behind; we were not approaching a new
home, only an indefinite spot in an unknown vacuum. . . .

. . . And even if our early hopes had lasted for a few
hours, the miseries of Ellis Island would have wiped them
out efficiently . . . We were shunted here and there, handled
and mishandled, kicked about and torn apart, in a way that
no farmer would allow his cattle to be treated. 'From here
on,' Father predicted with some strange foresight, 'we are
no longer men created in the image of God, but less than
dumb beasts.' . . .

[After arrival in Michigan] Then we all started out for . . .
our first house in America, which was situated in a Christian
neighborhood composed entirely of Hollanders, all of the
same faith we were. . . . We were outcasts. Our neighbors
pulled their kids away from us as if we were contaminated.
They only approached us when they had an old useless hunk
of furniture to dispose of at exorbitant prices, or when they
wanted to pry into our personal affairs to learn exactly why
we had to come to America and to their noble little street
to disgrace them . . . Whenever we stirred outdoors we heard
the singsong ditty shouted at us:

Dutchman, Dutchman, belly fulla straw,
Can't say nothin' but, ja, ja, ja . . .

This was usually accompanied with scratching gestures to
indicate that we had head lice. . . .

From then on, steadily, unflaggingly, almost unconsciously,
I started to hate those self-righteous Grand Rapids Dutch.
Afterwards, for many years I fought against my hatred, because it was a sin. . . . But it kept smoldering, and the more
I came to love America and Americans, the more did I come
to resent the Grand Rapids American-Dutch, whom ironically
enough I accepted as typical Americans for several years until
time and experience fortunately opened my eyes, but not
quite to the point of forgivingness. . . .

The day after Labor Day we children were sent to a

Christian school, one of the schools approved of and supported by our Dutch Christian Reformed church. . . . Whenever a dime was lost on the school grounds, we were accused of having stolen it. When a fence or banister was broken, we got the blame. . . . Over and over again we had to submit ourselves to the principal to be punished, to be questioned, to have our pockets searched for the things we had been accused of stealing, to have our palms struck with a ruler for assumed insults against the janitor, neighbors or older girls, of which we were completely innocent. . . .

Despite of everything, we were becoming Americanized. Naturally, we came in more frequent contact with real Americans now, those foolish people whose walks we shoveled, and who really must be slightly insane, because they were actually kind to us without any thought of gain. . . . They were the silly people who occasionally allowed us to swing in their swings, to pick apples from their trees, or to eat the slices of cake and pie that they gave us, because we were 'so cute' and our attempts at English were 'so darling.' . . .

Mother countered us by declaring that she on her part refused to see any of us become Americanized. . . . That conception of hers was based only on the people who lived close around us, those people of Dutch extraction who were so ashamed of being Dutch, but who lacked the courage or imagination to become American. People who suspected and distrusted their country of adoption, who simply aimed at bettering themselves financially, while they kept stubbornly opposing all mental and really spiritual growth. . . . Beneath a hard surface shell of religiosity they were undeviatingly materialistic and in a thousand petty ways. . . .

America was crowding closer. I started working in a drugstore. . . . Here I waited on people who seemed to have no idea of looking down on me, who graciously allowed me to serve them, and who even made small talk with me without shrinking away from my brogue. . . . Within a few weeks my entire conception of the American world had been radically changed and I was gathering unto myself a very unhealthy faith in humanity, and felt somewhat less called upon to keep myself separated from 'the world' as represented by these people. . . .

[A Dutch beggar] . . . leered fatuously. He sidled five

paces away . . . to say: 'Damned smug Dutchman. They're all alike.' He stood there now looking at me defiantly, and I found myself hurrying off that bridge . . . saying to myself almost violently: But I am becoming an American. And America has already become much more important to me than Holland. And making my way in America is much better and much more necessary to me than turning back to Holland. . . . I continued my way whistling beneath those trees and that bleak sky, past those American houses on that American street. And then I realized only one thing concretely, unmistakably: I didn't want to be walking anywhere else. And that realization was strong and positive enough to keep me whistling, but no longer defiantly.

PART FIVE

DECELERATION

From 1929

In America the great liberating idea of Protestantism—the freedom of conscience, the direct
responsibility of every individual before God—
had been revived by, and coincided with, the
great humanist ideas of eighteenth century liberalism."

Franz Schoenberner
The Inside Story of an Outsider

16

A New Type of Immigrant

> "I entered this country with a primitive feeling
> of boundless gratitude. It is the only region in
> the world where the concept of immigration is
> still kept alive to-day. To a European refugee it
> is paradise."
>
> Martin Gumpert
> *First Papers*

Nineteen twenty-nine! Clouds were gathering, but no one
sensed the approach of a storm that would usher in calamity
all over the world. In America it would unleash a depression
more severe than any America had experienced; in Europe it
would cause political upheavals, tyranny, persecution, and,
finally, war.

The quota law of 1929 and the fact that the depression was
of unusual severity had the effect of diminishing the desire of
Europeans to seek entrance to the United States. During some
of the depression years, the number of Europeans who returned
to their natal places exceeded the number of those who wished
to emigrate to the United States. Hitler's seizure of power
altered the picture. Three months after he had taken over the
German government, he moved to "purify" the universities and
research centers. Involved were forty percent of the teachers,
physicians, and scientists of Germany, and, after the *Anschluss*,
of Austria. Italy became infected when Mussolini joined Hitler's
band wagon. This new wave of persecution set a new exodus
into motion.

In addition to those who were admitted under the framework
of existing laws, "emigrés" were permitted to come here through
the Presidential Directive of 1945, the Displaced Persons Act
of 1948, the Refugee Relief Act of 1953, and the special authorization permitting the entry of thirty thousand victims of the
Hungarian Revolt in 1956. The total is held to be close to two
million.

These exiles were significantly different from the usual nineteenth century immigrants. First of all, many were educated Europeans who were either professional men, business men, or white-collar workers. Furthermore, since these people had no cause to cherish the recollection of the homelands which had rejected them, they were passionately grateful to America for providing asylum and eager to be accepted into the American family. Hence, their efforts were to learn English and to become Americanized with the utmost haste. Studies of refugee families have revealed the tendency among them to avoid immigrant neighborhoods, to prefer English newspapers, and to use the English language among themselves,[1] in distinct contrast to earlier immigrant groups who preferred to live in clusters and to retain their language habits. The fact that ninety-three percent of those who arrived before 1942 had achieved full citizenship by 1947 is taken as proof of their desire to identify themselves with America as quickly as possible.[2]

The haste with which they renounced their status as aliens, seems also to be reflected in their tendency to evaluate and judge their new environment as rapidly as possible. They did not wait to "recollect in tranquillity." If Sartre is right that the impulse to write one's memoirs is dictated by the desire to "inter . . . memories in a quiet cemetery," they seem to have wanted to bury their recollections as quickly as possible. Many of the reminiscences and impressions of these refugees have been available for more than twenty years, but some are either too personal or too chaotic to be of documentary value, except as proof of the mental stress to which these refugees had been subjected. The tendency among them is not to put the "I" into the foreground, but to compare the life they had known to the life they were living. These attempts to evaluate the American culture pattern are very searching, and more frequently than not they redound to the disadvantage of the world from which they came, without creating the impression that the motive is flattery. For the most part they reveal an objectivity that is indicative of a high degree of culture and mental discipline. Clearly the stimulus is a sincere attempt to uncover through deliberate thought and careful comparison the difference between diverse cultures. Where there is criticism, it is whimsical

1. Albert Q. Maisel, *They All Chose America* (New York, 1957), p. 268.
2. *Ibid.*, p. 277.

and indulgent, not cutting or taunting. The proof that the reactions of twentieth century appraisers are very favorable to
America, may be found not only in the writings of those who
came to live and die among us, but also in the evaluations of
two such different visitors as a Hindu student and a French
philosopher.

17

Comment from 1929

Carlos Bulosan
Poet, Writer
1914-

> America is not bound by geographical latitudes.
> America is not merely a land or an institution.
> America is in the hearts of men that died for
> freedom; it is also in the eyes of men that are
> building a new world. All of us, from the first
> Adams to the last Filipino, native born or alien,
> educated or illiterate—*We are America!*

A brother of Carlos Bulosan spoke these words; his brother
quotes him. Both experienced a kind of brutality during the
depression decade that sounds unbelievable to-day. His story
is a picture of the lives of all Filipinos on the West coast prior
to World War II. His countrymen, he tells us, "adventured into
the new land, for the opening of the United States to them was
one of the gratifying provisions of the peace treaty that cul-
minated the Spanish-American War." A ragged boy in his late
teens, he was drawn to what he considered a land of mythical
goodness, "where a poor boy like Abraham Lincoln could become
President." Landing in Seattle, he and a few more boys of his
age were dragged off by one of his countrymen into peonage as
cannery workers in Alaska. What awaited them in America was
sheer brutality, injustice, and discrimination. "Brown monkeys,"
as they were called, it was their fate to be hounded and spat
upon, to be cheated, beaten, and jailed without provocation.
When they "hopped a freight" from one fruit-picking job to
another, it was a certainty that if discovered, they would be
savagely mauled by railroad detectives and the police. They
were forced to live in red-light districts, where crime was a
daily occurrence, and where predacious characters helped to

deprive them of their wages through gambling and prostitution. Brutal beatings resulting in serious mutilation were all too frequent. Filipinos were barred from citizenship and from owner-ship of land. Many became criminals out of necessity; he too was briefly forced into thievery out of sheer desperation.

When he found he could write, he realized that he could no longer be silenced. His first acceptance by Harriet Monroe of *Poetry Magazine,* came just as he was forced to enter a hospital for an advanced case of tuberculosis. He also had a painful knee injury which would give him a stiff leg for the rest of his life and a serious impairment in one hand, both the result of brutal assault. During the two years in the hospital he educated him-self by reading voraciously. After leaving the hospital he went back to earlier attempts to organize a labor movement among Filipino fruit and vegetable pickers, and to organize them in a campaign to become naturalized. Congressman Vito Marcantonio of New York had proposed a bill to grant citizenship to Filipinos, but his bill was killed. The first ray of hope came as the result of Pearl Harbor and the proclamation by President Roosevelt that Filipinos could enter the armed forces. This event coincided with the publication of his first volume of poetry. While his brothers and friends enlisted in the newly formed Filipino units, he could only hope that, maimed as he was, he would be able to contribute "something to America's final fulfillment." Despite the barbarities that had been inflicted on him and his friends, he held fast to the conviction that it was "only in giving the best we have that we can become a part of America."

FROM *America is in the Heart**

We arrived in Seattle on a June day. My first sight of the approaching land was an exhilarating experience. . . . With a sudden surge of joy, I knew that I must find a home in this new land. . . . [There] we were sold for five dollars each to work in the fish canneries of Alaska . . . We were forced to sign a paper which stated that each of us owed the con-tractor twenty dollars for bedding and another twenty for luxuries. What these luxuries were, I never found out. It was the beginning of my life in America, the beginning of a long

*From *America is in the Heart* by Carlos Bulosan, copyright, 1943, 1946, Harcourt, Brace & World, Inc., and reprinted with their permission.

flight that carried me down the years fighting desperately to find peace in some corner of life. . . .

I had not seen this sort of brutality in the Philippines, but my first contact with it in America made me brave. . . . As time went on I became as ruthless as the worst of them, and I became afraid that I would never feel like a human being again. Yet no matter what bestiality encompassed my life, I felt sure that somewhere, sometime, I could break free. This faith kept me from completely succumbing to the degradation into which many of my countrymen had fallen. . . .

. . . Nick moved with my brother Macario and me to Hope Street, in the red-light district, where pimps and prostitutes were as numerous as the stars in the sky. It was a noisy and tragic street, where suicides and murders were a daily occurrence, but it was the only place in the city where we could find a room. I often wondered if I would be able to survive it, if I would be able to escape from it unscathed, and if the horrors in it would not shadow my whole life. . . .

I almost died within myself. I died many deaths in these surroundings, where man was indistinguishable from beast. . . . It took me a long time, then, to erase the outward scars of these years, but the deep, invisible scars inside me are not wholly healed and forgotten. They jarred my equilibrium now and then, and always, when I came face to face with brutality, I was afraid of what I would do to myself and to others. I was terribly afraid of myself, for it was the beast, the monster, the murderer of love and kindness that would raise its dark head to defy all that was good and beautiful in life. It was then that I would cry out for the resurrection of my childhood. . . .

Walking down the marble stairway of the hospital [to which he had taken a dying friend] I began to wonder at the paradox of America. José's tragedy was brought about by railroad detectives, yet he had done no harm of any consequence to the company. On the highway . . . motorists had refused to take a dying man. And yet in this hospital, among white people—Americans like those who had denied us—we had found refuge and tolerance. Why was America so kind and yet so cruel? Was there no way to simplifying things in this continent so that suffering would be minimized? . . .

One, day a Filipino came to Holtville with his American

wife and their child. It was blazing noon and the child was
hungry. The strangers went to a little restaurant and sat down
at a table. When they were refused service, they stayed on,
hoping for some consideration. But it was no use. Bewildered,
they walked outside; suddenly the child began to cry with
hunger. The Filipino went back to the restaurant and asked if
he could buy a bottle of milk for his child.

'It is only for my baby,' he said humbly.

The proprietor came out from behind the counter. 'For
your baby?' he shouted.

'Yes, sir,' said the Filipino.

The proprietor pushed him violently outside. 'If you say
that again in my place, I'll bash in your head!' he shouted
aloud so that he would attract attention. 'You goddam brown
monkeys have your nerve, marrying our women. Now get
out of this town!' . . .

I was afraid to leave the hospital. I knew that a perilous
life awaited me outside, that I would be inevitably caught in
its whirlpools. I had never known peace, except in the hospital,
where there was always something to eat and a place to sleep
on the cold nights. . . . On the outside life was alien and un-
friendly, and the summer days were long and the winter nights
were sharp with cold. I determined to face it again, but now
with an unswerving intellectual weapon. Maybe I could win
this time, and if I did—would I not create a legend of courage
and valor that other poor young men could emulate? . . .

A week after the fall of Bataan a letter came from a small
publisher. He wanted to publish an edition of my poems. Was
it possible that I would have a book at last? . . . The book was
a rush job and the binding was simple, but it was something
that had grown out of my heart. I knew that I would not
write the same way again. I had put certain things of myself
in it: the days of pain and anguish, of starvation and fear; my
hopes, desires, aspirations. All of myself in this little volume
of poems—and I would never be like that self again . . .

. . . I glanced out of the [bus] window again to look at
the broad land I had dreamed so much about, only to dis-
cover with astonishment that the American earth was like a
huge heart unfolding warmly to receive me. . . . It came to
me that no man—no one at all—could destroy my faith in
America again. It was something that had grown out of my

defeats and successes, something shaped by my struggles for a place in this vast land, digging my hands into the rich soil here and there, catching a freight to the north and to the south, seeking free meals in dingy gambling houses, reading a book that opened up worlds of heroic thoughts. It was something that grew out of the sacrifices and loneliness of my friends, of my brothers in America and my family in the Philippines— something that grew out of our desire to know America, and to become a part of her great tradition, and to contribute something toward her final fulfillment. I knew that no man could destroy my faith in America that had sprung from all our hopes and aspirations, *ever*.

Albert Einstein
Physicist, Teacher
1879-1955

> I do not consider myself the father of the release of atomic energy. My part in it was quite indirect. I did not, in fact, foresee that it would be released in my time. I believed only that it was theoretically possible. It became practical through the accidental discovery of chain reaction, and this was not something I could have predicted.

When Albert Einstein accepted the offer of the Institute for Advanced Study at Princeton to come to America in 1932, it was not with the intention of remaining here. But in 1933 the persecution of the Nazis became so menacing that he was persuaded to renounce his German citizenship prior to what was to be his final departure from Europe. He arrived on a visitor's visa. American laws require that immigration visas be secured from American consuls abroad. In order to qualify for permanent residence in America, he went to Bermuda, there to receive a permanent visa from the American consul. In 1941 he became an American citizen.

Like Joseph Priestley, who had come to America in 1794 after his discovery of nitrous oxide (laughing gas) in 1772, Einstein's major work was done before he decided he would make his home in the United States. (No other comparison is intended.) America could do little for him, except to assure him of what he said he had always sought—peace and quiet. He was an extremely retiring individual and had always avoided fanfare and publicity as much as possible. One of his biographers quoted him as saying: "By nature I am a lone traveler. I have never belonged to my country, my home, my friends, or even my immediate family with my whole heart."[1] Since World War I he had been an ardent pacifist and a dedicated believer in disarmament and world government. In Princeton he enjoyed his seclusion and the opportunity to indulge his "profoundly bohemian nature."[2]

A story is told of him which admittedly may be apocryphal:

> . . . one of his neighbors, the mother of a ten-year-old girl, noticed that the child often left the house and went to Einstein's home. The mother wondered at this, whereupon the child said: 'I had trouble with my homework in arithmetic. People said that at number 112 there lives a very big mathematician, who is also a very good man. I went to him and asked him to help me with my homework. He was very willing, and explained everything very well. It was easier to understand than when our teacher explained it in school. He said I should come whenever I find a problem too difficult.[3]

The important contribution he made during the American phase of his life was in the direction of hastening the end of the war. He affixed his signature to a letter to President Franklin D. Roosevelt, pointing out that some chemists at the Kaiser Wilhelm Institute in Berlin had succeeded in splitting the uranium atom and warning of the danger to the Allied cause if the Nazis developed this source of energy. President Roosevelt was aware of the work on atomic research, but it took Einstein's prestige to awaken him fully to the danger. The Manhattan Project was the result. When Einstein was told that the first atomic bomb had been exploded, he is supposed to have remarked: ". . . that the world was not ready for an atom bomb . . . [that] it would be like putting a razor in the hands of a three-year-old child."[4]

1. Peter Michelmore, *Einstein: Profile of the Man* (New York, 1953). pp. 81-82.

2. Philip Frank, *Einstein, His Life and Times* (New York, 1963). p. 294.

3. *Ibid.*, p. 297.

4. Michelmore, *op. cit.*, p. 230.

The New Americans

Albert Einstein wrote a series of autobiographical and philosophical essays in which he made scattered references to various aspects of American life. The only long comment is a homily on "The Negro Question." His feelings are in character with the reaction he is said to have experienced at being transported in a rickshaw by another human being.

FROM *Out of My Later Years**

I am writing as one who has lived among you in America only a little more than ten years. And I am writing seriously and warningly. Many readers may ask: What right has he to speak out about things which concern us alone, and which no newcomer should touch?

I do not think such a standpoint is justified. One who has grown up in an environment takes much for granted. On the other hand, one who has come to this country as a mature person may have a keen eye for everything peculiar and characteristic. I believe he should speak out freely on what he sees and feels, for by so doing he may perhaps prove himself useful.

What soon makes the new arrival devoted to this country is the democratic trait among the people. I am not thinking here so much of the democratic political constitution of this country, however highly it must be praised. I am thinking of the relationship between individual people and the attitude they maintain toward one another.

In the United States everyone feels assured of his worth as an individual. No one humbles himself before another person or class. Even the great difference in wealth, the superior power of a few, cannot undermine this healthy self-confidence and natural respect for the dignity of one's fellow-man.

There is, however, a somber point in the social outlook of Americans. Their sense of equality and human dignity is mainly limited to men of white skins. Even among these there are prejudices of which I as a Jew am clearly conscious; but they are unimportant in comparison with the attitude of the 'Whites' toward their fellow-citizens of darker complexion, particularly toward Negroes. The more I feel an American, the more this situation pains me. I can escape the feeling of complicity in it only by speaking out.

---

*Albert Einstein, *Out of My Later Years* (New York: Philosophical Library, Inc., 1950). Used by permission.

Many a sincere person will answer me: 'Our attitude towards Negroes is the result of unfavorable experience, which we have had by living side by side with Negroes in this country. They are not our equals in intelligence, sense of responsibility, reliability.

I am firmly convinced that whoever believes this suffers from a fatal misconception. Your ancestors dragged these black people from their homes by force; and in the white man's quest for wealth and an easy life they have been ruthlessly suppressed and exploited, degraded into slavery. The modern prejudice against Negroes is the result of the desire to maintain his unworthy condition. . . .

It would be foolish to despise tradition. But with our growing selfconsciousness and increasing intelligence we must begin to control tradition and assume a critical attitude toward it, if human relations are ever to change for the better. We must try to recognize what in our accepted tradition is damaging to our fate and dignity—and shape our lives accordingly.

What, however, can the man of good-will do to combat this deeply rooted prejudice? He must have the courage to set an example by word and deed, and must watch lest his children become influenced by this racial bias.

Eva Lips

> We had arrived for the purpose of preserving something; the ideals entrusted to our minds and hearts. These ideals consisted in the conviction that the elements of culture for which and by which we had lived, could remain constructive only in liberty. America offered them and us this liberty.

When Justice Cardozo inquired of Eva Lips how she liked America, she replied, she tells us: ". . . I feel like a Buddhist, reincarnated into another form of existence, only without having died in between." As exiles from Hitler's Germany, "liberty" had acquired for her and her husband a sharpened significance. He, an anthropologist and an authority on primitive law, had resigned a university post in Cologne, preferring exile to declaring allegiance to Hitler and his world order. When he came here in 1934 in response to an invitation from Columbia University to fill a post as visiting professor of anthropology, it was with the intention of making America their "New Homeland."

Though Mrs. Lips is highly emotional, even gushing, in her appreciation of freedom and liberty, her gratitude to her "new homeland" did not entirely blind her in regard to other aspects of our culture to which a recent European might be expected to react. As her husband's "partner and disciple," as she calls herself, she had cultivated a socio-anthropological viewpoint. Having accompanied him to Africa for four years, where he had codified the unwritten laws of some savage tribes, she was accustomed to surveying a culture from a special point of view. In order to "aid" herself, she says, she invented four categories into which she could fit the various American types: people who value success above anything else, whom she classified as "the Skyscraper People"; those who retain simple ideals and a simple outlook on life, as the "Corn, Cotton and Coal People"; recent Americans, whose appreciation of American values is as superficial as their knowledge of their own culture, as the "From Somewhere Americans"; those who have inherited a variety of ethnic traits and who have truly absorbed the concepts basic to American life, the "Outright Americans."

The Negro problem thrust itself on her attention when her husband accepted a teaching post at Howard University and she became the secretary of the department. She found that Negroes were refused permission to enter their apartment house and that some people did not hesitate to show their disdain of a white man who would teach at a Negro university.

As the author of a book meant to shock the American people into a realization of what Hitler's rise to power implied, she found herself in great demand as a lecturer to women's groups and religious organizations. It gave her the opportunity to travel all over the United States and to come into intimate contact with Americans.

Her experience as lecturer led to an enhanced respect for the American woman. What struck her as a unique characteristic of American women was that they combined a diversity of accomplishments—intelligence with good housekeeping, a profession with an interest in good grooming, civic prominence with devotion to home, husband, and children. Because the American woman retains her "womanly virtues," Mrs. Lips judged her "so far superior to most of her European sisters that singing her praise . . . has become my favorite occupation."

Like so many of the refugees of the twentieth century, Mr. and Mrs. Lips sought and obtained citizenship quickly.

FROM *Rebirth in Liberty**

I saw four groups shining out of the great reservoir, four groups whose members freely mingled with each other and sometimes even became merged into each other. Yet, they managed to retain most of their typical characteristics. I gave them these names: the Skyscraper People; the Corn, Cotton and Coal People; the From Somewhere People and the Outright Americans. . . .

The skyscraper men are the financiers and Big Business men of the United States and therewith of the world. . . . He does not want to be 'happy' in a contemplative, self-indulging way. Since he moves the wheels, he wants to be rewarded with those visible results which he terms 'success in life.' He would not understand a man who would tell him that his own great achievements are the result of thought. . . .

Under the sky lies the soil of the earth, and over it presides in America another characteristic group of men and women— the Corn, Cotton or Coal people who rule the farms, villages, small towns and cities. . . . They are the traders, shopkeepers and little manufacturers. They are the human element every-where. . . . [They] have time for a more reflective kind of human happiness.

. . . the From Somewhere people, luxuriate everywhere. . . . Culturally speaking, they have the least to offer to America. Those who 'at home' did not even touch the fringe of their native spiritual traditions and achievements are, naturally, incapable of bringing them as a fertilizer to American soil; nor can they, on the other hand, absorb fruitfully anything the New World offers them in the way of culture. . . .

. . . The Outright American is proud to be one of the mil-lions of all imaginable roots of origin who spread themselves over a territory which, as though symbolic of its population, presents a digest of the climates and beauties of all other

*Eva Lips, *Rebirth in Liberty* (New York: Flamingo Publishing Com-pany, Inc., 1942).

lands on earth. . . . Each . . . is typically American, just as are its people who have created that strange mixture of notions, habits and utterances known as the civilization of America. . . .

Like the drug stores, the cocktails, the foods, human ages also have no firmly contoured limits. Six-year-olds may sing on children's programs: 'I'll Never Love Again' grown-ups indulge in the 'funnies,' those remarkable manifestations of daily entertainment rivaled by the soap operas of the radio. . . . During my first American months I discovered some familiar things at unfamiliar places, like flowers, these children of the sun, being kept in ice boxes; or academic gowns worn by bandleaders or kindergarten graduates. . . .

We did not live in one world, [while working at Howard University] we lived in two. Each was perfectly ignorant of the other. Each did not want to have anything to do with the other. The Negroes hated the Whites *because they could not be like them.* The Whites excluded the Negroes from their sphere with cold disdain, *because it was done this way.* We stood between the two, helpless. We spent nights in Negro homes, listening to horror stories which, supposedly, reported 'facts from the South.' We spent other nights in white homes, listening to 'characterizations of the nigger mind.' . . .

America alone has produced the ideal blending of female virtue. It believes in a theory, which was always my own: that a so-called 'outstanding woman' begins to be 'important' only at the moment when she *adds* to the qualities and abilities of her average sister the special qualifications she claims for herself. A great poet who cannot cook does not impress me. A political woman who does not take care of her husband's buttons is a pitiful sight. A professional educator who neglects, over the theories on child psychology, her own offspring, is no gain to any nation. . . .

Our habits had changed first, from toothpaste to laundry soap. . . . The second step had been cultural. . . . All values we had known, all abstract conceptions, had been recoined. Our notions of profession and avocation; study and science; research and reading; Church and God; friendship and marriage; dwelling and hospitality; authority and respect; music and literature, had undergone a revolution.

Krishnalal Shridharani
Student, Journalist
1911-

> . . . Americans have a quaint habit of saying, 'Why
> don't you go home, then?' when foreigners don't
> like it here. But, I like it here, and I will be a sad
> man when I take your leave.

"Exhilarated . . ." "captured . . ." was the response of this
Hindu student to the American atmosphere. His observations
are quick and pungent and have nothing of the hackneyed
about them. To see America through his eyes is an "eye-opening"
experience. Most Indians, he explains, preferred to go to England to finish their education because the cost of an American
education is higher than its equivalent in England, and also
because Indians who returned from America were suspected
of having been converted to "dangerous ideas." But he wanted
to know more about those "dangerous ideas" and therefore in
1934 he elected to come here, despite the warnings that an
American education would be a hindrance to being given "a
swivel-chair government post" upon his return. He was twenty-
two, a graduate of Tagore's international university and his
choice was the School of Journalism at Columbia. Dangerous
ideas were not new to him because at seventeen he had been
arrested with other Gandhi followers. He had also won recognition as the author of a collection of poems.

He traveled through most of the United States and in some
places found himself stared at and even followed, but he did
not allow these gaucheries to spoil his liking for the United
States. Though sarcasm is not absent from his observations, his
over-all estimate was that "flaws were few and that, on the
contrary, there was much India could adopt that would benefit
the Indians."

A theory he advanced was that India is closer to the West
than to many peoples of the East. The West, he points out,
shares the mysticism of the Indians, and Christianity and Hindu-
ism are closer to each other in regard to non-violence than to
the Islamic religion, because in comparison to some of the

313

Islamic tribes even the most militant Christian would be considered a pacifist.

His attention roamed over all aspects of American life. As a cultured and sophisticated man, he allowed little that is characteristic of American life to escape his awareness. He took note of the "cult of youth," the sensitivity to age, the lack of leisure, the tendency to conform, the respect for "the so-called expert," the gullibility of some Americans who saw in every Indian a maharajah or a snake-charmer. He commented on drunkenness, apparently unknown in India, gum-chewing, which he compared with no little irony to betel-chewing in India, the prevalence of "blondes," the fact that a wife is frequently "the goods in her husband's shop window." However, his admiration for some of the distinctive facets of American thinking far outweighed his criticism.

When, after eight years, he left America, it was with great regret and with the hope that some of the features of the American pattern of life could be transplanted to his homeland.

FROM *My India, My America**

When I decided to come to the United States, it was against the advice and counsel of my elders. . . . My speculations were based on the idea that the United States was gradually but surely becoming the center of Western civilization. . . . Not only will the United States emerge from the present conflict as the strongest nation in the world, but it will also outgrow its inferiority feelings with reference to Europe, and stand out the bulwark of western culture, the 'arsenal of democracy.' . . .

I also learned that American training can make a democrat out of a Hindu hierarchist. . . . On every hand there were men who could set examples for the caste-conscious Hindu, examples of self-reliance, ruggedness, boldness. A man could start from scratch, he could even return to an ancient land ready to blaze new trails. . . .

It is when nature does the right thing in the right way at the right time that America is devastatingly beautiful. Witness her wheat fields. Once I took a picture of them, standing on

---

*Krishnalal Shridharani, *My India, My America* (New York: Duell, Sloan & Pearce, 1941). By permission of Meredith Press.

the running board of a Chevrolet in Kansas, and I was caught in the act—to our mutual astonishment—by a farmer who stared at me across the drooping, pregnant heads of his golden protectorate. I wanted to say that I had no designs upon his sunny realm. . . . I was simply a man from a rice-growing country who was impressed. . . .

. . . I fell utterly in love with the American scene [beyond New York] and felt that if there was 'heaven on earth' it was right here. This was before I had heard anyone talk of 'God's country.' Not that I did not see flaws in the masterpiece corporately drawn by a vigorous and pioneering people. Especially I noticed with dismay the junkyards, the dump-heaps, the abandoned houses and factories, and I felt that an economy which makes it cheaper to build anew than to mend or amend the half-used must be essentially a wasteful economy. But such flaws were few, and I was glad for the people of the United States, even if all along that pilgrimage I felt a deep pang in my heart—a pang that sprang from the renewed realization of the comparative misfortune of my own people and the strong desire to remake India in the American image. . . .

The Hindu student of American culture can take back home a pointer or two from the American scene. I, for my part, have decided that the idea that the state owes a job to the citizen is full of dynamite strong enough to arouse the slumbering masses of India. If the slogan, 'Your starvation is partly the fault of the government,' can repeatedly be brought to the attention of every adult of India, I think the impact of this alone would bring about that change that would spell freedom. . . .

One of the pleasantest folkways over here is the American's inclination to go out of his way to be nice to others in small matters of every-day living. How often one hears: 'What a beautiful tie!' 'He's a good guy.' . . . 'Now you tell us, because you know all about it.' What makes it pleasanter is that there is not the slightest element of flattery on one hand or of snobbery on the other; it merely manifests the tacit recognition that one not only does not lose anything by being nice to others but, on the contrary, adds to the total happiness of one's fellow beings in a world which is quite full of frustrations anyway. . . .

I was once riding with the president of a big city's Chamber of Commerce en route to addressing his group, and I noticed that his chauffeur contradicted him right and left on national affairs and international politics. That could happen only in America. Both the boss and the chauffeur contribute to the Average American.

Laura Fermi
Wife of Enrico Fermi
1907-

> Everybody is talking about the atomic bomb, of course! . . . People of good judgment abstain from any technical comment, and realize that it would be vain to seek who is the first author in a work which is the result of a collaboration. All, however, are perplexed and appalled by its dreadful effects. . . . For my part I recommend you to God, Who alone can judge you morally.

These words came from Enrico Fermi's sister in Italy after the atomic explosions over Hiroshima and Nagasaki. A refugee from Italy because of his wife's Jewish birth, Enrico Fermi was the first in America to achieve a chain reaction in 1942. He was one of the team of physicists who developed the atomic bomb at Los Alamos. While the *leitmotif* of Laura Fermi's story is her life with Enrico Fermi, it ineluctably reveals the reactions of an intelligent European and those of her genius husband to an environment which represented, for her at least, a complete break from the culture in which she had been raised—in which a resident of Rome was more likely to say: "Sono Romana" than: "Sono Italiana." Despite her disapproval of Mussolini, she had had no quarrel with their way of life until the tightening of the Fascist laws.

In 1938, however, came the race laws, the *Manifesto della Razza*. The offer of a teaching post at Columbia University coupled with the Nobel award, offered the opportunity to escape. With their children the Fermis proceeded to Stockholm, where Laura Fermi danced with a prince, and from there embarked for New York. She was thirty-one; he thirty-seven. It was Enrico Fermi's fifth trip to America and her second. She had accompanied him in 1930, when he had accepted an invitation from the University of Michigan at Ann Arbor. He returned in the summers of 1933, 1935, 1936, and 1937, but she chose to remain in Italy. She admits that on her first trip she had failed to grasp "the significance of America and its great institutions," whereas he immediately liked America and its people, and grew to appreciate them more and more. After each trip "he would talk of going to the United States, of escaping from a dictatorship into a Democracy," but she was always against it and did not consider it "a change for the best." She liked life in Rome and felt that she belonged to it. Though the American people had struck her as kind and hospitable, America bewildered her; she missed the "European refinement in the American way of life." Furthermore, she was alienated by what she considered symptoms of "primeval instincts" and "primeval cruelty."

Her acclimatization began in New York, continued in Leonia, Chicago, and Los Alamos, which for two and a half years was "Los Alamos" only to those living there, and "Site Y" to the few outsiders who knew about its existence. "Fermi" as she often refers to her husband, plunged happily into his work; the children's adaptation proceeded with the speed usual for children. The children became their parents' teachers. Enrico Fermi loved "gadgets" and gave her a step-on garbage-can as a "never forgiven" Christmas gift. But he avoided gardening and found urgent work in the laboratory whenever she asked him to mow or water the lawn. He had worked on "fission" in Italy and was soon deep in secret work; he took "mysterious" trips. From 1940 to 1945, Laura Fermi, who had studied General Science at the University of Rome, was shut out from any knowledge of what he was doing.

Despite the fact that he was engaged in war work, they were designated enemy aliens between 1941 and 1944, when both became citizens. In 1944 she joined him at "site Y," where he was stationed. They disappeared from the world for two and a half years. Scientists from all parts of the United States and from almost all European coutries, whom General Leslie Groves is supposed to have spoken of as "the largest collection of crackpots ever seen," were assembled there. All were under the jurisdiction of the army. Not until the bombs had been dropped, she says, did the scientists realize what a monstrous weapon they had brought into the world. After the war Enrico Fermi went back to teaching and research.

In discussing Americanization, Laura Fermi raises several thoughtful questions. Is it enough to learn the language and the customs and to understand American institutions? Can one become Americanized without being able to identify with the spirit of American History? Is it necessary to transfer one's love of Dante to Shakespeare and to make a "bonfire of Garibaldi and Mazzini"? After sixteen years of residence in America, she was still unsure of herself, for she concluded with this question: "Can I truly say that I am Americanized?" But after Enrico Fermi's untimely death in 1954, at fifty-two, she remained with her children in America.

FROM *Atoms in the Family**

The process of Americanization should have started for me in the summer of 1930, when Enrico and I spent our first two months in the United States. . . . I was overwhelmed by the huge city [New York] that attempted to grow into the air, toward the skies as well as on the land; by the gray, untidy city that did not know the joy of chattering fountains in the midst of squares or the surprise of an unexpected sight at the turn of a meandering street. In the subway, awed by its efficiency and speed but depressed by its white-tiled, latrine-like stations, I stared into human eyes that belonged to unknown human races; I saw features described in courses of anthropology; I apprehended with a shock the existence of tattoos, not in recitals of exotic story-tellers, but on the bare arms of summer riders, in the most civilized city in the world. . . .

Who would not like a country where everybody is kind, hospitable and helpful to foreigners, where nobody laughs at them for their awkwardness and their mistakes? However, when I now reexamine my feelings at that time, I realize that I had not grasped the significance of America and its

* Reprinted from *Atoms in the Family* by Laura Fermi by permission of The University of Chicago Press. Copyright 1954 by the University of Chicago. Copyright 1954 under the International Copyright Union. Published 1954. Ninth impression 1961. Composed and printed by The University of Chicago Press, Chicago, Illinois, U.S.A.

great institutions. . . . I mistook their spontaneity, their lack of constraint and inhibitions, for immaturity. I did not realize that the European refinement, which I missed in the American way of life, may well have been an indication of decadence; that in the United States that refinement of the few had been replaced by higher living standards of the masses; that by accepting the principles that all men are born equal and have the same right to happiness, the Americans had renounced many of the old country's privileges. . . .

. . . It was the morning of January 2, 1939. . . . Soon the New York skyline appeared in the gray sky, dim at first, then sharply jagged, and the Statue of Liberty moved toward us, a cold, huge woman of metal, who had no message yet to give me.

But Enrico said, as a smile lit his face tanned by the sea: 'We have founded the American branch of the Fermi family.' . . .

. . . One set of objects never lost its appeal for Enrico: the gadgets. To him they represent the never ending quest for saving labor, the material proof of human progress, the product of a technology which he considers the symbol, the salvation and the promise of America. He has never lost interest in gadgets, and although parsimonious by nature and education, he is always ready to buy one more; from the step-on garbage can, his never-forgotten present of my first Christmas in the United States, through electric razor and electric saw, to the lately acquired television set, we have gone through purchase and use of all available and most automatic household equipment. . . .

In the process of Americanization, however, there is more than learning language and customs and setting one's self to do whatever Americans can do. There is more than understanding the living situations, the pattern of schools, the social and political trends. There is the absorbing of the background. . . . And there is the switch of heroes. . . . If I still miss them . . . and still marvel at the vastness of America, at newly discovered sights, at the mention of some great name still unheard of by me, if I fail to understand the humor in Charles Addams' cartoons, can I truly say that I am Americanized? . . .

For a while I could follow the progress of research at that

distance which a layman finds himself from specialists. . . .
Soon, however, a voluntary system of censorship was established, and the lid of secrecy fell over nuclear physics. . . .
Enrico often went on mysterious trips. . . . On his return I
was left alone with my speculations on the color of the mud
under his shoes or on the amount of dust on his suit. . . .

Hungarian-born physicist Leo Szilard felt more strongly than
anyone else in this matter of double responsibility of the
scientists toward the government and of the government
toward that part of science that might become useful to the
military. . . . In July 1939, he and another Hungarian-born
physicist, Eugene Wigner, conferred with Einstein in Princeton. . . . The three men decided that they would prepare a
letter to President Roosevelt and that Einstein would sign
it, being by far the most prominent of all the scientists in the
United States. Szilard then asked economist Alexander Sachs
to deliver Einstein's letter to the President. On October 11th,
Roosevelt received Sachs, read Einstein's missive, and listened
to Sachs' explanations. At once the President appointed an
'Advisory Committee on Uranium.'

Why were the persons acting this drama all foreign born?
. . . In Italy, I reflected, no foreigner could have succeeded
. . . These people, these Hungarian-, German- and Italianborn knew the organization in dictatorial countries; it *occurred*
to them that there might be ties between research and military
applications, that in Germany all scientific work might have
been enrolled in the war effort. That is why President
Roosevelt received his first warning from persons like Einstein, Szilard, Wigner and Teller while American-born andraised physicists had not yet found the door out of their ivory
tower . . .

. . . Los Alamos had caused the war to end abruptly, perhaps six months, perhaps a year, sooner than it would otherwise. Los Alamos had saved the lives of thousands of
American soldiers. The whole world was hailing the great
discovery that their husbands had given to America. The
wives' elation was justified. When among the praising voices
some arose that deprecated the bomb, and words like 'barbarism,' 'horror,' 'the crime of Hiroshima,' 'the mass murder'
were heard from several directions, the wives sobered. They
wondered, they probed their consciences, but found no answer
to their doubts. . . .

To moral questions there are no universal answers. The range of reactions among our husbands was wide. Some felt that a rapidly ending war more than compensated for the destruction at Hiroshima and Nagasaki. Some told themselves that evil lies in the will to wage wars, not in discovery of new weapons. Some said the atomic bomb should never have been built; researchers should have stopped working when they realized that the bomb was feasible. Enrico did not think this would have been a sensible solution. It is no good trying to stop knowledge from going forward. . . . Worse evils could be conceived than giving it [the bomb] to the Americans.

Erna Barschak
Psychologist, Teacher

"When do you think I may be called an American?" I asked a friend the other day. I was not joking, I was very serious. "I try so hard to adapt myself to the American way of life. I am a movie fan, I understand something about the funnies, I turn the radio on all day long, I have attended a baseball game. What else do I need to become fully adjusted to the American way of life?"

The core of Erna Barschak's observation on American life centers on the differences between the American and European culture patterns. Hers is not the usual subjective document, for she supplies only the scantiest personal details. Her attempt of comparing divergent cultures patterns is reminiscent of Frances Trollope, whose archetypical *Domestic Manners of the Americans* offered her view of the American scene at the beginning of the nineteenth century. But unlike Mr. Trollope, who surveyed a frontier society from the incomparably superior level of the cultured Englishwoman subsisting in a cultural wilderness, Miss Barschak is indulgent, and frequently approves of our "manners" and habits. In her attitude of benevolent, though sometimes amused appreciation, she follows a course chosen by many of the more recent refugees, whose critical inclinations may have been disarmed by their gratitude to America.

Erna Barschak found refuge in the United States in 1940.

A psychologist and holder of the Ph.D. degree from the University of Tübingen, she had filled a university post before the advent of of the Nazis. Within a year after arrival she had secured an appointment to teach psychology at a college in Ohio. There she was able to study the societal pattern as it reflected itself in the behavior of men, women, students, and children. After five years she felt qualified to present her views of the traits and habits of the genus Americanus in the mid-twentieth century.

Some of comments are shrewd, others amusing, and some merely innocuous. Only some can be listed: American people (including some American animals) are more friendly than Europeans. (Maurice Hindus was surprised to find that American dogs were conspicuously more amiable than Russian dogs during the "normal" pre-depression decade, but that they had become more surly during the depression years.) Even turkeys seemed to want to be sociable, for they followed her around to the point of annoyance. On buses she found conversation to be inevitable (which she did not seem to disdain, perhaps because it was grist for her mill). Yet she noted that Americans frown on personal questions and remarks of a personal nature. Like the Hindu, Krishnalal Shridharani, she approved of pleasant comments on one's appearance. She was favorably impressed with the fastidiousness of American women, but spoke disdainfully of the tendency to wear costume jewelry, a reaction many Europeans share. The widespread use of cosmetics, even among young children (who like to paint their fingernails), caught her attention. She noted the tendency of young couples to move frequently, the desire for a string of bathrooms, even when the home is a modest one, the love of picnics and the "hot dogs," the passion for driving, the disinclination for walking, the differences in table manners (that knife again!), the "aseptic" kitchens, the waste of food, the addiction to milk and ice cream, for which she offers an interesting explanation. The taste in home furnishings reminded her of "the nice postcards you can get in the drug stores." She noted the craving for popularity and the tendency towards conforming, even among college students, who, she found, want to look alike, unlike the Europeans, who strive for distinction.

One aspect of American life that evoked her admiration is the friendship that exists between American parents and children. The love, understanding, and respect which the American parents lavish on their children, impressed her as paying "dividends." The fact that American parents do not reprimand their children in public, that they prefer to convince rather than to punish, struck her favorably. She was impressed by the initiative and independence of young children. She also approved of the aims of American education to establish patterns for social behavior and intelligent leadership in contrast to European education, which emphasizes training for future careers solely.

Miss Barschak shares with other twentieth century newcomers the tendency to avoid sharp criticism and to appreciate the fact that in spite of the rejection by her homeland, she found acceptance and considerate treatment in the United States.

FROM *My American Adventure**

Going down the ship's gangway to the Custom's Office on the pier was a dream-like walk. To think that I had arrived safely in the New World! America meant a new life in safety, meant no more bombs [as in London], no more Gestapo terror, no more threat of Nazi cruelty. . . .

. . . for the first time I felt how badly prepared we European intellectuals were for living in 'another world.' Why had I not learned to keep house, to cook, to sew? I could find a job immediately if only I knew what every other woman in the world was supposed to know! . . .

Here for the first time I came across a serious problem which puzzles me even now, once in a while. What are the standards by which American employers. . . . measure the suitability of an applicant? In Europe . . . a pleasant appearance, a slim figure, a charming personality are of little or no importance. I know of some very successful woman professors and social workers to whom the term 'charming personality' could never be applied. Who cared? Careful grooming, on the other hand, might be considered by a prospective European employer as suspicious, as an indication of other than scholarly interests, of 'worldly inclinations,' interest in hunting for a husband instead of hunting for a job. What did count in the U.S.A.? . . .

. . . If you have seen three modern American living rooms of

---

*Erna Barschak, *My American Adventure* (New York: Ives Washburn, Inc., 1945). Used by permission of the publisher.

families in the middle income brackets, you need not see more. You know all of them: 'Good Housekeeping Model,' 1940; Macy's '265 dollars.' This is the usual pattern from San Francisco to Maine: chintz-covered couch, matching chairs . . . matching curtains, a low table with a bowl or a strange pottery animal with a green plant instead of a tail, sometimes a small table with the newest best sellers or magazines. . . .

. . . The Americans seem not to be 'sentimental' or possessive at all about most of their belongings. Friends borrow and wear one another's undergarments, stockings, dresses, even formal ones, hats, furcoats, overshoes and gloves. . . . I am not quite sure if American kindness and generosity include the exchange of autos or fishing rods or a tennis raquet. . . .

. . . In approaching her chores, the American housewife thinks: 'It's not amusing, it's dull, but it has to be done. Let's get on with the job!' And I have often admired, too, her ability to do jobs which in most European countries housewives leave to experts: fixing electric bulbs, repairing short circuits, hanging curtains, taking off storm windows, putting in screens—and enjoying all the gadgets she can lay her hands on . . .

The strangest symptom of this American escapism is the quite customary idea of providing a picnic place in the garden for parties. Think of it! Americans who have the most up-to-date kitchen in the world, who are more hospitable than other people, invite guests for dinner, and offer them as the greatest of all treats wieners roasted in their own garden! . . .

The unwritten law of conformity results in one of the outstanding differences between the American college student and his European counterpart. Europeans, especially the intellectuals, want to differ in every respect from their fellow men. . . . But in the U.S.A. to be different among adults as well as among adolescents is to be queer, odd, unpopular. And popularity is after all something which most Americans are craving for, especially college students! . . .

I am not certain, being as I said no 'animal psychologist,' about environmental influences on the behavior of animals. I found, however, that animals in England behave with much restraint and quietness; English cats avoid foreigners; English dogs don't bark at them frequently; English cattle pay little attention to passers-by. These American turkeys certainly were persistent, inquisitive, gregarious and very friendly. Could there really be any relationship between the animals and the spirit of the country . . .? . . .

Certain professions develop certain personality traits. Professorial absentmindedness is proverbial. So is the philosophic attitude of shoemakers, but I wonder if anyone has ever tried to evaluate the influence of occupation on bus drivers. They definitely have a special gift of dealing with people. Among the many fine men I have met on the American lines, I want to mention a few local drivers who impressed me as having that particular friendliness and human consideration which is one of the greatest assets of the American way of life. . . .

But this emphasis on food may have another origin. Food certainly acts as compensation. It may even be a cure against boredom. Why not escape in food? Why not in steak, or Southern fried chicken, or in ice cream? It seems to me that many Americans escape from the disappointments of daily life in ice cream. Let's make a survey! I'm sure we may find a sponsor among the food-producing concerns in this food-minded country. . . .

Homesickness is more widespread in America than in the Old World. The homesickness of American soldiers has been openly discussed. All books by war correspondents mention the longing of young Americans for home and parents. . . .

To me, brought up under the 'benevolent dictatorship' of father and mother, as was my whole generation in Central Europe, the comradeship and mutual understanding between children and parents in the United States is one of the greatest assets of American life. To me it seems to be the best guarantee for the survival of freedom and democracy.

Martin Gumpert
Physician, Man of Letters
1897-1962

The transformation of a European into an American is a harsh experience in the twentieth century. Is it at all thinkable? Can we and shall we surrender ourselves in this way? What happens to us?

325

Thomas Mann referred to Martin Gumpert (allegedly his physician), as "homo literatus." Four of Dr. Gumpert's books were published in translation in America. A refugee of the Hitler era, he draws an extremely perceptive view of the problems which awaited those emigrés, as he calls himself, who, in middle age, were forced to seek new and uncertain careers in strange lands. Rather than an autobiography, Martin Gumpert offers a de-personalized account of a mass odyssey in which he was a participant. He was one of the "doctors and businessmen" and one of "the nervous, frightened, bald-headed professors" who quailed before the task of having to re-educate himself in order to qualify for a license to practice medicine. He speaks for all who experienced the awful insecurity and embarrassment of having to learn English in a desperate hurry, via night school, cheap moving pictures, teachers supplied by social agencies. He speaks as an individual only when he offers his version of how American life struck an observant and intelligent European during that era in the world's history. He found "no gold in the streets," but he traveled widely; he was received by President Franklin D. Roosevelt. As Thomas Mann remarked in his introduction to Dr. Gumpert's volume, he looked at America with "grateful but not servile eyes."

Evidently he studied the reactions of the most recent European newcomers to America and pondered deeply over the characteristics that distinguish the American scene from the European. It is significant that he advocates greater regimentation of immigrants. His jaundiced eye is reserved for Europe; the more benevolent glance comes to rest on America. His comments touch on all spheres of our way of life: American children, for whom America is, in his vision, "Paradise"; American women, whom he saw as forming an "American matriarchate." He commented on the relationship between men and women, which struck him as distinctive for "its excess of emotional independence," "too little passion," "too little time for love," all of which seemed to him to cause "a lack," which he judged responsible for "the dangerous spread of psychoanalysis."

It was to be expected that as a physician he would comment on American medicine. Because of the high cost of good medical care, he favored socialized medicine. He admitted that the "official rules of medical ethics are stricter than in Europe, but pointed out that they are not often observed, that "skill and even knowledge are at a much higher level than in Europe . . . and yet the physician lacks the guidance of instinct." He took note of the situation of the Negro, to whom, like so many of the foreign-born, he was sympathetic, of our legal system, of American religion, capitalism, and other props of our society.

Because his estimate is based on an environmental framework, a sociological tinge is hard to avoid. However, his observations reveal a psychological rather than a sociological bias. Though he formed his convictions very quickly—in less than six years of residence in America—there is no hint of glibness or superficiality. In the freshness, originality, and good will, if not in romantic optimism, his remarks seem in some ways to be reminiscent of Crevecoeur's prototypical attempt to assess the meaning of "Americanism" in an earlier and more fluid society where newcomers could take a warm welcome for granted.

FROM *First Papers**

We have been preceded by millions, disappointed and hunted, rebellious and hungry for joy. They settled the coasts, drove their axes into the forests, navigated the streams, founded cities and States, created liberty and power for themselves. They began to love the soil that bred their children. . . . But they soon saw that time and space, weather and wind here followed a rhythm of their own . . . that this was a land of its own, shaping their faces, changing their looks, their language, their gait, their food, their thoughts, containing all the elements—wealth, mental growth, historical traditions and the innate creative values of a strong new young nation. It was through this revolutionary process of forgetting and reshaping, of melting down and creating anew that there arose—America. . . .

. . . much remains to be done to complete a realistic and unprejudiced picture of the capacity for Americanization among the many national units. At the same time there should be studies—and this should not be difficult of attainment— as to where men are needed and where they would be superfluous, whither members of certain groups should turn, where the soil is ripe for settlement or industry. . . .

---

*Martin Gumpert, *First Papers* (New York: Duell, Sloan & Pierce, 1941). Used by permission of Meredith Press.

One often hears that a great regimentation of immigrants would run counter to democratic principles. That is not necessarily true. Education for Americanism begins with the first step toward immigration. . . . America is no longer a colonial structure where one can put one's European traditions and ideas of its own. We have come late and we have much to catch up with. . . .

. . . For the first time in years we find people who receive petitioners with friendly decency, who show patience and sympathy even when they are unable to do anything. We find here what with some imagination one might take to be the picture of European civilization—respect and tolerance, courtesy and serenity, a desire for education and advancement. Nowhere is there the arrogant superiority of the insider towards the outsider. . . .

America had its prehistoric period, when the Indians hunted over its plains and prairies; it had its classical antiquity with the attainment of its national independence, the founding of its national ideas, its immortal constitution of world-historical significance. America, finally, had its Middle Ages with the chaos of the Civil War, the delimiting of its borders, the ruthless exploitation by a new breed of robber barons, the formation of classes, the shaping of a national character and a national culture. And perhaps one is not far wrong in placing the close of the American Middle Ages in the year 1940, or at least in the years that followed the first World War. . . .

. . . Nations often associate their ideals with a definite age level. The French have long shown a curious affinity for old age, the Germans for men "in their prime," the Americans for childhood. The 'Century of the child'—that is a phrase coined in America. Undoubtedly there is a close connection between this and the supremacy of women which plays such an important role in all public and social functions: With all the progressive cultural consequences that follow in its wake, the American matriarchate is an archaic phenomenon of the kind we see with all young nations at the beginning of their evolution. . . .

The transformation of this country begins in the schools. From these new generations now growing to maturity, a dynamic force will emanate—a force that will achieve recognition. America has the most broadly planned educational system of the civilized world. . . . Whoever wants to know where democracy is still alive has only to take a good look at these young people. . . .

Americans have not yet passed through a period of genuine romanticism. The pioneer age, the 'Gay Nineties' will not serve as equivalents. What is lacking is the yearning, the pain, the irony, the mood . . . that in Europe make a loving heart soft and gentle and tender, sad and happy. . . . there is no doubt that this is a lack which is felt to be a lack. Otherwise psychoanalysis could not have found so vehement an interest and so dangerous a spread in this country. . . . Nowhere but in New York have I found so many people hanging around in bars, lonely and alone, trying to submerge their domestic problems in countless drinks, and eager to talk about themselves to some understanding strangers. . . .

Our customs and ways, our emotions must be as strange to them [to Negroes] as theirs are to us. But since our civilization is the way into freedom for them, they are much more patient and reasonable than we. Their attitude toward the white man seems a mixture of admiration and pity. It is the manner in which cautious guards treat wild beasts in their care—half devotion, half careful tension, lest something unexpected happen the very next moment. The porters in the Pullman cars and the women watching over their little white angels in Central Park have almost the same kind of maternal and almost ecstatic loving-kindness. . . .

The dignity of the Americans requires no external insignia. . . . Democratic informality is not synonymous with lack of form—. . . it is no primitive semibarbaric state, such as it often seemed to us across the ocean. Dignity has its spiritual and moral standards even in shirt-sleeves, and it is this civil dignity that has become the moral fundament of the American people. It is possible to slap the boss on the shoulder, while still submitting to his authority. . . .

It is a question of decency, just how one wishes to thank America. . . . Whoever needs the much-discussed boon of liberty to breathe and finds it here again—he is an American. And whoever fails at least to try to strike off the rusty chains of his past commits a sin against himself.

Jacques Maritain
Philosopher, Teacher
1882-

> It is not money, it is *work* which holds sway over
> American civilization. . . . There is no materialism,
> I think, in the astonishing, countless initiatives of
> fraternal help which are the daily bread of the
> American people, or in the profound feeling of
> obligation toward others which exists in them,
> especially toward any people who are in distress.

One of the most favorable statements on America and the
Americans comes from Jacques Maritain, the French neo-Thomist
philosopher. As he himself stresses, his study was not meant to
be "systematic, complete and supposedly 'scientific.'" He was
well acquainted with America, having spent many years here
between 1933 and 1956, teaching and lecturing at Princeton
University, the University of Chicago, the University of Notre
Dame, and at Hunter College. Having developed a deep affection and admiration for America, which, he says, were shared
by his wife, he offers his testimony to what "I love in America."
A paean to such traits as American generosity, moral sense,
spirituality, eagerness for knowledge, it also offers observations
from which it is obvious that some contradictory aspects of our
culture did not escape him. However, Mr. Maritain is never
censorious and he does not castigate. He can only regret that
Americans have created an image that is not flattering to ourselves.

Such weaknesses as sensitivity to criticism, lack of patience
with ourselves (not with others), inner insecurity, are mentioned
in the manner of the understanding psychoanalyst. Thus, boast-
ing becomes a cover-up for "too much modesty" and aggressive-
ness a mask for inner insecurity. We are presented as being in
many respects woefully misunderstood.

Like many Europeans, he recognizes the race question to be
a peculiarly American concern. But here, too, he explains its
continuing presence on the basis of psychological factors which
must be treated with patience. In taking note of the leaning
toward anti-intellectualism, he speaks of it merely as something

"which offers little cause for elation." Though he seems to disapprove of what he called "the experiential approach," which insists on "all factual data, all points of view and all possible opinions" (clearly too much to him), his chiding is gentle. Ascribing it to too much "ideological modesty" he warns about "a serious risk: the risk of intellectual isolation, of making the American people non-communicable to other nations and walling them up in themselves."

Even when discussing our brand of capitalism, which, as a follower of the medieval philosophy of Thomas Aquinas, he cannot favor, his criticism is carefully sheathed. He observes consolingly, that "the big organism," as he calls our giant enterprises, has already become "more socially minded though not out of Christian love, but because the democratic spirit demands it."

In spite of his lenitive attitude, his shrewdness and Gallic logic are only half-concealed. He touches lightly on such of our characteristics as "the horror of doing nothing," the disregard of the need for leisure, and the contradiction between the insistence on romantic love in marriage coupled with the "pursuit of individual self-realization."

The fact that Jacques Maritain is undoubtedly of gentle temperament and that he does feel affection for America would seem to be the reason for treating us with such consideration. But the suspicion lingers that many of our behavioral traits, even some of our cherished convictions, would appear illogical and naive if the protective coloring Mr. Maritain imparts were swept aside.

His comforting appraisal should be a balm to the most sensitive Americans.

FROM *Reflections on America**

. . . few things, to my mind, are as sickening as the stock remarks with which so many persons in Europe, who are themselves far from despising the earthly goods of this world, reproach this country with its so-called materialism. The power of this fable is so great that sometimes you yourself are taken in by it. . . . Well, all this talk about American

---

*Jacques Maritain, *Reflections on America* (New York: Charles Scribner's Sons, 1958). By special permission of Charles Scribner's Sons.

materialism is no more than a curtain of silly gossip and slander . . .

Americans like to give. Of course, there is the exemption from taxes for gifts directed to the common welfare; but this very law about taxes would not have been possible if the astute legislator did not know that as a rule the American people are aware of the fact that it is better to give than to receive. . . .

The first [weakness of Americans] I shall mention is by no means a weakness. I am alluding to the fact that the American people are anxious to have their country loved; they need to be loved. (You will never find such a need in an Englishman. As to Frenchmen, they are so sure in advance that everybody loves them that they don't feel any particular anxiety about the matter. But they are very much shocked when they realize it is not true.) Well, this desire to have America loved is the mark of a soul which lies open to the sense of human brotherhood; it plays an important part, I think, in the general psychology of this country. . . .

When they are abroad it seems that they feel unhappy, afraid of meeting people, shy. And, as a result, they tend to become arrogant. Where are their cordial, genial, cheerful manners? They left them behind, in the native climate of the big country. One is led to think that each individual needs his home, his natural environment so much that abroad he feels estranged from himself. . . .

. . . what we witness when we consider in a general way the race question in America, is the spectacle of a nation which struggles doggedly against itself, or, more accurately against large segments of its own people, against a certain legacy of evil in its mores, and against the demons of the human heart— in order to free itself of abuses which are repellent to its own spirit, and to raise its entire practical behavior to the levels of the tenets and principles in which it believes and in the strength of which it was born. . . .

. . . the perpetual arrival of a new first generation of immigrants, as well as to the arrival of the first colonists, one might say that the tears and sufferings of so many unfortunates have been and ceaselessly are a stream fecundating the soil of the New World and preparing for America's grandeur. . . . The tears and sufferings of the persecuted and unfortunates are transmuted into a perpetual effort to improve human destiny and to make life bearable; they are transfigured into optimism and creativity. . . .

For the time being there is indeed in American ways . . . a particular point which offers little cause for elation, namely the attitude of public opinion toward intellectuals, especially toward artists. . . . Here . . . their opinions carry less weight than that of prominent businessmen; furthermore, and this is more serious, they seem to arouse some suspicion, and communion between the beholder and the artist is lacking in the very place where it should exist, namely, in that area which . . . may be called the enlightened public. . . .

The power of big money is still big itself, very big indeed. And the tremendous power of corporations and corporate management, in proportion as it grows, must, as a matter of public interest, be lawfully counterbalanced and regulated by various other powers. . . . The gradual realization of the American ideal of equal opportunity for all, and progress in social justice, will be the work of generations. But the road is open, the guiding spirit on which the whole ritual of economy finally depends has changed; a rupture with the old forms of the industrial regime has taken place.

. . . the truth is that America is taking leave of capitalism, not through any sudden, violent and destructive revolution, but through steady, constructive—and unsystematic transmutation. . . .

Work, which is a fundamental necessity of our existence, is not an end in itself. We work in order to improve human life. But will this very improvement, in ourselves and in others, only consist in working again and working more? . . . Certain kinds of repose, in which the mind is supremely active, and reaches, however imperfectly, some fruition of immortality through its contact with truth, or with Eternal Love, are better than work. . . .

There is one thing that America knows well, and that she teaches as a great and precious lesson to those who come in contact with her astounding adventure: it is the value and dignity of the common man, the value and dignity of the people . . . America knows that the common man has a right to the 'pursuit of happiness': the pursuit of the elementary conditions and possessions which are the prerequisites of a free life, and the denial of which, suffered by such mul-

titudes, is a horrible wound in the flesh of humanity; . . .
Here heroism is required, not to overcome tragedy, but to
bring to a successful conclusion the formidable adventure
begun in this country with the Pilgrim Fathers and the pioneers and continued in the great days of the Declaration
of Independence and the Revolutionary War.

Franz Schoenberner
Editor, Humanist
1892-

> The experience of exile is highly valuable for a
> thinking individual. . . . Having renounced the
> citizenship of your birth, you have renounced
> nationality in itself; you are henceforth a citizen of
> the world, and the only citizenship you can
> acquire with good conscience is that of a nation
> from all nations, foreshadowing the great com-
> munity of mankind.

As the decade of the 1930s unreeled itself, Franz Schoenberner, editor of the political satirical weekly, *Simplicissimus,*
had two choices: to continue to expose the fallacies of Nazism
by means of the printed word and the cartoon, or to surrender
and become a disciple of Hitler. He chose to continue his policy of sarcasm and ridicule until forced to seek exile first in
Switzerland, then in France. For eight years he and his companion, who later became his wife, led an existence reminiscent
of Kafka's nightmares.

He spoke no English when they reached the United States
in 1941 through the aid of the International Rescue Committee.
Here "guardian angels," his designation for those who had
smoothed the way for their emigration and who guided them
during the process of acclimatization, took over. It surprised
him to find that American churches were behind such a secular and practical endeavor as relocation of refugees. As the son
of a minister, he was aware that in Germany the church had
remained "entirely isolated from the true reality of life." One
of his comments on the American scene reveals his astonishment to find American theologicans combining theological

scholarship with intellectual interests, versatility, liberal political views, and practical sense.

They were heartened by the kindness, sympathy, and tact that was shown them, not only by those who had undertaken to be officially responsible for them, but also by individuals not directly connected with the rescue movement. Everyone was eager to help; but, though his ideas, which he hoped to turn into a source of income, were received with enthusiasm, nothing tangible developed. His observation that the dislike of Americans to say "No" inspired unwarranted hopes, has been affirmed by others whose experiences were similar.

It was through the unflagging efforts of his two "background angels" that he finally found himself on the road to self-sufficiency. Starting as a clerk in the office of a church-sponsored group, he was sent by the organization on a speaking tour as soon as it was decided that he had learned enough English. By that time he had achieved publication in one of the better magazines. Traveling as far west as Lake Tahoe and addressing groups in large and small communities proved to be an education in Americanization. The trip through the heartland of America provided new insights and a new surprise—that people living in small and far away places were so well informed and so deeply concerned with the problems of the times.

In 1944 he joined the Office of War Information (OWI) as one of the German editors. He had also begun to write his first book and it was to be in English. It was soon to be followed by another.

As the first decade of life in America came to an end, misfortune was lurking in the not too far distance. One evening he requested of a young neighbor that he turn his radio lower and was knocked down. The result was that he found himself completely paralyzed below his neck. He still had his head, as a nurse pointed out, but only his head. The thoughts that crowded his consciousness during eighteen weeks in a hospital, became the subect of still another book and provide further illumination of his thoughts in regard to life in America. The fact that he refused to look upon this accident as "a typical American barbarism," (as one of his friends suggested) but, instead, as an example of "life's unfathomable irrationality," is an indication of his sentiments to America and its people.

The New Americans

FROM *The Inside Story of an Outsider**

It is no coincidence that the founding fathers of the American nation, its leaders of the revolution against England, were men of English descent like Washington and Jefferson and Franklin, or real Englishmen like Thomas Paine. . . . The others were and are all 'damned foreigners,' only of longer or shorter standing, which does not seem to make much difference. The record shows that among the most prominent Americans of all times, from the War of Independence to World War II, there were always quite a number of statesmen and generals, of artists and scientists, of leaders in commerce and industry and social progress who were only first-, second-, or third generation Americans—whether the Sons or Daughters of the American Revolution like it or not. . .

I had eagerly anticipated the impressive moment when, standing on deck, I would take a last look at Europe, this haunted and haunting continent . . . I did not expect to find milk and honey; but there was hope that this second exodus, this narrow escape from servitude or death, would prove more successful than the first one; that in the new world overseas I would be allowed to live and die, perhaps not in peace, but as a freeman. . . .

Never before had I found so many real friends as I made here (without the help of Dale Carnegie) during my first days on a foreign continent, a stranger among strangers, hardly able to understand or to make myself understood in their language. The real story of such a miracle, composed of the cumulative effect of innumerable small but important acts and gestures, would make a whole book. But at least, in order to prevent the reproach of sentimental prejudice in favor of this country, I tried to make believable the miraculous fact that immediately, at first sight, I saw America at her very best. . . .

. . . since my first acquaintance with the English language my logical mind had instinctively resented the fact that there were practically no universal rules of pronunciation, as in all other languages I knew. It looked to me as if you had to be introduced personally to every word, because exactly the same combination of letters could mean two or three different

---

*Franz Schoenberner, *The Inside Story of an Outsider* (New York: The Macmillan Company, 1949). Used by permission of the publishers.

sounds or vice versa, not to speak of the strangely annoying phenomenon that obviously Latin, Greek or French words were mostly accentuated in a way which made them unrecognizable to me. I heartily enjoyed the famous definition that the English language is composed of foreign words which are mispronounced. . . .

In the course of the first months, having the same experiences again and again, I had learned to understand that being optimistic and feeling 'fine' was a sort of religion with Americans, the ritual of which had to be performed under any circumstances. To keep me happy with some vague hopes was for them at the same time a means of keeping themselves happy. After all, it is rather depressing to admit that you cannot do anything for a person whom you would really like to help. The idea of the American promise, whether or not it can be kept, must remain intact. . . .

It seems to me that, . . . generally speaking, the small-town atmosphere is here less stagnant than in Europe, if only because of the nomadic instinct which keeps a large part of the American population, and not only the millions of migratory workers, continuously on the move. . . . People are coming and going, especially young people, and even the really indigenous population cannot help taking notice of the outside world. . . .

It is true that there was an inner affinity between the best spiritual heritage of America and my own world of thought. The rational idealism and humanism of the 'fathers of the American Constitution' was based upon the great liberal and liberating ideas of the late eighteenth century, the century of Enlightenment. . . . Perhaps I am a case of arrested development, but I must confess that my basic principles and convictions, my whole approach to moral, political or social and economic problems is still determined by this humanistic and rational idealism which, in its essence, combines the most precious elements of the Greco-Roman and Judeo-Christian heritage of Western culture.

FROM *You Still Have Your Head**

The writer had often wondered when and why the turning

*Franz Schoenberner, *You Still Have Your Head* (New York: The Macmillan Company, 1957). Used by permission of the publishers.

of the tide began—this total change in America's mental and psychological attitude toward its intelligentsia—which, as it lost more and more of its former prestige, finally became so inured to the general air of humorous contempt that it began to deride itself. . . . Was it, perhaps, that the era of the Founding Fathers had been something of a Periclean Age, not only because it was formed and guided by great ideas but also because its democratic ideals had been translated into political reality under the leadership of an intellectual elite or even of a few truly great men, exactly as in Athens democracy had been the highest form of oligarchy? And could it be said that the great change, the transvaluation of all values, or certainly the devaluation of intellect and cultural values, had begun with the end of this noble era when, as successor to John Quincy Adams, the simple farmer-general from Tennessee, 'Andy Jackson,' a 'man of the people,' was swept into the White House by a groundswell of rough western pioneers and backwoodsmen who took their democracy straight, like their liquor, and as literally as only illiterates can do? . . .

Could it be that by a cruel irony the noble experiment of general and universal education inaugurated by Jefferson with the most utopian hopes and the most generous intent had somehow miscarried, because the precious privilege of the few, when it was made accessible to everybody, even to those who had never asked for it, necessarily lost its value and fell gradually more and more into disrespect? . . .

He had known from the start, and had discerned more and more clearly in the course of ten years, that there were also different worlds in the American universe, some of them rather dark and wild and violent like the catastrophes of nature with its tornadoes and hurricanes, its earthquakes, floods and droughts which time and again would suddenly smash the most perfect technical pattern of civilized human existence by an outburst of elemental destructiveness.

Bibliography

Adamic, Louis. *Dynamite: The Story of Class Violence in America.* New York, 1934.
———. *My America.* New York, 1938.
———. *Two-Way Passage.* New York, 1941.
———. *What's Your Name.* New York, 1942.
———. *Dinner at the White House.* New York, 1946.
Bojer, Johann. *The Emigrants.* New York, 1925.
Bremer, Frederica. *America in the Fifties.* New York, 1924.
Brissenden, Paul F. *The I.W.W. A Study of American Syndicalism.* New York, 1919.
Bryce, James. *American Commonwealth.* New York, 1922.
Burlingame, Roger. *The American Conscience.* New York, 1957.
Burr, Anna Robeson. *Autobiography.* Boston, 1909.
Cahan, Abraham. *The Rise of David Levinsky.* New York 1917.
Curti, Merle. *Growth of American Thought.* New York, 1951.
David, Henry. *History of the Haymarket Affair.* New York, 1936.
Davie, M. R. *Refugees in America.* New York, 1947.
Dickens, Charles. *American Notes for General Circulation.* London, 1842.
Drinnon, Richard. *Rebel in Paradise.* Chicago, 1961.
Ernst, Robert. *Immigrant Life in New York City.* New York, 1949.
Felix, David. *Protest.* Bloomington, 1965.
Filler, Louis. *Crusaders for American Liberalism.* Yellow Springs, Ohio, 1961.
Frank, Philipp. *Einstein, His Life and Times.* New York, 1963.
Gamio, Manuel. *The Mexican Immigrant.* Chicago, 1931.
Glazer, Nathan & Moynihan, Daniel Patrick. *Beyond the Melting Pot.* Cambridge, 1963.
Gold, Michael. *Jews Without Money.* New York, 1930.
Goldberg, Harvey (ed.). *American Radicals.* New York, 1957.
Goldman, Eric F. *Rendezvous with Destiny.* New York, 1950.
———. *The Crucial Decade.* New York, 1956.
Handlin, Oscar. *Immigration as a Factor in American History.* Englewood Cliffs, N. J., 1950.

Bibliography

———. *Boston's Immigrants*. Cambridge, 1941.

———. *The Uprooted*. Boston, 1951.

Hansen, Marcus Lee. *The Immigrant in American History*. Cambridge, 1940.

Harrington, Michael. *The Other America*. New York, 1962.

Herberg, Will. *Protestant, Catholic and Jew in America*. New York, 1955.

Higham, John. *Strangers in the Land*. New Brunswick, N. J., 1955.

Howe, Helen. *The Gentle Americans*. New York, 1966.

Joll, James. *The Anarchists*. Boston, 1964.

Jones, Maldwyn J. *American Immigration*. Chicago, 1960.

Kent, D. P. *The Refugee Intellectuals*. New York, 1953.

Maisel, Albert Q. *They All Chose America*. New York, 1957.

Martineau, Harriet. *Society in America*. London, 1837.

Maurois, André. *From the New Freedom to the New Frontier*. New York, 1963.

Michelmore, Peter. *Einstein: Profile of the Man*. New York, 1953.

Moberg, Vilhelm. *The Emigrants*. New York, 1951.

———. *Unto a Good Land*. New York, 1954.

———. *The Last Letter Home*. New York, 1961.

Münsterberg, Hugo. *The Americans*. Boston, 1904.

Musmanno, Michael. *The Italians in America*. New York, 1965.

Pascal, Roy. *Design and Truth in Autobiography*. Cambridge, 1960.

Pisani, L. F., *The Italians in America*. New York, 1957.

Pryce-Jones, A. (ed.). *The American Imagination*. New York, 1960.

Rayback, J. G. *A History of American Labor*. New York, 1959.

Riis, Jacob A. *How the Other Half Lives*. New York, 1890.

———. *Battle with the Slum*. New York, 1902.

Rischin, Moses. *The Promised City*. Boston, 1962.

Rolvaag, Ole Edvart. *Giants in the Earth*. New York, 1927.

Roucek, J. S. & Brown, F. J. *One America*. New York, 1937.

Robison, Sophia M. *Refugees at Work*. New York, 1942.

Safford, Victor. *Immigration Problems*. New York, 1925.

Saloutos, Theodore. *They Remember America*. Berkeley, 1956.

Saveth, Norman E. *American Historians and European Immigrants*. New York, 1948.

Shannon, William V. *The Irish in America*. New York, 1963.

Siegfried, André. *America Comes of Age*. New York, 1927.

Smith, William C. *Americans in the Making.* New York, 1939.

Solomon, Barbara M. *Ancestors and Immigrants.* Cambridge, 1956.

Stephenson, G. M. *A History of American Immigration,* Cambridge, 1956.

Taft, Philip. *The A.F. of L. Under Gompers.* New York, 1957.

Wittke, Carl F. *We Who Built America.* New York, 1939.

Zahler, Helene. *The American Paradox.* New York, 1964.

ADDITIONAL AUTOBIOGRAPHIES BY IMMIGRANTS

Antin, Benjamin. *The Man from the 22nd.*
Bercovici, Conrad. *It's the Gypsy in Me.*
Bogen, Boris D. *Born a Jew.*
Borgenicht, Louis. *The Happiest Man.*
Bridges, Horace. *On Becoming an American.*
Brown, Demetra Vaka. *A Child of the Orient.*
Brown, Fred Kenyon. *Through the Mill.*
———. *Through the School.*
Buaken, Manuel. *I Have Lived with the American People.*
Clarke, J. I. C. *My Life and Memories.*
Cohen, Rose G. *Out of the Shadow.*
Davis, James J. *Iron Puddler.*
Edstrom, David. *Testament of Caliban.*
Gatti-Casazza, Giulio. *Memories of the Opera.*
Genthe, Arnold. *As I Remember.*
Hasanovitz, Elizabeth. *One of Them.*
Hassler, Frederick R. *Memoirs.*
Hurok, S. *Impresario.*
Irvine, Alexander F. *From the Bottom Up.*
Kohut, Rebecca. *My Portion.*
Lang, Lucy Robins. *Tomorrow is Beautiful.*
Lowe, Pardee. *Father and Glorious Descendant.*
Mattson, Hans. *The Story of an Emigrant.*
Muir, John. *Story of My Boyhood and Youth.*
Mukerji, Dhan Gopal. *Caste and Outcast.*
Shaw, Anna Howard. *Story of a Pioneer.*
Sikorsky, I. *Story of the Winged-S.*
Sone, Monica. *Nisei Daughter.*
Thorek, Max. *A Surgeon's World.*
Vitkauskas, Arejas. *An Immigrant's Story.*

Bibliography

Waksman, Selman. *My Life with the Microbes.*
Waldman, Louis. *Labor Lawyer.*
Weinstein, Gregory. *The Ardent Eighties and After.*
Yezierska, Anzia. *Red Ribbon on a White Horse.*
Zweig, Stefan D. *The World of Yesterday.*